ESOP Valuation

Second Edition

ESOP Valuation

Second Edition

Edited by Scott S. Rodrick

The National Center for Employee Ownership
Oakland, California

ESOP Valuation, Second Edition
Editing and book design by Scott S. Rodrick

The National Center for Employee Ownership
1736 Franklin Street, 8th Floor
Oakland, CA 94612
(510) 208-1300
(510) 272-9510 (fax)
E-mail: *nceo@nceo.org*
Web: *http://www.nceo.org/*

First printed August 1999; reprinted December 1999
Second edition, January 2001
Reprinted with minor changes, July 2003

ISBN: 0-926902-69-5

Contents

Preface

For business owners, managers, professional advisors, and fiduciaries involved with an employee stock ownership plan (ESOP) in a closely held company, the determination of the stock's fair market value for ESOP purposes is a crucial issue. This book collects the most noteworthy articles on ESOP valuation from the *Journal of Employee Ownership Law and Finance,* the only professional journal in the U.S. devoted to employee ownership. Published quarterly by the National Center for Employee Ownership (NCEO), the *Journal* draws upon leading authorities to deliver timely, accurate, and thorough information on ESOPs, stock options, related incentive plans, and employee participation programs.

The articles reprinted here originally appeared between 1995 and 2000.* Each one has been reviewed and updated as needed for this publication. Some of the older articles as well as the most recent ones did not need to be updated aside from a few words inserted here or there; the following, however, were substantially revised: "An Introduction to ESOP Valuation," "Enhancing Shareholder Value in Negotiated ESOP Transactions," and "ESOP Valuation and Financial Advisory Analysis Due Diligence Checklist."

The articles in this book cover a wide range of issues, from ESOP valuation basics to multi-investor buyouts to S corporations. Valuation is a somewhat controversial area of ESOP practice, and so we include articles on valuation ethics and on how to evaluate an appraiser. We hope that you find this book useful and that it assists you in working with ESOPs.

Second Edition

The second edition added an important new article on "Shifting Control in an ESOP Context" (no. 12), which discusses multi-stage transactions in which the ESOP begins with a minority interest and gradually acquires a controlling interest. A few minor edits were made in other chapters. Finally, the book was reformatted in a smaller, easier-to-hold page size.

Second Edition, 2003 Reprint

This 2003 reprint of the second edition includes an update at the end of "Shifting Control in an ESOP Context" and updates to the author biographies for several articles.

---

* Articles 1, 2, 3, 4, 5, 13, and 14 appeared in the winter 1995 issue; article 6 in the summer 1995 issue; article 7 in the winter 1999 issue; article 8 in the summer 1996 issue; article 9 in the fall 1997 issue; article 10 in the summer 1999 issue; article 11 in the fall 1998 issue; and article 12 in the spring 2000 issue.

1

An Introduction to ESOP Valuation

John W. Murphy
John P. Murphy

Valuing corporate stock is possibly the single most important component in employee stock ownership plan (ESOP) transactions. Whether a company is planning to implement an ESOP or already has a plan in place, an accurate and defensible valuation is the logical first step in transactions involving the corporation, an ESOP, and the ESOP participants. This article discusses the framework for conducting a supportable valuation, and focuses on basic factors to be considered, valuation approaches and methods, selecting capitalization and discount rates, selecting premiums and discounts, common valuation errors, and regulatory issues.

Valuing corporate stock is possibly the single most important component in employee stock ownership plan (ESOP) transactions. Whether a company is planning to implement an ESOP or already has a plan in place, an accurate and defensible valuation is the logical first step in transactions involving the corporation, an ESOP, and the ESOP participants.

Under Internal Revenue Code Section 401(a)(28)(C), a closely held company that has an ESOP must conduct an independent appraisal of its shares each time the plan acquires stock and as of the end of each plan year thereafter. Both existing Internal Revenue Service (IRS) regulations[1] and proposed Department of Labor (DOL) regulations[2] use fair market value as the appropriate standard to be applied in ESOP valuations. As defined by the IRS, the phrase "fair market value" means the price at which a property would change hands between a willing seller and a willing buyer, when the former is under no compulsion to sell and the latter is under no compulsion to buy, and both parties have reasonable knowledge of the relevant facts.[3] Business owners who have spent years building their closely held corporations often have only a vague idea of what their company is worth. Although many will gladly offer their opinion, their concept of value, which can be emotionally charged, is usually not the same as the company's fair market value. More importantly, the owner's opinion of value does not meet the applicable legal and regulatory requirements, even if it is accurate.

John W. Murphy, CBA, is the president, and John P. Murphy, CBA, is the senior vice president of Atlantic Management Company, Inc., a Portsmouth, New Hampshire-based firm that provides business valuation ESOP advisory services to closely held companies and their principals.

Factors to Consider

Because the fair market value cannot be determined as a mathematical certainty, it is critical that the valuation analysis be based on pertinent information that is accurate, objective, and comprehensive. Only then can a defensible conclusion be reached as to the fair market value of a company being appraised. To ensure the thoroughness of the analysis, the valuation of the company's outstanding common stock should follow the guidelines set forth in Revenue Ruling 59-60.[4] (Revenue Ruling 83-120 provides special methods for valuing closely held preferred stock.) Revenue Ruling 59-60 was issued by the IRS in 1959 to provide guidance in valuing closely held stock for estate and gift tax purposes. In 1965, the IRS broadened the scope of Revenue Ruling 59-60 with the issuance of Revenue Rulings 65-192 and 65-193. These rulings indicated that the general approach, methods, and factors outlined in Revenue Ruling 59-60 applied to valuations of closely held stock for income tax and other tax purposes. Further, Revenue Ruling 59-60 was deemed appropriate in determining the fair market value of business interests of any type, and of intangible assets for all tax purposes. Proposed DOL regulations issued in 1983 relied heavily on Revenue Ruling 59-60 as well.

Revenue Ruling 59-60 spells out a number of factors to be considered when the stock of a closely held corporation is valued:[5]

- The nature of the business and the history of the enterprise from its inception,
- The economic outlook and the condition and outlook of the industry in particular,
- The book value of the stock and the financial condition of the company,
- The earning capacity of the company,
- The dividend-paying capacity of the company,
- Whether or not the enterprise has goodwill or other intangible value,
- Sales of the stock and the size of the block of stock to be appraised, and
- The market price of stocks of corporations engaged in the same or a similar business and having their stocks actively traded in a free and open market.

Is one factor more important than another? According to the IRS, the relative weight afforded a particular factor depends upon the nature of the corporation's business.[6]

When valuations are conducted in connection with ESOP transactions, they should also comply with proposed U.S. Department of Labor regulations.[7] In that regard, the valuation analysis must also take into consideration the following two factors.[8]

Marketability The first factor is the marketability, or lack thereof, of the securities. Where the trust is the purchaser of securities that are subject to "put" rights and such rights are taken into account in reducing the discount for lack of marketability, such assessment shall include consideration of the extent to which such rights are enforceable, as well as the company's ability to meet its obligations with respect to the "put" rights, taking into consideration the company's financial strength and liquidity.

Control Premium The second factor is whether or not the seller would be able to obtain a control premium from an unrelated third party with regard to the block of securities being valued, provided that in cases where a control premium is taken into account: (1) actual control, both in form and substance, is passed to the purchaser with the sale, or will be passed to the purchaser within a reasonable time pursuant to a binding agreement in effect at the time of the sale; and (2) it is reasonable to assume that the purchaser's control will not be dissipated within a short period of time after the acquisition.

Having identified the basic factors that must be considered in every ESOP valuation, we will now take a closer look at each factor.

The Nature and History of the Company

The nature and history of the company provide a multidimensional picture of the company and its operations. Within this framework, the appraiser looks at how the company arrived at its present position and how it was operating around the valuation date in terms of product line, customers, competition, employees, management, business facilities, opportunities, and problems. The results of this analysis will bring to light such points as growth or decline in the market, the depth of management, potential risks to the company from changes in technology, and how the company is positioned for future growth. Significant events in the company's history are noted, as are changes in the way it does business. Keep in mind that one of the main reasons for analyzing the past is as a guide in projecting the future. Therefore, events that are unlikely to recur should be discounted.

Economic Outlook and the Condition and Outlook of the Industry

A study of the economic outlook looks at current and future economic conditions as they affect the company, its industry, and the environment in which the company operates. General economic factors are analyzed to see what affect they may have regionally and nationally, while short- and long-range industry forecasts are prepared to project cyclical patterns and other trends. For example, if the industry is experiencing rapid changes in its technology, how well is the company positioned to keep up with these changes and maintain a competitive position?

Book Value of the Stock and the Financial Condition of the Company

The financial analysis begins with a careful review of the company's balance sheet around the valuation date and for a representative number of previous years. As discussed in Revenue Ruling 59-60, the company's balance sheet for two or more years should be obtained;[9] however, a five- or six-year period is usually analyzed if the information is available. When this information is set up in comparative format, patterns, trends, and changes emerge that provide an insight behind the numbers and suggest a starting point for further inquiry.

Earning Capacity of the Company

An equally thorough examination of the company's comparative income and expense data is made covering the same years as the balance sheets. The purpose of this examination is to arrive at the true historical earning capacity of the business, which is used in projecting future earning capacity.

It is usually necessary to adjust the income and expense statements of the company being valued to arrive at its true earning capacity.[10] With the adjusted earnings in hand for a representative period of time, the appraiser can develop an earnings base with which to approach value. Whereas past performance is one indication of future performance, trends in earnings should be considered along with any changes that have occurred that may influence how the company can be expected to perform in the future.

Using financial statements prepared in a comparative format, the appraiser looks for extraordinary or nonrecurring items of income and expense that may be adjusted in determining earning capacity. These could include losses from closing an unprofitable plant, one-time costs of computerizing the business, or similar items that are unlikely to recur. Close attention is paid to substituting a more conservative straight-line method for depreciation for the accelerated methods allowable for income tax purposes, and to items that are personal in nature and being charged to the business, such as vacations, health club memberships, or rent paid to maintain an apartment for so-called business associates. An officer's salary is examined to determine whether it is excessive in terms of what a non-owner would be paid for the same job. Other salary accounts are also examined to determine whether the company is paying salaries to other family members who are either not employed in the business or earning more than a nonfamily member would be paid. As mentioned before, income and expenses related to nonoperating assets are also eliminated from the statements.

Dividend-Paying Capacity of the Company

If the valuation is of a controlling interest, dividend-paying capacity is more important than the actual dividends paid,[11] because the controlling stockholder often takes out cash in other ways (compensation, related party leases, etc.) that leave less earnings to be distributed in the form of dividends. However, in valuing a minority interest, the actual dividends paid are more important than the dividend-paying capacity, because the minority stockholder generally cannot force a company to pay dividends, even if it has the capacity to do so.[12]

Existence of Goodwill or Other Intangible Value

The existence of goodwill, and its value, is a function of the amount by which earnings exceed a fair return on the company's net tangible assets. Goodwill is usually thought of in terms of a company's operating characteristics: quality of management, reputation, trade name, or location. However, these characteristics can be quantified only by their contribution to earnings. If a company has other intangibles, such as patents, these would be valued separately and not lumped into the goodwill factor.

Most often the appraiser is concerned with arriving at the value of a going concern in its entirety and does not value goodwill separately. Thus, the characteristics that make up goodwill are factored into the overall assessment of the company, and the value of their contribution to the company as a whole is a matter of judgment. There are notable exceptions, however—such as a valuation to allocate a sale price—when goodwill is valued separately. This brings us to the sometimes controversial "formula method" contained in Internal Revenue Service A.R.M. 34.

A.R.M. 34 was issued in 1920 to provide a rule of thumb in arriving at the loss of goodwill value in connection with the impact of prohibition on breweries. It used one computation to arrive at the dollar amount of excess earnings and another to convert that amount to a value for goodwill. Revenue Ruling 65-192, mentioned earlier, attempted to clarify and restrict the use of the formula method by stating that it has no valid application in determining the fair market value of corporate stocks or other business interests unless it is necessary to value the intangible assets of the corporation or of other business interests. And even then, it continues, the formula method is to be used only when there is no better method available.

A frequently encountered problem with this method is the rates used by inexperienced practitioners. When this method was introduced, the respective rates cited were from 8% to 10% for tangible assets and from 15% to 20% for excess earnings.[13] Now, 80 years later, appraisals are still being done by using this method and these same rates. While this method, with modifications, may be used as a reasonableness test, it generally should not be used on a stand-alone basis in ESOP valuations.

Previous Sales of Stock

Prior sales of the company's common stock can be an excellent indicator of value if the transactions occurred relatively close to the valuation date and the transactions were at arm's length.

Market Price of Stocks of Corporations Engaged in the Same Business

Valuing a closely held company in relation to the trading prices of guideline public companies is one of the most useful techniques available to the appraiser. It is also one of the most complex.

A careful analysis of the guideline companies is required to develop various investor ratios that relate the market price of each of the guidelines around the valuation date to such factors as earnings per share, price/earnings ratio, dividend yield, and book value. By using these investor ratios as a guide, together with all other pertinent information, the appraiser is able to develop indicated values for the subject company.

Approaches to Business Valuation

No single formula can be used to determine the value of every closely held company in every situation. Therefore, a number of generally accepted approaches and methods for valuing closely held companies have been developed, none of which is necessarily superior to the others. The selection of valuation approaches and methods depends on the purpose of the engagement, the standard of value being determined, the type of company being valued, available data, and other factors. The following discussion summarizes the three most generally accepted valuation approaches, and the valuation methods employed within each method.

Asset-Based Approach

In a limited number of situations, a company's worth can be measured by reference to the net value of its underlying assets. This approach consists of the adjusted book value method and the liquidation value method. Both of these methods determine value on the basis of a hypothetical sale of the company's assets, rather than focusing on its earnings potential, and are generally used if the subject company (1) is an investment or holding type of company with significant tangible assets; (2) has no established earnings history or a volatile earnings history; or (3) is not able to continue as a going concern. The application of these methods is also more appropriate when a controlling interest is being valued rather than a minority interest, because a minority shareholder typically cannot cause a sale of the company's assets.

Adjusted Book Value Method The adjusted book value method involves adjusting the company's assets and liabilities to their appraised values to determine the value of the company. A key consideration in the adjusted book value method is to recast the current balance sheet data to bring it from an accounting basis to an economic basis. This involves such adjustments as substituting an appraised value of fixed assets, revising inventory figures to market value, and determining the value of any intangibles that exist in the company but that do not appear on its balance sheet. Liabilities also may require adjustment to record such items as contingent liabilities. A further adjustment may be required to reflect the potential income tax implications from a presumed sale of the assets.

Liquidation Value Method The liquidation value method involves discounting the net proceeds from liquidating the company's assets and paying off its liabilities to determine the value of the company. In situations in which a company has had a history of losses or where the sole owner-manager has died and the company's future is in doubt, it is reasonable to value the company on the basis of the likelihood of liquidation. In these cases, the adjusted book value is further adjusted to factor in the costs of liquidation and the potential income tax implications of disposing of the company's assets.

Market Approach

The market approach consists of an analysis of previous sales of the company's stock, sales of privately held companies similar to the subject company, and sales of stock of publicly traded companies similar to the subject company.

Previous Sales of the Company's Stock Previous sales of the company's stock offer perhaps the most reliable indication of a company's fair market value, provided the transactions were for reasonable consideration and at arm's length. Details of the transactions should be carefully examined in light of the willing seller–willing buyer concept of value to rule out isolated sales made under distress conditions or bargain sales to employees or family, which would not be considered arm's length transactions.

Where valid transactions have occurred, the terms of the transaction should be taken into consideration. For example, if payment for the stock was received in the form of a note, or cash and a note, the face value of the note would be discounted to its net present value at the time of the transaction to arrive at fair market value. Another factor to be taken into consideration is the size of the block of stock being valued. A controlling interest, with its added element of value, would command a premium, while a minority interest may be subject to a discount.

Sales of Closely Held Companies The value also may be based on recent sales of closely held companies that are similar to the subject company. Although this method has a strong conceptual appeal, the availability of adequate, reliable, and timely information on actual sales of private companies is often difficult to obtain or simply not available.

Sales of Stock of Publicly Traded Companies Finally, fair market value can be determined by reference to the trading prices of stocks of public companies engaged in the same or a similar business as the subject company. The Internal Revenue Service strongly supports the use of this method when an active market for a closely held company's stock does not exist. As stated in Revenue Ruling 59-60, "the prices of stocks which are traded in volume in a free and active market by informed persons best reflect the consensus of the investing public as to what the future holds for the corporations and industries represented. When a stock is closely held, is traded infrequently, or is traded in an erratic market, some other measure of value must be used. In many instances, the next best measure may be found in the prices at which the stocks of companies engaged in the same or similar line of business are selling in a free and open market."[14]

In determining whether a particular company should be considered a guideline company from a valuation perspective, a number of important factors must be considered: products, markets, earnings, dividend-paying capacity, book value, position in the industry, capital structure, credit status, depth of management, nature of the competition, personnel experience, and maturity of the business.[15]

Additional guidance as to the issue of comparability is presented in *Estate of Hall v. Commissioner* (92 T.C. No. 19, 1989). This case focused on the valuation of closely held shares of Hallmark Cards, Inc. Because only one greeting card company was publicly traded, it was deemed reasonable to develop guideline company data on the basis of companies subject to similar economic conditions, namely consumer spending patterns. Under that parameter, the public companies used in the Hall case included A.T. Cross, Avon, Coca Cola, Lenox, and Papercraft.

Once suitable guideline companies have been identified, a number of valuation methods can be used to develop a range of indicated values. Some of the more common methods include price to earnings, price to gross cash flow, price to dividends, price to revenues, price to book value, and price to net asset value ratios.

In these methods, the market price of each guideline company's common stock is divided by the appropriate benefit stream to arrive at a multiple. After adjustment for differences between the guideline companies and the subject company in terms of size, sales and earnings trends, depth of management, market diversification, and scope of marketing area, the multiples are then applied to the subject company's applicable benefit streams to arrive at an indication of value.

Income Approach

Although a number of methods are included in the income approach, the two most commonly used are the capitalization of earnings method and the discounted cash flow method.

Capitalization of Earnings Method The capitalization of earnings method develops an indicated value on the basis of the company's historic earnings and tends to be more appropriate when a company's current operations are indicative of its future operations. The indicated value is determined by dividing a historical earnings stream by a capitalization rate.

Depending on the history of the company, it may be appropriate to use only the most current earnings or a weighted average of historical earnings for a number of years. Selecting an appropriate earnings base is another area in which judgment comes into play, as the common practice of indiscriminately using five-year average earnings or three-year average earnings can significantly distort the valuation conclusion. One must keep in mind that in discussing earnings, we are concerned with the amount that would be available to be paid out in dividends or reinvested in the company. In other words, we are looking at after-tax earnings. In the same vein, when adjustments are required to add back such items as nonrecurring expenses or excess officers' salaries, the add-backs are made on an after-tax basis.

Discounted Cash Flow Method The discounted cash flow method develops an indicated value on the basis of the company's projected future cash flows and tends to be more appropriate when future returns are expected to be different from current operations. In this instance, the indicated value is determined by discounting future cash flows to their present worth by using a discount rate that reflects both the current market rate of return and the risks inherent in the specific investment.

Selecting Capitalization and Discount Rates

A capitalization rate is any divisor, usually expressed as a percentage, that is used to convert an earnings stream into value. It is usually derived by subtracting the subject company's expected long-term average growth rate from its discount rate. On the basis of this premise, a company's capitalization rate is usually lower than its discount rate.

A discount rate represents the rate of return an informed investor would expect to receive on an investment in the subject company, given the degree of risk inherent in that investment. Unlike a capitalization rate, a discount rate is not used as a divisor to determine a company's value. Rather, the discount rate is used as a base to determine present value factors, which are then used to discount a future benefit stream (i.e., cash flow or earnings) to present value.

Some of the factors that must be considered in developing the discount rate include the nature of the business and its outlook at the valuation date, the risks involved, and the stability of earnings. This is clearly an area where all pertinent factors that have a bearing on value must be considered, which makes it one of the most difficult tasks in the valuation process.

In constructing a discount rate, the starting point is usually the rate of return available on "risk-free" investments. The second layer adjusts upward to a return on "moderate-risk" investments, and the final layer represents a risk premium that reflects the degree of risk in the company. In other words, the risk premium quantifies the appraiser's assessment of the company itself as an investment: its outlook, the outlook for the industry as a whole, the quality and depth of management, the company's financial strength, and its competitive position. Only after all these factors have been considered can an appropriate discount rate be constructed.

In practice, the discount rate is often derived from a compilation of the following variables:

Risk-Free Rate of Return

Risk-free rate of return is the return an investor could obtain from a low-risk, guaranteed investment, where such return is normally equivalent to the yield to maturity of long-term U.S. Treasury bonds. Typically the rate is based on the 30-year Treasury bond yield in effect at the end of the company's fiscal or calendar year.

Equity Risk Premium

Equity risk premium is the additional return earned on stocks by an average equity investor in excess of the return on long-term Treasury bonds. Although there are many sources from which this premium can be determined, it is often based on data published in Ibbotson Associates' *Stocks, Bonds, Bills, and Inflation Yearbooks,*[16] which is probably the most well-known and widely used source.

Risk Premium for Size

Risk premium for size represents the additional risk associated with an investment in a smaller closely held company compared with an investment in a larger company and recognizes that investors typically demand a higher return from companies that are smaller in sales and capitalization. As with the equity risk premium, this premium is generally based on research compiled by Ibbotson Associates, which measures the difference between monthly small stock total returns and monthly common stock total returns.[17] The small stock total return combines the return earned by companies listed in the smallest 20% of the New York Stock Exchange with companies generally similar in size and capitalization that are listed on the American Stock Exchange or are traded in the over-the-counter markets. The common stock total return is based on the Standard & Poor's Composite Index.

Risk Premium for Other Risk Factors

Risk premium for other risk factors represents the additional risk associated with an investment in a smaller closely held company compared with an investment in an average Standard & Poor's 500 company. This includes such factors as industry risk, financial risk, diversification risk (products, customer base, geographic location, etc.), and additional operational risks (management depth, competence, etc.).

There have been a number of attempts to standardize a range of discount rates by associating a particular risk premium with identifiable operating characteristics, such as the age of the business, the volatility of earnings, and "key-man" versus second-line management issues. Although these benchmarks are useful in pointing out a general direction, the appraiser must rely on judgment and common sense in weighing the relative importance of the various factors.

Tax Shield

Subject to limits under current tax law, companies can deduct amounts that represent the combined principal and interest used to repay an ESOP loan.[18] The allowable deduction of the loan principal provides tax advantages to the corporation, which is often referred to as a "tax shield." These tax advantages preclude a dollar-for-dollar reduction of the outstanding ESOP loan from the preliminary value as determined on a debt-free basis.

Premiums and Discounts

Depending on the valuation methods used, the facts and circumstances surrounding the subject company, and the ownership interest that is being valued, the indicated values often require additional adjustments to arrive at a final conclusion of value. This brings us to the subject of premiums and discounts.

Control Premium

A controlling interest in a closely held corporation is generally held to be worth more than its proportionate share of the value of all the outstanding shares. The rationale for applying a control premium stems from Revenue Ruling 59-60, which states "the size of the block of stock itself is a relevant factor to be considered. Although it is true that a minority interest in an unlisted corporation's stock is more difficult to sell than a similar block of listed stock, it is equally true that control of a corporation, either actual or in effect, representing as it does an added element of value, may justify a higher value for a specific block of stock."[19] The added element of value is measured by a premium that attaches to the shares that have control. In practice, the premium can be quantified by reference to prices paid in the public market for a control position in a corporation whose stocks had previously traded as minority interests.

The magnitude of a control premium is influenced by the shareholder's ability to exercise any or all of a variety of rights typically associated with control. Some of the more common benefits of control include:[20]

- Electing directors and appointing management;
- Determining management compensation and perquisites;
- Setting policy and changing the course of business;
- Acquiring or liquidating assets;
- Making acquisitions of other companies;
- Liquidating, dissolving, selling, or recapitalizing the company;
- Selling or acquiring treasury shares;
- Registering the company's stock for a public offering;
- Declaring and paying dividends; and
- Changing the articles of incorporation or bylaws.

Several firms follow these transactions and publish studies on control premiums. Among the more widely used studies are the *Control Premium*

Study and *Mergerstat Review,* both published by Houlihan Lokey Howard & Zukin of Los Angeles, California. Table 1 shows the average and median control premiums paid between 1980 and 1997 as shown in the *Mergerstat Review Study.*[21]

Table 1. Percent Premium Paid Over Market Price

Year of Buyout	Number of Transactions	Average Premium Paid over Market	Median Premium Paid over Market
1980	169	49.9%	44.6%
1981	166	48.0%	41.9%
1982	176	47.4%	43.5%
1983	168	37.7%	34.0%
1984	199	37.9%	34.4%
1985	331	37.1%	27.7%
1986	333	38.2%	29.9%
1987	237	38.3%	30.8%
1988	410	41.9%	30.9%
1989	303	41.0%	29.0%
1990	175	42.0%	32.0%
1991	137	35.1%	29.4%
1992	142	41.0%	34.7%
1993	173	38.7%	33.0%
1994	260	41.9%	35.0%
1995	324	44.7%	29.2%
1996	381	36.6%	27.3%
1997	487	35.7%	27.5%

Minority Discount

A minority interest in a closely held corporation is generally held to be worth less than its proportionate share of the value of all the outstanding shares. This is because minority shareholders generally cannot effect control of the company. The magnitude of a minority discount depends on the shareholder's inability to exercise any or all of a variety of rights typically associated with control, as discussed previously.

The *Mergerstat Review* study provides the average and median control premiums. From this, an implied minority discount can be determined by using the median control premiums paid as a basis (table 2).[22]

Marketability Discount

In contrast to shares of stock in public companies that have an active market, ownership interests in closely held companies are typically not readily marketable. Consequently, it is often appropriate to apply a discount to the

Table 2. Implied Minority Interest Discount

Year of Buyout	Number of Transactions	Implied Minority Interest Discount
1980	169	30.8%
1981	166	29.5%
1982	176	30.3%
1983	168	25.4%
1984	199	25.6%
1985	331	21.7%
1986	333	23.0%
1987	237	23.5%
1988	410	23.6%
1989	303	22.5%
1990	175	24.2%
1991	137	22.7%
1992	142	25.8%
1993	173	24.8%
1994	260	25.9%
1995	324	22.6%
1996	381	21.5%
1997	487	21.6%

value of the closely held shares to reflect the reduction in value attributed to the lack of marketability.

This position is supported by IRS Revenue Ruling 77-287, which addresses the reduced value inherent in unregistered shares of a corporation relative to otherwise identical registered shares in the same corporation.[23]

Rather than selecting an arbitrary discount to quantify lack of marketability, the experienced appraiser derives a discount by reference to a number of factors, including prevailing discounts on restricted stocks and the cost of creating a public market in the stock. A greater or lesser discount is permitted on the basis of the impact of factors such as:

- Restrictions on transfer;
- A buy-sell agreement;
- The prospect of a public offering or sale of the company;
- A put option;
- The market available that may be interested in purchasing shares; and
- Dividends or partnership payouts.

When the shares under valuation are owned by an ESOP, the following factors also are taken into consideration.

Put Option

A put option requires the company to repurchase an ESOP participant's shares of stock upon distribution after termination of employment under a fair valuation formula.[24] Note that the ESOT often has the right to purchase the departing participant's stock, but the put option is with the company, and not the ESOT. In assessing the impact of the put option on marketability, it is necessary to consider factors such as the terms of the put option itself, the corporation's history of honoring its put commitment, and the corporation's ability to honor future put commitments.

It should be noted that the mere existence of a put option does not automatically permit reduction of the discount for lack of marketability. The corporation may have a history of repurchasing the departing participants' stock using a promissory note instead of cash. In that case, the lack of liquidity associated with the promissory note usually warrants a marketability discount.

Repurchase Liability

Repurchase liability is a liability whereby a closely held company is required to offer to repurchase stock distributed to an ESOP participant at the stock's then-current fair market value. This liability is determined by a number of factors, including but not limited to the size of the annual contribution to the ESOT by the company, the change in the fair market value of the stock, the vesting schedule for each participant, the ages of the participants, the number of employees in the plan, employee turnover rates, and the method of distribution of the participant's account balance.

In practice, the circumstances surrounding the participant's departure from the company determine the timing of ESOP distributions. Effective for securities acquired by an ESOT after December 31, 1986, vested benefits usually must begin to be distributed in the plan year following the plan year that a participant either retires, becomes disabled, or passes away. If the participant departs for any other reason, the company may delay the distribution of benefits until the sixth plan year after the plan year in which the employee left the company.[25]

Diversification Requirements

Effective for securities acquired by an ESOT after December 31, 1986, the ESOT must provide eligible employees an opportunity to diversify their plan holdings by either (1) distributing cash or stock to the employee within 90 days of the period in which the diversification election may be made, (2) offering the employee at least three investment options other than employer stock, or (3) permitting the transfer of funds to another retirement plan that provides for diversified investment options. Participants in the ESOT who have reached age 55 and completed ten years of participation in the ESOP have the right to request that up to 25% of their account balance be diversified. Up to 50% of their account balance can be diversified if participants have reached age 60 and participated in the ESOP for ten years.[26]

Common Valuation Errors

A valuation might yield indefensible results for a number of reasons. As cited by the IRS in instructional material used to train their audit personnel,[27] some errors that often occur are as follows:

- Failing to obtain adequate background information on the company, the industry, and the economic environment in which the company operates;
- Valuing the company solely on the basis of its financial statements;
- Using financial statements for only one or two years instead of a five-year or more period, which would be more representative of a normal business cycle;
- Failing to consider the company's working capital position;
- Ignoring the existence of intangible assets or other off-balance sheet value;
- Failing to adjust income statements to arrive at true earning capacity;
- Basing a valuation on a single method without considering other methods;
- Using incorrect methods given the facts and circumstances;
- Disregarding prior arm's length sales of the company's stock;
- Failure to consider trading prices of public companies in the same or a similar business;
- Capitalizing an earnings base that arbitrarily ignores loss years;
- Failure to apply a minority interest discount or control premium when appropriate; and
- Incorrect application of a discount for lack of marketability in relation to the terms of the "put" provision.

Considering the critical role of valuation in ESOP transactions, it goes without saying that the appraiser must make every effort to avoid errors in theory or methodology that would invalidate the conclusion of value.

Federal Challenges to ESOP Valuations

Having discussed the factors to be considered in the valuation process, the various approaches and methods available to the appraiser, and the application of discounts and premiums, let us take a look at the more common situations giving rise to challenges by the IRS and DOL to ESOP valuations:

- Do-it-yourself valuations in which the corporation or one of its employees determines the value of the corporate stock;
- Use of the corporation's regular accounting firm, which often lacks the necessary independence;
- Having the valuation done by a person or firm not thoroughly experienced in ESOP valuations;
- Use of unconventional valuation methods that are not acceptable to IRS and DOL;
- Failure to adequately document the valuation analysis; and
- Basing an ESOP transaction on a valuation that is out of date at the time of the transaction.

Regulatory Issues

Two of the most important issues surrounding the valuation of a company for either implementation or maintenance of an ESOP are adequate consideration and the qualifications of the valuation firm.

Adequate Consideration

By law, an ESOT cannot pay more than adequate consideration for the employer stock it purchases.[28] The proposed DOL regulations establish a two-part test for determining what is adequate consideration: (1) the consideration must reflect fair market value, and (2) the valuation must be made in good faith.

Appraiser Qualifications

In determining who is qualified to perform the valuation, ESOP trustees or other fiduciaries are faced with searching through various sections of the Internal Revenue Code, the Employee Retirement Income Security Act of 1974 (ERISA), the proposed Department of Labor Regulations, and the proposed Internal Revenue Service ESOP Examination Guidelines.

Basically, that search would reveal that a qualified appraiser is one who (1) holds himself or herself out to the public as an appraiser or performs appraisals on a regular basis and is qualified to make appraisals of the type of property being appraised; and (2) is independent with respect to the corporation and the other parties to the ESOP transaction other than the ESOP.

In terms of qualifications, the amount of credibility the IRS or DOL attaches to the conclusion of fair market value is greatly influenced by their assessment of the expertise demonstrated by the individual or firm doing the appraisal.[29] The same can be said for the independence of the appraiser. To satisfy the independence criteria, the valuation cannot be done by:[30]

- The taxpayer that maintains the ESOP;
- A party to the transaction in which the ESOP acquired property;
- An employee of the taxpayer that maintains the ESOP; or
- An individual or firm regularly used by the taxpayer maintaining the ESOP who does not perform a majority of his or her appraisals for entities other than the taxpayer maintaining the ESOP.

Conclusion

At the risk of belaboring the point, it bears repeating that business valuation is a complex and time-consuming process. To reach a sound conclusion, the appraiser's analysis must include all pertinent factors that have a bearing on value.

The goal of the appraisal process is to develop a supportable conclusion of value—a conclusion that represents economic reality; that can withstand challenges from the Internal Revenue Service, the Department of Labor, or other entities; and that meets the accepted definition of fair market value.

Notes

1. Revenue Ruling 59-60.
2. U.S. Department of Labor, Proposed Regulation Relating to the Definition of Adequate Consideration, 29 C.F.R. Part 2510 (DOL Proposed Regulation).
3. Revenue Ruling 59-60, § 2.02.
4. The purpose of Revenue Ruling 59-60 is to outline and review in general the approach, methods, and factors to be considered in valuing shares of the capital stock of closely held corporations for estate tax and gift tax purposes. The methods discussed in the ruling apply likewise to the valuation of corporate stocks on which market quotations are either unavailable or are of such scarcity that they do not reflect the fair market value.
5. Revenue Ruling 59-60, § 4.01.
6. Revenue Ruling 59-60, § 5.

7. DOL Proposed Regulation.
8. Ibid.
9. Revenue Ruling 59-60, § 4.02(c).
10. Revenue Ruling 59-60, § 4.02(d).
11. Revenue Ruling 59-60, § 4.02(e).
12. Ibid.
13. A.R.M. 34 indicates that for businesses put out of existence by the prohibition law, the return on tangible assets is 10%, and the percentage for capitalization of the return upon intangibles is 20%. However, it also states that the valuation of goodwill for businesses that consist of the manufacture or sale of standard articles of everyday necessity not subject to violent fluctuations where the hazard is not so great, the return on tangible assets might be reduced to 8% or 9%, and the percentage for capitalization of the return upon intangibles might be reduced to 15%.
14. Revenue Ruling 59-60, § 3.03.
15. *Tallichet v. Commissioner* (33 T.C.M.1133, 1974); *Estate of Victor P. Clarke* (35 T.C.M. 1482, 1976).
16. Ibbotson Associates, *Stocks, Bonds, Bills, and Inflation: 1998 Yearbook,* Chicago, 1998.
17. Ibid.
18. Internal Revenue Code ("Code") § 404(a)(9)(A)-(B). It should be noted that a deduction for ESOP contributions applied to the principal repayment of an ESOP loan may be taken up to 25% of the total compensation of all employees under the ESOP.
19. Revenue Ruling 59-60, § 4.02(g).
20. Shannon P. Pratt, *Valuing a Business: The Analysis and Appraisal of Closely Held Companies,* 3nd ed. (Homewood, Ill.:-Irwin 1996), 44-45.
21. *Mergerstat Review 1997* (Los Angeles, CA: Houlihan Lokey Howard & Zukin, 1998).
22. Jay E. Fishman, Shannon P. Pratt, J. Clifford Griffith, and D. Keith Wilson, *Guide To Business Valuations,* 8th ed. (Fort Worth: Practitioners Publishing Company, 1998), 8–11.
23. Revenue Ruling 77-287. The purpose of this ruling is to provide information and guidance for the valuation of securities that cannot be immediately resold because they are restricted from resale pursuant to Federal securities laws.
24. Code § 409(h)(1)(B).
25. Code § 409(o)(A).
26. Code § 401(a)(28)(B).
27. *Internal Revenue Service Valuation Guide for Income, Estate and Gift Taxes: Valuation Training for Appeals Officers* (Chicago: Commerce Clearing House, 1994).
28. DOL Proposed Regulation.
29. *Donovan v. Cunningham,* 716 F.2d 1455 (5th Cir. 1983).
30. DOL Proposed Regulation.

2

Valuation Issues in Multi-Investor ESOP LBOs

Susan L. Mueller
Judith C. Gehr

The U.S. Department of Labor (DOL) has advanced the position that common stock should be allocated in the same percentage as each investor's dollar contribution to the purchase price and that the nonrecourse debt contributed by the ESOP should be treated as cash for purposes of determining each party's contribution. The DOL hoped that the court would rule on this "dollar-for-dollar" allocation proposal in Reich v. Valley National Bank of Arizona (the Kroy case). This article discusses why applying the DOL's position literally would essentially eliminate non-ESOP participation in LBOs. It also shows how the DOL's position can be adjusted to consider timing and risk of cash flows to the various investors to assure that the ESOP receives adequate consideration for its investment and that the non-ESOP investors receive returns in line with market rates on investments similar in risk. In addition, the article addresses how the level of value (control or minority interest) affects adequate consideration.

By its nature, a company buyout uses leverage and requires the cooperative participation of various investor groups, each with its own agenda. These investor groups may include company management, outside equity investors, lenders, and, for the purposes of this article, an employee stock ownership plan (ESOP).

In transactions not involving ESOPs, each party is free to attempt to maximize its returns through negotiation with the other parties to the transaction. When an ESOP participates in the transaction, the Employee Retirement Income Security Act (ERISA) and the Internal Revenue Code impose certain constraints on the structuring process. For example, the ESOP must pay no more than adequate consideration for the stock it purchases. All parties must make certain the ESOP is not a "loser," or the transaction will not withstand regulatory scrutiny.

Recent U.S. Department of Labor (DOL) letters,[1] litigation,[2] and the lack of a final version of the proposed regulation[3] relating to adequate consideration from the DOL have impeded multi-investor ESOP leveraged buyouts (LBOs). Standards of appraisal practice are dynamic and have been evolving for many years. With the filing of *Reich v. Valley National Bank of Arizona* (the "Kroy case"), the appraisal industry felt increased urgency to formalize practice standards.[4]

Susan L. Mueller, CFP, CFA, is a principal in The Phoenix Group Inc., a business appraisal firm in Cincinnati, Ohio. She has practiced in the field of valuation, including ESOP appraisals, since 1988. Judith Gehr, MBA, is a Chartered Financial Analyst.

The Basic Issue

In the Kroy case, the DOL alleged that Valley National Bank, trustee of the Kroy Inc. ESOP, breached its fiduciary duties under ERISA. Specifically, the DOL alleged that failure of the bank to make a good-faith determination of the fair market value of the Kroy stock caused the ESOP to receive less than adequate consideration for its investment.

The DOL based part of its argument on the ESOP's having paid a share of the purchase price in excess of its share of post-transaction common stock ownership. In connection with this allegation, the DOL had expected the court to rule on its "dollar-for-dollar" position. The court found that the trustee had violated its fiduciary duty by not conducting an independent investigation in good faith. The court ruled that the ESOP had, indeed, not received adequate consideration for its investment, but based its findings on the use of an *investment value* standard rather than a *fair market value* standard as prescribed in ERISA. In addition, the ESOP price included a premium for control, and the fiduciary had made no attempt to determine if the ESOP would have "control in fact." The court declined to rule on the "dollar-for-dollar" position.

In August 1993, the court rendered a decision in the Kroy case. Before this, DOL Solicitor Robert Davis strongly asserted the DOL's position on equity allocation: "I will state it quite bluntly right now, that if the ESOP is responsible for 90 percent of the purchase price of the company they should get 90 percent of the common stock."[5] Although the DOL anticipated the Kroy case would resolve the dollar-for-dollar equity allocation issue, much as *Dole v. Farnum* was to have settled the issue of post-transaction debt, it did not.[6] The decision did provide a set of points to guide ESOP fiduciaries in their decisions and sparked a strong response in the appraisal industry.

This article states the position commonly held in the appraisal industry that the DOL's dollar-for-dollar position is untenable in a capital market context.[7] However, when the dollar-for-dollar method is adjusted for timing and risk, it creates an equity allocation among the ESOP LBO investors that meets the DOL's definition of adequate consideration and is fair from a financial point of view to the ESOP participants and beneficiaries and others in the transaction. This article also addresses how the application of adequate consideration is affected by whether fair market value (FMV) is found on a control basis or on a minority basis.

Equity Allocation in an ESOP LBO

In most equity buyout transactions involving multiple classes of investors, each class attempts to gain an advantage. Advantages are generally achieved by a preferential purchase price and rate of return, or by ownership attributes. All investors negotiate an infinite variety of alternatives until an agreement is reached that is fair to all parties, i.e., that assures they will earn a rate of return adequate to compensate them for the risk inherent in their investment.

Parties to a leveraged ESOP transaction include, at a minimum, the ESOP, the company, and the lender. In addition, leveraged ESOP transactions often include company management and outside equity investors (e.g., venture capitalists).

Adequate Consideration

The statutory definition of "adequate consideration," the standard imposed on ESOP valuations, has two major components: "in the case of an asset other than a security for which there is a generally recognized market, [adequate consideration is] the fair market value[8] of the asset as determined in good faith[9] by the trustee or named fiduciary pursuant to the terms of the plan and in accordance with regulations promulgated by the Secretary of Labor."[10] Compliance with both the fair market value and the good faith requirements ensures that the ESOP has been established and will operate for the exclusive benefit of the participants.

The non-ESOP investors are not bound by the FMV standard. In most cases they will consider unique facts and circumstances such as special synergies or talents of the buyer. The resulting valuation uses investment value,[11] not FMV. Investment value is usually higher than FMV. Nevertheless, all investors must be certain that the ESOP pays no more than adequate consideration.

The Fairness Standard

The adequate consideration standard places constraints on advantages that the non-ESOP parties can gain vis-à-vis the ESOP. The transaction must be fair to the ESOP from a financial perspective. First of all, the ESOP must not pay more than FMV for its investment. Additionally, the ESOP's investment must be "fair" relative to the other parties to the transaction. In other words, even if the ESOP pays no more than FMV, the deal is unfair if the ESOP pays relatively more than the non-ESOP participants, taking into account each party's contribution to the transaction, level of risk, and expected return.

Contributions of Investors The ESOP brings many advantages to a multi-investor transaction. Principal payments on ESOP debt are tax-deductible within certain limits, as are, in C corporations, dividend payments used to reduce the debt. The note must be nonrecourse to the ESOP.

The tax deductibility of debt principal and dividends improves cash flow compared to an LBO without an ESOP, shortening the term needed for debt repayment and saving interest dollars. In some cases, the ESOP participants contribute wage concessions and/or changes to existing benefit plans.

The seller can benefit from the tax-deferral provisions of Section 1042, assuming that the ESOP holds at least 30% of the equity and the company is a closely held C corporation; in this case, the selling price may be lower than if the ESOP did not participate. The Section 1042 tax deferral may also be available to the private non-ESOP equity investors as an exit vehicle.

Management investors in an ESOP LBO bring strategic and operational expertise that is vital in maintaining a competitive and profitable entity. Management generally invests a percentage of the necessary cash.

Outside equity investors contribute equity capital. This equity provides a cushion that makes the deal more attractive for lenders to participate in and may lead to lower interest rates.

Lenders contribute debt capital, usually collateralized by the company, that enables the transaction to be consummated. Without the debt, the ESOP would be unable to participate, and the ESOP-related advantages would be lost.

The company contributes its collateral guarantee to the lender. The ESOP's equity investment in the sponsoring company requires the company to service the debt and repurchase ESOP shares from participants. The company's viability as a long-term investment affects the final determination of FMV.

Risk Incurred by Investors All investors incur risk associated with the performance of the highly leveraged company following the consummation of the deal. The level of risk incurred by each party depends, in part, on the attributes of the transaction-related documents (loan covenants and shareholder agreements) that define the priority of cash flows, priority in liquidation, voting rights, put options, buy/sell restrictions, and other features.

Many of these factors are dictated by ESOP regulators. The company must guarantee the ESOP debt, and the loan must be without recourse against the ESOP. The stock (if it is not publicly traded) must be common stock with voting and dividend rights at least equal to the classes of common stock having the greatest voting power and dividend rights, or preferred stock that is convertible into such common stock.

Principal and interest payments on the ESOP debt cannot be eliminated without endangering the company's going-concern status; each principal payment increases the value of the ESOP's equity position. Often, loan covenants stipulate that no dividends can be paid to the non-ESOP investors until the ESOP debt is fully repaid.

If the company stock held by the ESOP is not readily tradable, the employer must provide a put option. Upon retirement or termination, the ESOP participant can "put" the stock to the company at the most recent appraised value. The terms and conditions of the redemption are spelled out in the plan documents. This put option offers ESOP participants marketability, provided the company has the resources to honor the put, but furnishes no protection against inability to redeem the put. Non-ESOP equity investors can obtain similar marketability by incorporating an agreement as to time of sale or marketability into their documents. Venture capitalists generally will not participate unless they have an exit route by way of an initial public offering (IPO), a put option, or a buy/sell agreement guaranteeing marketability.

While management's cash investment often comprises a relatively small portion of the overall transaction, it is generally significant relative to the managers' personal resources. Tying management returns to performance targets via incentive stock helps ensure that management's full energies will be devoted to enhancing shareholder value.

Outside equity investors bear the highest risk because they receive residual cash flows. Lenders usually assume the least amount of risk because they have first claim on cash flows.

Return Requirements of Investors Returns required by the investors in a multi-investor LBO are based on returns concurrently available in the capital markets on investments comparable in risk. Providers of capital require returns that will compensate them for the time value of their money plus the risk inherent in the specific investment. They will not invest unless they can expect to earn the required rate of return. Lenders demand the lowest return because their investment is least risky, whereas outside equity investors demand the highest return.

The DOL's "Dollar-for-Dollar" Allocation Position

Since the early 1980s, the DOL has contended that an ESOP does not pay no more than adequate consideration in multi-investor situations involving ESOPs unless a "dollar-for-dollar" rule is applied. The DOL's position is that if the ESOP invests 80% of the total dollars invested, the ESOP should receive 80% of the common shares after conversion of all subordinate classes of stock. This position has been reiterated on numerous occasions, including orally[12] and through DOL advisory opinions,[13] but has never been decided by a court.

The DOL's position is at odds with the reality of capital markets. It is based on the assumption that the ESOP's contribution of debt is the equivalent of a cash contribution. This assumption ignores the effect the debt has on the post-deal equity value. Because the note is nonrecourse to the ESOP, the company must guarantee the debt. If all investors contributed cash, the post-deal value would equal the pre-deal value. Because the ESOP contributes nonrecourse debt, upon completion of the transaction the pre-deal value is immediately reduced by the market value of the debt obligation. The impact of the ESOP debt is the same as the effect of financing real estate with debt—the value of the equity is the total investment value less the amount of the debt.

The following example demonstrates the flaw in the DOL's position. Assume XYZ Company is purchased by an ESOP and an outside investor group for $100 million. The ESOP contributes $80 million in the form of a nonrecourse note; the outside investors contribute $20 million in cash. Assume the present value of the ESOP tax savings (deductibility of principal) and interest savings (reduced borrowing rate) is $20 million. The post-deal value of the equity is $40 million ($100 million + $20 million – $80 million). If the ESOP receives 80% of the value, it means the outside investors receive an investment worth $8 million for their contribution of $20 million cash—an immediate capital loss of $12 million. Clearly, no rational investor would enter into such a transaction.[14] This method ignores the burden of the nonrecourse debt and the differences in risk/return profile of the investor classes.

Strictly applying the dollar-for-dollar standard, unadjusted for timing and risk, as advocated by the DOL would eliminate non-ESOP equity participation in LBOs. This is contrary to the intent of Congress (as stated in ERISA) of encouraging such transactions to foster employee ownership. In addition, it appears to be contrary to the concept of adequate consideration. Fair market value is based on market forces, and the good faith requirement charges the ESOP trustee with determining value based on the facts and circumstances of the specific case.

Alternative Allocation Methods[15]

Several allocation methods have been proposed by the DOL and various practitioners. Some allocation methods are based on each party's contribution to the transaction without considering differences in timing and risk of future cash flows. An alternative method allocates equity based on equating the present value of future cash flows discounted at the appropriate risk-adjusted rate of return, with the initial contribution of each party.

Methods Not Adjusted for Timing and Risk

Methods not adjusted for timing and risk are discussed below and summarized in table 1. The first two, Face Value and Discounted ESOP Note, do not differentiate between the debt contribution of the ESOP and the cash contribution of other investors and are shown to be unfair to the non-ESOP investors. In the last two methods, Quantification of Benefits and Allocation of Debt, both parties' contributions are put on a cash equivalent basis. All examples assume two parties to the transaction: the ESOP and an outside investor group.

Employee concessions should be considered in determining equity allocation. Concessions may include lower wages for a period of time or the conversion of the assets of an existing pension plan into an ESOP. For simplicity, our examples assume that there are no such concessions.

Face Value This method is similar to the DOL's dollar-for-dollar position. The ESOP note is treated as cash, and the ESOP receives a pro-rata share of the equity based on the pre-deal equity value. If company XYZ is purchased for $100 million and the ESOP contributes a nonrecourse note with a face value of $80 million, the ESOP receives 80% of the equity.

Discounted ESOP Note This method is similar to the face value method, except that the market value of the ESOP note is used rather than the face value. The market value is usually lower than the face value because of the preferred borrowing rate.

To illustrate, assume XYZ Company is purchased for $100 million, with the ESOP contributing a nonrecourse note with a face value of $80 million and a fair market value of $60 million. The non-ESOP investors contribute $20 million in cash. The fair market value of total capital is $80 million, and the ESOP's share is 75%. As table 1 shows, this method results in outside investors paying $20 million for an investment worth $10 million. This method, like the Face Value method, is flawed by its lack of realism. Rational non-ESOP equity investors will not participate in such a transaction.

Table 1. Allocation Methods Not Adjusted for Timing and Risk ($ in millions)

Purchase Price (FMV Pre-Deal)	$100
ESOP Note: Face Value	$ 80
Outside Cash	$ 20
ESOP Benefits (tax shield + interest rate)	$ 20
ESOP Note: Market Value (Face - Benefits)	$ 60
Debt/Equity Ratio Post-Deal (Market Value)	1.5
Post-Deal Value:	
Purchase Price	$100
Plus ESOP Benefits	20
Less ESOP Debt	(80)
Value	$ 40

	ESOP			Outside Investor Group		
Allocation Method:	Share of Deal	Equity Value	Gain (Loss)	Share of Deal	Equity Value	Gain (Loss)
Face Value	80%	$32	$12	20%	$ 8	$(12)
Discounted ESOP Note	75%	$30	$10	25%	$10	$(10)
Quantify ESOP Benefits	50%	$20	$ 0	50%	$20	$ 0
Allocation of Debt	50%	$20	$ 0	50%	$20	$ 0

Quantification of Benefits This method allocates equity based on the cash equivalent contributions of each party. The ESOP often contributes tax and interest rate benefits, and the outside equity investors contribute cash. In the above example, the present value of the ESOP benefits is $20 million, and the outside investors contribute $20 million in cash. The equity would be allocated equally between the ESOP and the outside investors.

Table 1 shows that this allocation method is equitable to both the ESOP and the outside equity investors. Each party receives an investment with a dollar value commensurate with its cash equivalent contribution.

Allocation of Debt This allocation method is based on the percentage of total capital supported by the equity contribution of each party. The example in table 1 shows a post-deal debt to equity ratio of 1.5 to 1 ($60 million market value of debt, $40 million market value of equity). Because the outside investors contribute $20 million in cash, their equity will support $30 million in debt, or $50 million in total capital. Their share of the $100 million purchase price is 50%. As table 1 illustrates, this allocation method is fair to all investors and is in line with economic reality.

Adjusted for Timing and Risk

The Allocation of Future Cash Flows method, illustrated in table 2, takes into account the differences in risk and required return between the equity

Table 2. Allocation of Future Cash Flows ($ in millions)

Purchase Price	$100	
Growth Rate	15%	
Terminal Value (Selling Price)	$266	
ESOP Note: Face Value	$ 80	
ESOP Note: Term (Years)	7	
Note Principal and Interest Payments	$ 15	
	ESOP	**Outside Group**
Allocation of Terminal Value	50%	50%
Sale Proceeds	$133	$133
Annual Cash Flows:		
Initial Outlay	$(80)	$(20)
Year 1	$ 15	$ 0
Year 2	$ 15	$ 0
Year 3	$ 15	$ 0
Year 4	$ 15	$ 0
Year 5	$ 15	$ 0
Year 6	$ 15	$ 0
Year 7	$148	$133
Internal Rate of Return	24%	31%

held by the ESOP and the equity held by the outside investors, as well as the differences in timing of cash receipts by each party. Cash receipts consist of dividends and capital appreciation.

In our example, during the term of the ESOP loan, all cash flows go to the ESOP for repaying principal and interest on the note. The outside investors are proscribed by loan covenants from receiving any cash distributions until the note has been repaid. After the note has been repaid, the company can be sold and the proceeds divided between the shareholders.

Assume the ESOP contributed 80% of the purchase price (based on the face value of the note), but received 100% of the cash flows over the term of the note. It follows that the outside equity investors are entitled to more than 20% of the final distribution. Exactly what percentage that should be depends on the expected capital appreciation and the rate of return each party requires to participate in the deal. The key to achieving the proper allocation is to determine the appropriate rate of return for each participant based on alternative capital market investments of similar risk.

Table 2 shows the interim and terminal cash flows for XYZ Company, assuming a seven-year note at a rate of 8% per annum. For the first seven years, all cash flows go to the ESOP for debt service. The company value grows at a compound annual rate of 15%, and equals $266 million at the end of the seventh year. An allocation of 50% of the terminal value to the ESOP and 50% to the outside investors provides the ESOP with a return of about 24% and the outside investors with a return of about 31%. If the returns are equivalent to market returns on investments of comparable risk, both will invest in the transaction and both will pay fair market value.

This allocation method bridges the gap between economic reality and the DOL's untenable position on dollar-for-dollar equity allocation. This method conforms to the DOL dollar-for-dollar method if the cash flows are adjusted for timing and risk. By definition, the dollars contributed equal the present value of future cash flows discounted at the required rate of return. In other words, if investors contribute $1 in equity they expect to receive a percentage of the proceeds with a fair value of $1. Fair value is determined by discounting future cash receipts at the investor's required rate of return. If all parties receive their required returns, the allocation of total cash flows must equal the initial proportions contributed by each party. As long as both parties earn the required rate of return, the allocation is in line with the original contribution.

Value Basis—Control or Minority

The degree of control purchased by the ESOP is integral to the determination of FMV. An ESOP trustee must determine if the ESOP will have a controlling interest or a minority interest. To the extent the ESOP will have control, a premium may be appropriate. The premium a third party would be willing to pay for control is not indicative of what the ESOP should pay unless the ESOP can exercise exactly the same degree of control as the third-party investor.

A controlling interest is usually worth more than a minority interest in the same class of stock in a company. This is because ownership of a controlling interest confers certain prerogatives: the right to acquire or liquidate assets, appoint directors, determine salaries and benefits, set dividend policy, set operating and strategic priorities, and sell or recapitalize the company.

The value of a controlling interest depends upon the ability to exercise the prerogatives of control, not on the absolute size of the block. An ownership interest of more than 50% does not automatically confer control. In some states, a supermajority is required for certain activities such as change in ownership, while a simple majority suffices for other activities. Control is not an all-or-nothing position; there are varying degrees of control.

A control premium is "the additional value inherent in the control interest, as contrasted to a minority interest, that reflects its power of control."[16] By definition, the minority interest discount is the reverse of the control premium.

James A. Abate[17] has suggested that the control premium can be quantified as the difference in value between the business operated as is and operated as the controlling party would operate it.[18] Ironically, this implies that a poorly run business will get a high control premium and a well run business will get a low control premium. For the financial buyer, defined here as one who pays fair market value, the better a company is run, the fewer the opportunities for improvement and the lower the control premium. In the extreme, the control premium would be zero; that is, cash flows to all shareholders would already have been maximized.

The appropriate control premium, which can vary with time and circumstances, can also be quantified by analyzing data observed in the public markets. By comparing prices paid for acquisitions of entire companies with the trading prices of companies on a minority interest basis, we derive estimates of control premiums.[19] However, one must beware of direct extrapolation, because any premium paid is dependent on the specific facts and circumstances. A buyer in the public market is generally a strategic buyer. That is, the premium is based on expected synergies or investment value. This is not an appropriate benchmark for a control premium for an ESOP, which must base its price on FMV.

Types of Control

The DOL's proposed regulations on adequate consideration state that an ESOP may pay a control premium only if the plan obtains control "both in form and in substance," and that the premium must be consistent with what a hypothetical third party would pay. Control in form is defined by percentage ownership of the shares outstanding. Control in substance must be viewed in the context of the ESOP plan document; the corporate articles of incorporation, bylaws, and governance structure; and the facts and circumstances unique to the transaction.

ESOPs in closely held companies are required by law to pass through voting rights on shares allocated to the plan participants in matters concerning sale of the company's assets, merger, recapitalization, etc. The DOL has taken the position that unallocated shares must be voted by the trustee. Passing through voting rights is not sufficient to establish control if the plan fiduciaries have the power to resell the ESOP shares to a third party without the approval of the plan participants. If members of corporate management serve as plan fiduciaries, it raises the suspicion that the ESOP may not have control in fact. Control that will be dissipated within a short period of time after the transaction does not warrant a premium. Similarly, an agreement with the employer to sell shares to the ESOP in increments that will cumulate in a controlling interest must be binding, and control must pass to the ESOP within a reasonable period of time.

Both the courts and the DOL's proposed regulations recognize that an ESOP may hold control in theory. They have defined control in form—voting control. Neither the courts nor the DOL have explained how an ESOP can hold control in fact. This lack of clear guidance places the onus on the appraiser and the trustee to document in the written report the basis for using a control premium. Decisions to value stock on a control basis or a minority basis create controversy among appraisers. The facts and circumstances of each individual transaction as well as prevailing law affect this decision.

Empirical evidence is lacking to support the claim that ESOP participants can hold and exercise control "in fact." For example, in the American Avents case, the vote was passed through to the participants on an offer to sell the company. The participants overwhelmingly voted no; the independent trustee voted yes. The court upheld the decision of the trustee. The ESOP participants' prerogative of control—the vote—was set aside.[20]

Unlike the DOL, the Internal Revenue Service (IRS) does not distinguish between numerical control and actual control.[21] The IRS considers ownership of more than 50% of the stock by an ESOP to be prima facie evidence of "control." This places the IRS's point of view in direct conflict with the DOL's point of view.

Conclusion

Equity allocation in ESOP LBOs will continue to be the focus of intense DOL scrutiny and, perhaps, litigation and adverse advisory opinions. It is likely that the DOL will again test its dollar-for-dollar equity allocation position in court. The authors are optimistic, based on the findings in the Kroy case, that ESOP LBOs valued at the present time that follow appraisal industry standards and that have equity allocated on sound financial and capital market principles will not be set aside by the courts. However, all investors in an ESOP LBO transaction must, through their actions, meet or exceed both the letter and spirit of the law when arriving at a final price and equity allocation that is fair to all parties.

The applicability of control premiums to the ESOP's ownership position remains controversial within the appraisal industry. The DOL's proposed regulation on adequate consideration explicitly provides for the application of a control premium to the extent that a hypothetical (per the definition of FMV) third party would be willing to pay it, provided the ESOP has control "in form" and "in fact." Great care must be taken in applying control premiums extrapolated from the capital markets to ESOPs. In all ESOP LBOs, as in all valuations, particular attention must be paid to evidentiary facts and circumstances.

Notes

1. *Blue Bell, Inc.* (Labor Department Letter Closing Case of November 26, 1984), 12 BNA Pension Reporter 52 (1985); *Raymond International, Inc.* (Labor Department Opinion Letter of September 12, 1983), 11 BNA Pension Reporter 1494 (1984); *Scott & Fetzer,* 12 BNA Pension Reporter 1182 (1985).

2. *Reich v. Valley National Bank of Arizona,* 837 F. Supp. 1259 (S.D.N.Y. 1993); *Dole v. Farnum,* No. 90-0371 (D.C.R.I.; case voluntarily dismissed).

3. Proposed Regulation Relating to the Definition of Adequate Consideration, 29 CFR Part 2510.

4. See the following: Standards Board of the Appraisal Foundation. *Uniform Standards of Professional Appraisal Practice,* 1994 ed. (The Appraisal Foundation, 1994); *Principles of Appraisal Practice and Code of Ethics,* rev. ed. (Washington, D.C.: The American Society of Appraisers, 1994); *Business Appraisal Standards,* pub. no. P-311a (Institute of Business Appraisers, Inc., 1993); Michael A. Gregory, "Why Appraisers Should Be Concerned With Standards," *Business Valuation Review* 13, no. 1 (March 1994), 33-35.

5. *Reich v. Valley National Bank of Arizona,* 837 F. Supp. at 1299.

6. See Gregory K. Brown, Marilyn H. Marchetti, and John E. (Jack) Curtis, *The Kroy Decision: A Reality Check for ERISA Fiduciaries,* this journal 6, no. 2 (spring 1994): 51-52. The present authors disagree with the opinion expressed in David R. Johanson, ed., *1993 Legislative, Regulatory and Case Law Developments: A Year In Review* (Washington, D.C.: The ESOP Association, 1994), 10, that the Kroy case did settle the issue.

7. Richard S. Braun, "ESOP Valuations," Chapter 8 in James H. Zukin, *Financial Valuation: Businesses and Business Interests* (New York: Maxwell MacMillan, 1990), 8-10; O. Kit Lokey, "Adequate Consideration Requirements," *The 1987 ESOP Association Convention* (Washington, D.C.: The ESOP Association, [1987]), 356-57; Richard May, "The Use of Employee Stock Ownership Plans in Conjunc-

tion with Leveraged Buyouts Involving Multiple Investors," *The 1987 ESOP Association Convention* (Washington, D.C.: The ESOP Association, [1987]), 364-65, 368; Louis A. Paone, "The Use of ESOPs in Leveraged Buyout Transactions," *The 1989 ESOP Association Convention* (Washington, D.C.: The ESOP Association, [1989]), 188; Gregory P. Range, "Advanced Valuation Issues in ESOP Leveraged Buyouts," Chapter 10 in Robert W. Smiley Jr. and Ronald J. Gilbert, *Employee Stock Ownership Plans* (New York: Maxwell Macmillan/Rosenfield Launer, 1989), 10-21; Joseph S. Schuchert, "Adequate Consideration Determination in Leveraged ESOP Transactions," *The 1986 ESOP Association Convention* (Washington, D.C.: The ESOP Association, [1986]), 189, 203; James H. Zukin, "An Approach to Equity Allocation," *The 1987 ESOP Association Convention* (Washington, D.C.: The ESOP Association, [1987]), 382.

8. Fair market value (FMV) is the basic standard that defines a company's value for all transaction participants in an ESOP LBO. Fair market value, as defined by Congress in ERISA, means "the price at which an asset would change hands between a willing buyer and a willing seller when the former is not under any compulsion to buy and the latter is not under any compulsion to sell, and both parties are able, as well as willing, to trade and are well informed about the asset and the market for such asset." This is the definition adopted by the DOL in its proposed regulation relating to the definition of adequate consideration. Both definitions are based on IRS Revenue Ruling 59-60, which established the basis for valuation of closely held securities for gift and estate tax purposes and was later amended and expanded to apply to other tax purposes. In line with frequent court decisions, Revenue Ruling 59-60 specifies that the buyer is a hypothetical buyer and the seller is a hypothetical seller. The DOL is proposing two additions to the fair market value standard for purposes of Section 3(18)(B) of ERISA and Section 8477(a)(2)(B) of the Federal Employees' Retirement System Act of 1986 (FERSA): namely, that fair market value (1) must be determined as of the date of the transaction and (2) must be presented in written documentation meeting certain requirements (a statement of the purpose of the valuation, a statement of the relative weight accorded different valuation methodologies employed, and a statement of the effective date of the valuation).

9. Good faith is an objective standard of conduct. To fulfill the good faith requirement, a trustee must base the determination of fair market value on "prudent investigation of the circumstances prevailing at the time of the valuation, and the application of sound business principles of evaluation." In addition, the fiduciary must be independent of all parties to the transaction or rely on an independent appraiser. The good faith standard allows the ESOP fiduciary to rely on an outside appraiser to determine fair market value. However, the fiduciary must confirm the appraised value and ensure that the underlying assumptions are consistent with the industry outlook and with management's expectations. Courts have held fiduciaries responsible for inadequate diligence and lack of prudence in accepting the appraiser's value, maintaining that "a pure heart and an empty head are not enough." *Donovan v. Cunningham*, 716 F.2d 1455, 1467 (5th Cir. 1983).

10. Proposed Regulation on Adequate Consideration, 29 CFR § 2510.3-18 (b)(1)(i)(A).

11. Investment value may be higher than fair market value since its basic premise includes a specific buyer that may be willing to pay more for the acquisition based on synergistic elements unknown to the seller. There may be several valid reasons for investment value to differ from fair market value. A particular owner or prospective owner's estimates of future earning power, perception of the degree of

risk, tax status, or synergies with other operations owned or controlled may differ considerably from the consensus viewpoint of a hypothetical buyer.

12. *Reich v. Valley National Bank of Arizona; Dole v. Farnum.*

13. *Blue Bell, Inc.* (Labor Department Letter Closing Case of November 26, 1984), 12 BNA Pension Reporter 52 (1985); *Raymond International, Inc.* (Labor Department Opinion Letter of September 12, 1983), 11 BNA Pension Reporter 1494 (1984); *Scott & Fetzer,* 12 BNA Pension Reporter 1182 (1985).

14. The interested reader can find additional information on equity allocation methods in the following:

    Braun, Richard S. "ESOP Valuations." Chapter 8 in James H. Zukin, *Financial Valuation: Businesses and Business Interests.* New York: Maxwell MacMillan, 1990.

    Lokey, O. Kit. "Adequate Consideration Requirements." *The 1987 ESOP Association Convention,* 353-358. Washington, D.C.: The ESOP Association, [1987].

    May, Richard. "The Use of Employee Stock Ownership Plans in Conjunction with Leveraged Buyouts Involving Multiple Investors." *The 1987 ESOP Association Convention,* 359-368. Washington, D.C.: The ESOP Association, [1987].

    Paone, Louis A. "The Use of ESOPs in Leveraged Buyout Transactions." *The 1989 ESOP Association Convention,* 183-207. Washington, D.C.: The ESOP Association, [1989].

    Range, Gregory P. "Advanced Valuation Issues in ESOP Leveraged Buyouts." Chapter 10 in Robert W. Smiley Jr. and Ronald J. Gilbert, *Employee Stock Ownership Plans.* New York: Maxwell Macmillan/Rosenfield Launer, 1989.

    Schuchert, Joseph S. "Adequate Consideration Determination in Leveraged ESOP Transactions," *The 1986 ESOP Association Convention,* 179-207. Washington, D.C.: The ESOP Association, [1986].

    Zukin, James H. "An Approach to Equity Allocation." *The 1987 ESOP Association Convention,* 369-395. Washington D.C.: The ESOP Association, [1987].

15. Ibid.

16. Shannon Pratt, *Valuing a Business: The Analysis and Appraisal of Closely Held Companies,* 2nd ed. (Homewood, IL: Dow Jones-Irwin, 1989), 398.

17. James A. Abate, "Discounts and Premiums in the Valuation Process," speech delivered at the IBA National Conference on Appraising Closely Held Businesses, Orlando, Florida, January 1994.

18. Management salaries and "perks" are a common source of incremental earnings and cash flows. The tax-adjusted difference between total compensation for current management and an industry benchmark should be added to earnings. It is important to consider factors such as the company's attractiveness to new management and requirements for unique characteristics that would affect compensation. For example, suppose that XYZ company earns $200,000 after taxes and is valued at $1 million (a capitalization rate of 20%). The owner of XYZ company earns $200,000 per year in salary and benefits. A new manager with comparable experience can be employed for $100,000, which would increase XYZ's after-tax earnings to $260,000. The company would now be worth $1.3 million, and the control premium would be 30%.

19. Sources of this information include data published in *Mergerstat Review, Mergers & Acquisitions, HLHZ Control Premium Study,* and many other publications.

20. *Central Trust Company v. American Avents Corp.*, 11 E.B.C. 1850 (D.C. Ohio 1988). In this case, the court apparently asserted that the voting rights rules of Internal Revenue Code Section 409(e) were applicable to the pass-through of a tender decision to ESOP participants.
21. Andy Fedders, U. S. Internal Revenue Service, speech delivered at the Ohio ESOP Association Meeting, Columbus, Ohio, November 19, 1993.

Bibliography

Brown, Gregory K., John E. Curtis, Jr., and Marilyn H. Marchetti. "The Kroy Decision: A Reality Check for ERISA Fiduciaries." This journal 6, no. 2 (spring 1994): 29-64.

ERISA Advisory Council Ad Hoc Work Group On Employee Stock Ownership Plans. "The Participation of Leveraged Employee Stock Ownership Plans in Multi-Investor Leveraged Buyouts." *The 1988 ESOP Association Convention*, 175-184. Washington, D.C.: The ESOP Association, [1988].

Fishman, Jay E., J. Clifford Griffith, Shannon P. Pratt, and D. Keith Wilson. *Guide to Business Valuations*. 4th ed. Texas: Practitioners Publishing Company, 1994.

Gougis, Chester A., "ESOP Valuation Issues Before, During and After the Transaction." *The 1987 ESOP Association Convention*, 348-351. Washington, D.C.: The ESOP Association, [1987].

Johanson, David R., ed. *1993 Legislative, Regulatory and Case Law Developments: A Year in Review*. Washington, D.C.: The ESOP Association, 1993.

Kaplan, Jared. "Fiduciary and Related Concerns In ESOP Leveraged Buyouts." *The 1993 ESOP Association Convention*, 95-115. Washington, D.C.: The ESOP Association, [1993].

Lokey, O. Kit. "Adequate Consideration Requirements." *The 1987 ESOP Association Convention*, 353-358. Washington, D.C.: The ESOP Association, [1987].

May, Richard. "The Use of Employee Stock Ownership Plans in Conjunction with Leveraged Buyouts Involving Multiple Investors." *The 1987 ESOP Association Convention*, 359-368. Washington, D.C.: The ESOP Association, [1987].

Neece, Roger N. "The New Role of the Independent Financial Advisor in Multi-Investor Leveraged ESOP Transactions." *The 1989 ESOP Association Convention*, 353-360. Washington, D.C.: The ESOP Association, [1989].

Paone, Louis A. "The Use of ESOP's in Leveraged Buyout Transactions." *The 1989 ESOP Association Convention*, 183-207. Washington, D.C.: The ESOP Association, [1989].

Pratt, Shannon. *Valuing a Business: The Analysis and Appraisal of Closely Held Companies*. 2nd ed. Homewood, IL: Dow Jones-Irwin, 1989.

Reich v. Valley National Bank of Arizona, 837 F. Supp. (S.D.N.Y. 1993), 1259-1312.

Roberts, James O. "Recent Court Case Developments." Presentation to the American Society of Appraisers International Appraisal Conference, 1994.

Schuchert, Joseph S. "Adequate Consideration Determination in Leveraged ESOP Transactions," *The 1986 ESOP Association Convention*, 179-207. Washington, D.C.: The ESOP Association, [1986].

Smiley, Robert W. Jr., and Ronald J. Gilbert. *Employee Stock Ownership Plans*. New York: Maxwell Macmillan/Rosenfield Launer, 1989.

Smiley, Robert W. Jr., Ronald J. Gilbert, and David M. Binns. *Employee Stock Ownership Plans: 1994 Yearbook.* New York: Warren Gorham Lamont, 1993.

Stocks, Bonds, Bills and Inflation: 1994 Yearbook. Illinois: Ibbotson Associates, 1994.

U.S. Department of Labor. *Proposed Regulation Relating to the Definition of Adequate Consideration.* 29 CFR Part 2510.

Valuing ESOP Shares. Washington, D.C.: The ESOP Association, 1989.

Vogel, Mark A. "The Use of Leveraged ESOPs to Acquire Employer Securities." *The 1989 ESOP Association Convention,* 147-182. Washington, D.C.: The ESOP Association, [1989].

Zukin, James H. "An Approach to Equity Allocation." *The 1987 ESOP Association Convention,* 369-395. Washington, D.C.: The ESOP Association, [1987].

———. *Financial Valuation: Businesses and Business Interests.* New York: Maxwell MacMillan, 1990.

Zukin, James H., John G. Mavredakis, and Jack W. Berka. *Financial Valuation: Businesses and Business Interests: 1993/1994 Update with Cumulative Index.* New York: Warren Gorham Lamont, 1993.

3

Accounting Rules Cause Controversy

Kenneth W. Patton

In 1993, the American Institute of Certified Public Accountants implemented a change in accounting for companies with leveraged employee stock ownership plans (ESOPs). This change created controversy in the business appraisal community. The new accounting rules reduce the number of shares outstanding after a leveraged ESOP transaction for purposes of calculating earnings per share. If the appraiser uses the lower number of shares in calculating fair market value, he or she will have ignored critical underlying economic realities. The author states that all shares held in the ESOP, regardless of whether they are deemed suspense shares, should be considered outstanding.

The American Institute of Certified Public Accountants (AICPA), with the issuance of Statement of Position (SOP) 93-6,[1] created controversy in the appraisal profession[2] that bears close scrutiny in the valuation of shares of stock in leveraged employee stock ownership plans (ESOPs). In essence, the new accounting rules provide for a change in the manner in which the number of outstanding shares is calculated when the ESOP has certain types of indebtedness. Before SOP 93-6, all shares owned by the ESOP were considered outstanding. The new accounting rules require that shares pledged to secure loans to the ESOP by a third party will not be considered outstanding. Because business appraisers reach a conclusion of value on a per share basis, does this change in accounting rules automatically mean that valuation conclusions will change? Is a change in valuation per share appropriate if nothing has happened to change the underlying economics of the transaction? This article proposes that the accounting changes do not affect fair market value and that appraisers would be in error to use the lower number of shares in calculating the conclusion of fair market value on a per share basis.

Background

The Old Rules: SOP 76-3

Before SOP 93-6, accounting for ESOPs was governed by SOP 76-3. Under SOP 76-3, shares of a business were considered outstanding whether or not

Kenneth W. Patton, ASA, is the president of Mercer Capital Management, Inc., one of the leading independent business appraisal firms in the U.S. and one of the leading appraisers of securities held by ESOPs.

they were pledged to any lender. For purposes of calculating the number of shares outstanding, this treated debts of the ESOP similarly to the debts of any other shareholder. Unlike other shareholder debt, however, the loans to the ESOP were recorded on the balance sheet if the debt was guaranteed by the company sponsoring the ESOP or if contributions were the sole source of repayment. ESOP debt was also reported as a reduction in equity. If an ESOP borrowed funds to acquire shares, the amount of debt would rise, the book value would fall by the amount of the debt, and the number of shares would remain constant. Business appraisers would calculate the value per share using all of the shares.

The New Rules: SOP 93-6

The AICPA deemed appropriate a revision in the accounting rules due to the growing complexity and popularity of ESOPs, particularly those employing third-party debt (bank loans or loans from selling shareholders) to acquire existing or newly issued shares. SOP 93-6 provides a comprehensive framework for ESOP accounting issues, most of which do not affect valuation. SOP 93-6 is effective for fiscal years beginning after December 15, 1993. As a practical matter, appraisers began encountering the changes in a substantial number of ESOP plans for the fiscal year ending December 31, 1994.

New Accounting Rules Under SOP 93-6

Although SOP 93-6 covers a wide variety of issues related to leveraged ESOP plans, the following are the most relevant from the perspective of valuing the shares owned by the plan. These rules are taken directly from the SOP.[3]

1. Employers should report the issuance of new shares or the sale of treasury shares to the ESOP when the issuance or sale occurs and should report a corresponding charge to unearned ESOP shares, a contra-equity account.
2. Employers should credit unearned ESOP shares as the shares are committed to be released based on the cost of the shares to the ESOP. The difference between the fair value of the shares committed to be released and the cost of those shares to the ESOP should be charged or credited to additional paid-in capital.
3. Employers should report redemptions of ESOP shares as purchases of treasury stock.
4. Employers should report loans from outside lenders to ESOPs as liabilities in their balance sheets and should report interest cost on the

debt. Employers with internally leveraged ESOPs should not report the loan receivable from the ESOP as an asset and should not report the ESOP's debt from the employer as a liability.

5. For earnings-per-share (EPS) computations, ESOP shares that have been committed to be released should be considered outstanding. ESOP shares that have not been committed to be released should not be considered outstanding.

Which Shares Are Outstanding

The key change is rule number 5 above. When an ESOP borrows money, the debt is typically collateralized by shares in the employer company. These shares are held in a suspense account and are called "suspense shares" in accounting terminology. As the debt is repaid from employer contributions or dividends, the suspense shares are released and allocated to the individual accounts of the appropriate employees as of the ESOP's fiscal year-end. Under SOP 93-6, the shares would be considered outstanding when there is a legal obligation to release them. Shares that had not been committed to be released would not be considered outstanding.

Fair Value Versus Fair Market Value

SOP 93-6 further addresses share valuation by noting that it is necessary to determine the fair value of the employer securities on at least an annual basis. "Fair value" is a phrase that has decidedly different meanings to accountants on one hand and to business appraisers on the other. To accountants, fair value is a concept used in recording asset values. To business appraisers, fair value is a standard of value relating to a legal concept found in state law that applies to certain corporate transactions. In turn, both of these concepts of fair value are distinct from the standard of value known as "fair market value," which is commonly accepted for the valuation of shares held in an ESOP. The potential for differences in the conclusion of value using fair value (as defined by business appraisers) is significant when compared to conclusions reached using fair market value. The SOP does not appear to support a change in the standard of value for valuing shares in ESOPs; however, the mingling of terminology can be confusing.

An Example of SOP 93-6's Impact on Valuation

Assessing the impact on valuation on a per-share basis can best be done with an example. Consider the following for a hypothetical company named ABC Inc. The pertinent facts before implementing the ESOP are as follows (table 1):

Table 1. ABC Inc. Before ESOP Implementation

Number of Shares Outstanding	10,000		
Adjusted Book Value	$1,000,000		
Ongoing After-Tax Earning Power	$ 200,000		
Projected Annual ESOP Contribution	$ 50,000		
Price/Earnings Multiple	6		
VALUATION CALCULATIONS:			
	Valuation	*Weight*	*Product*
Adjusted Book Value	$1,000,000	30%	$ 300,000
Earnings Capitalization Method	$1,200,000	70%	$ 840,000
Initial Indication of Value			$1,140,000
Discount for Lack of Marketability (15%)			$ (171,000)
Conclusion of Value			$ 969,000
Number of Shares Outstanding			÷ 10,000
Conclusion of Value per Share			$ 96.90

The shares are appraised on a non-marketable minority interest basis for $96.90 per share before the transaction. Simplistically, the valuation might place a 30% weight on adjusted book value ($1,000,000) and a 70% weight on an earning capitalization method ($1,200,000), which yields $1,140,000 before a discount for lack of marketability. Assuming the discount for lack of marketability to be 15%, the dollar value would be $969,000, or $96.90 per share.

Assume that 30% of the existing shares (3,000) are sold to the ESOP for $96.90 per share, or $290,700, which is financed by a bank loan guaranteed by the company that is in turn collateralized by the stock sold to the ESOP. The book value is immediately reduced by $290,700, and under the new accounting rules (SOP 93-6) the number of shares is reduced to 7,000.

Valuation Example Under SOP 76-3 (The Old Rules)

It is helpful to look at the implications for fair market value after the ESOP transaction under SOP 76-3 as compared to SOP 93-6. Appraisal practice under SOP 76-3 leaves the number of shares outstanding unchanged at 10,000, instead of reducing them as under the new rules. Using the example above, the appraiser might be faced with the following circumstances one year after the transaction (table 2).

Again, assuming the same simplistic approach and weightings, the dollar value is $82.79 per share. A 30% weighting is applied to an adjusted book value of $908,800. The earnings value of $1,002,000 (6 times $167,000) is weighted 70%. The weighted average of $974,040 is discounted by 15% for lack of marketability, resulting in an aggregate fair market value of $827,934 for the 10,000 shares. The fair market value is thus $82.79 per share. The decline in value is due to the debt incurred by the ESOP, which affects both adjusted book value and earnings. The stock value could eventually increase as debt is repaid; however, the earnings reduction could prove permanent as the need to repay the debt is replaced by a need for liquidity in the ESOP.

Table 2. Valuation for ABC Inc. Under SOP 76-3 After ESOP Implementation

Number of Shares Outstanding	10,000
Adjusted Book Value	$908,800[4]
Ongoing After-Tax Earning Power	$167,000[5]
Annual ESOP Contribution	$ 50,000
Price/Earnings Multiple	6

VALUATION CALCULATIONS:

	Valuation	*Weight*	*Product*
Adjusted Book Value	$ 908,800	30%	$ 272,640
Earnings Capitalization Method	$1,002,000	70%	$ 701,400
Initial Indication of Value			$ 974,040
Discount for Lack of Marketability (15%)			$(146,106)
Conclusion of Value			$ 827,934
Number of Shares Outstanding			÷ 10,000
Conclusion of Value per Share			$ 82.79

Valuation Example Under SOP 93-6 (The New Rules)

Table 2 illustrates the situation facing the appraiser if SOP 93-6 is used to determine fair market value.

The aggregate fair market value is $827,934, just as under SOP 76-3. The only difference is a reduction in the number of shares outstanding to 7,429, which increases the fair market value per share to $111.45 ($827,934 divided by 7,429).

Issues Raised by SOP 93-6

As shown above, fair market value per share goes down using the accounting rules of SOP 73-6 and goes up under SOP 93-6. Yet absolutely nothing has changed in the economics of the transaction. Because ESOPs are governed by the Employee Retirement Income Security Act (ERISA), which expressly proscribes the ESOP from paying more than adequate consideration when acquiring shares, it is imperative that appraisers have a clear understanding of the economics of the transaction and their translation into fair market value.

Table 3. Valuation for ABC Inc. Under SOP 93-6 After ESOP Implementation

Number of Shares Outstanding	7,429[6]		
Adjusted Book Value	$908,800		
Ongoing After-Tax Earning Power	$167,000		
Annual ESOP Contribution	$ 50,000		
Price/Earnings Multiple	6		
VALUATION CALCULATIONS:			
	Valuation	*Weight*	*Product*
Adjusted Book Value	$ 908,800	30%	$ 272,640
Earnings Capitalization Method	$1,002,000	70%	$ 701,400
Initial Indication of Value			$ 974,040
Discount for Lack of Marketability (15%)			$(146,106)
Conclusion of Value			$ 827,934
Number of Shares Outstanding			÷ 7,429
Conclusion of Value per Share			$ 111.45

The author believes it is appropriate to examine several important aspects of a typical leveraged ESOP, which often owns a minority interest in a company. SOP 93-6 details the accounting treatment for debt that is incurred to acquire the shares. As the debt is paid, the "penalty" to equity is reduced on the balance sheet. The earnings statement continues to absorb any contributions to the ESOP, regardless of the contribution's purpose—to pay debt, acquire shares, or build liquidity in the plan. In a very real sense, one accounting treatment is transitory (balance sheet), while the other may be permanent. It is the second factor, which reduces earnings because of the increase in compensation expense, that has the most immediate impact on value to other shareholders and to ESOP participants.

Economic Impact of the Transaction

The valuation analyst must look at the underlying economics of the transaction to determine fair market value both before and after the transaction is completed. The critical question appears to be whether the suspense shares are common stock equivalents for economic purposes, even though the AICPA has now deemed that they are not for financial reporting purposes. A common stock equivalent is defined as follows: "although certain securities are not actually common stock, the terms and/or conditions under which they were issued usually contain provisions that enable the holder to become a common stockholder."[7]

If the terms of the financial instrument or changing financial conditions result in more common shares, the existing shareholders' equity is diluted. From an economic perspective, emphasis should be placed on the substance of a security or transaction to determine if it is indeed dilutive. A second perspective on dilution can be found in the following description of dilution: "The value of a common stock is said to be diluted if there is an increase in the number of shares without a corresponding increase in assets and earning power."[8]

If earning power is initially affected by the requirements to make contributions for debt and then to provide liquidity for the plan, it appears that the plan is holding shares that will ultimately make a claim on earnings without any offset to earnings. This would meet the above definition of dilution and should be considered in any valuation.

The contractual debt obligations of the ESOP and employer are certain. Payment terms are specified and can be modified only by mutual consent of the lender and the borrower(s). The debt is never contingent on future events. This is unlike other potentially dilutive circumstances, such as out-of-the-money stock options or options that require performance by the individual or the company. The company will have to pay the debt even to the financial detriment of the other shareholders. Furthermore, the suspense shares would also have the right to vote and receive dividends.

Conclusion

Given the relative certainty of the payments, which release suspense shares, and the long-term impact of ESOP contributions on earnings, it is apparent that the substantive criteria for having an economically dilutive transaction have been met. For purposes of determining fair market value, the shares held in the suspense account of the ESOP should therefore still be considered outstanding immediately after the completion of the leveraged ESOP. Consequently, the reduction in the number of shares determined by SOP 93-6 should not be used in calculating earnings per share for valuation purposes.

Notes

1. American Society of Certified Public Accountants, *Statement of Position 93-6, Employers' Accounting for Employee Stock Ownership Plans* (November 22, 1993).
2. E.g., in the panel discussion on "Emerging Problems for ESOPs" at the National Center for Employee Ownership's 13th Annual Conference on Employee Ownership and Participation, Cleveland, Ohio, April 8, 1994.

3. *Statement of Position 93-6*, pp. v–vi.
4. The adjusted book value of $908,800 at one year after the transaction is calculated by adding one year's net income of $167,000 to the beginning adjusted book value of $1,000,000, minus the original ESOP debt of $290,700, plus the payment of debt of $32,500. We have assumed a seven-year fully amortizing loan.
5. The ongoing earning power of $167,000 is based upon the original estimate of $200,000, minus the new ESOP contribution of $50,000, plus the tax effect of $17,000.
6. The revised number of shares is based upon the original number of 10,000, minus the 3,000 purchased by the ESOP, plus the 429 shares to be released from the loan payment.
7. Martin A. Miller, *Miller Comprehensive GAAP Guide* (New York: Harcourt Brace Jovanovich, 1988), p. 13.03.
8. Benjamin Graham, David L. Dodd, and Sidney Cottle, *Security Analysis: Principles and Techniques*, (New York: McGraw-Hill, 1962), p. 615.

Editorial Note for the 1999 Reprint

Although the author wrote this article in response to a controversy that arose in 1994, his analysis is still current. Kathryn F. Aschwald of Columbia Financial Advisors, a past chair of the ESOP Association's Advisory Committee on Valuation, wrote as follows shortly before the republication of this article in 1999: "The ESOP Association's Advisory Committee on Valuation supports the author's position regarding the use of all shares outstanding in determining fair market value for ESOP appraisal purposes."

4

Enhancing Shareholder Value in Negotiated ESOP Transactions

Brad Van Horn

ESOPs are intended to give employees a share in the company and in its future equity growth; however, that share is, in many cases, not a share of common stock. Many ESOP transactions in C corporations use various forms of dividend-paying stock, such as convertible preferred stock or so-called "super-common" stock. There are numerous scenarios under which forming an ESOP with common stock is not feasible, or under which the transaction would be unacceptable to the seller if it relied on transferring common stock to employees. This article explains why many ESOPs are structured to use dividend-paying rather than common stock in C corporations, and explores the differences that exist within an S corporation structure.

Have you ever been involved in an aggressively negotiated transaction in which the selling shareholder wanted to sell shares to an employee stock ownership plan (ESOP) and trust? For example, imagine that a company having a single owner and a value of $10,000,000 (on a marketable minority basis[1]) desires to sell 30% of the common stock for $3,500,000. If the underlying common stock has a fair market value of $3,000,000 (and not $3,500,000, as desired by the owner) how can the transaction be structured so that the value received by employees is enhanced; hence, the ESOP can justifiably pay $3,500,000?

In situations such as this, the owner sometimes walks away from the ESOP transaction rather than receive a less-than-desired price for his or her shares. The "right" value (or fair market value) has become the "wrong" value (i.e., unacceptable to the owner). The owner's objectives are unsatisfied, and the employees do not receive an equity interest in their company. No one wins.

Solving the Problem of When the "Right" Value Is the "Wrong" Value

Many owners are, for obvious reasons, interested in receiving as high a price as possible from a buyer. In fact, one of the reasons that an independent appraisal of the company is required in an ESOP transaction is to protect the

---

Brad Van Horn, MBA, CPA, is a managing director of ComStock Valuation Advisors, Inc., a national valuation firm specializing in ESOP transactions.

employees from paying too high a price in a negotiated sale with an aggressive seller. The independent appraiser must be careful to take all relevant factors into consideration when arriving at a valuation conclusion. Placing too high a value on the stock could result in an indefensible position which, under audit by the U.S. Department of Labor or the Internal Revenue Service, might result in an unwinding of the transaction with severe financial penalties to both the company and the selling shareholder. If that value were deemed to have been more than the fair market value of the stock, the entire transaction would be classified as an illegal "prohibited transaction."

A Solution: Using Convertible Preferred or Super-Common Stock

Better alternatives exist to enhance the value being purchased by the ESOP without creating an untenable valuation conclusion. One solution that solves this problem in a C corporation is structuring a new dividend-paying stock that the ESOP buys. This new stock can be a convertible preferred stock, or can take the form of a class of "super-common" stock.[2] Owners can fairly demand more money when the stock being purchased carries a dividend, in part because the employees receive less risk. The dividend paid to the ESOP represents a priority claim on the cash flows of the business before any distributions are made to non-ESOP shareholders.

Using convertible preferred stock can create certain problems, discussed later in this article. Assuming for the moment that a super-common stock is used, the company is then recapitalized before the ESOP transaction so that a mix of 70% common stock and 30% super-common stock is substituted for the existing class of common stock.[3] A loan can then be made that permits the ESOP to purchase the super-common stock from the owner. The company pays tax-deductible dividends on the super-common stock; these dividends will be received only by the ESOP. The ESOP, in turn, can use the dividends it receives to repay its loan from the company.

An Example of Super-Common Stock

Using a hypothetical example, a class of super-common stock created as a result of the recapitalization might have the following characteristics:

- The stock has a stated value of $100.00 per share.
- The stock pays a dividend of 6.25%, or $6.25 per share, which is cumulative for a three-year period immediately following the ESOP transaction.
- The stock has the same voting rights as the common stock.
- The stock has a preference in liquidation to receive its stated value per share plus all cumulative and unpaid dividends.

- *(Optional)* The super-common stock has a minimum guaranteed floor value that the company must honor when the stock is put back to the company.[4]

Value of the Super-Common Stock The market value of the super-common stock being purchased by the ESOP trust is comprised of the sum of the value of the underlying common stock (based on an appraisal of the business) and the present value of the dividend payments to be received by the ESOP over the three-year period.

Value of the Floor Put Right If a minimum guaranteed floor value is structured as part of the super-common stock, the value of this floor put right can be determined with option pricing techniques.[5]

Comparative Valuation Examples Illustrating the Use of Super-Common Stock

The following examples use as a starting point a "Base Case" in which neither preferred nor super-common stock is used to enhance the value of the shares being sold. In the Base Case (table 1), the owner has sold 30% of the total common shares outstanding to the ESOP, retaining a 70% ownership interest. Because a dividend-paying stock is not used in the Base Case, the owner receives $3,000,000 from selling stock to the ESOP.

In Case 2 (table 1), a 30% ownership interest is again sold to the ESOP using a dividend-paying super-common stock with the characteristics outlined above. The dividend on the stock produces a present value of $500,000 over a three-year period, allowing the ESOP to pay $3,500,000 instead of $3,000,000. In our hypothetical case study, the owner agrees to this transaction, and the employees are able to obtain a much-desired employee benefit. Notice, however, that the transaction involves the sale of 35% of the value of the company and only 30% of the stock ownership. Whenever this situation occurs, the incremental 5% value being sold has a dilutive impact on the remaining non-ESOP shares. This topic is discussed later in this article.

Table 1. Valuation in a Sale of the Company Using Common Stock (the Base Case) and Dividend-Paying Super-Common Stock (Case 2)

	Base Case	Case 2
Value of Company (Minority Basis)	$10,000,000	$10,000,000
Percentage Sold	30%	30%
Cash Proceeds from Sale of Equity	$ 3,000,000	$ 3,000,000
Cash Proceeds from Dividend Value	0	500,000
Total Cash Proceeds	$ 3,000,000	$ 3,500,000
Cash Proceeds as a Percentage of Total Value	30%	35%

If the case study's assumptions are changed so that the owner desires $3,000,000 in cash proceeds but would like to minimize the percentage ownership being sold to the ESOP, some interesting results can be achieved. Case 3 (table 2) shows how an owner could sell a 25% ownership interest in the company but still receive 30% of the value of the company by using a dividend of 6.25% for a four (rather than three) year period. The value of the dividend as a percentage of the value of the underlying common stock being purchased is 22%, which represents a reasonable premium. The calculation of the reasonableness of the net "dividend premium" is important from the perspective of the Internal Revenue Service. Structuring a transaction with an unreasonably high dividend premium can also have significant adverse consequences to both the company and the selling shareholder.

Case 4 (table 2) takes this example a step further, showing the owner selling a 21% ownership interest in the company and receiving 31% of the value of the company by extending the dividend period to 10 years. In Case 4, the value of the dividend is 45% of the value of the underlying common stock being purchased, which may be excessive and therefore inappropriate. The premium paid in ESOP transactions reflected by the dividend must be reasonable. Whether or not a dividend is considered reasonable depends on the facts and circumstances of each case. Careful analysis should be performed regarding all significant risks and opportunities related to the particular investment. However, an important generalization is that dividends represent a return on the ESOP's investment. If the ESOP must receive too high a dollar return (through the payment of the dividend) in order to justify its investment, then the investment might not be considered "prudent." This reasonableness test effectively limits the extent to which an owner can receive cash in an ESOP transaction but sell relatively little equity.

Table 2. Valuation Using Stock Paying a 6.25% Dividend (Case 3) and Stock Paying Dividends Over 10 Years (Case 4)

	Case 3	Case 4
Value of Company (Minority Basis)	$10,000,000	$10,000,000
Percentage Sold	25%	21%
Cash Proceeds from Sale of Equity	$ 2,500,000	$ 2,100,000
Cash Proceeds from Dividend Value	540,000	950,000
Total Cash Proceeds	$ 3,040,000	$ 3,050,000
Cash Proceeds as a Percent of Total Value	30%	31%
Dividend Value as a Percent of Stock Value	22%	45%*
Dividend Rate on Convertible Preferred Stock	6.25%	6.25%
Number of Years Dividend Is Paid to ESOP	4	10

* The premium of 45% being paid for the dividends may be considered excessive, depending on the facts and circumstances of each case. If that were deemed to be true in this case, a 10-year dividend period would not be appropriate.

Problems Solved Through Using Dividends

The use of a dividend-paying stock is a well-documented way to solve other problems encountered in transactions in which owners want to sell stock to their employees.

Deduction Limits Dividends used to pay principal or interest on an ESOP loan are not considered "annual additions" because they are earnings of the plan, not contributions. The employer can deduct from taxable income such dividends (to the extent they are reasonable) if they are used to make principal and interest payments on the ESOP loan used to buy the securities on which the dividends were paid. (However, the dividends must be considered part of the tax base when computing the alternative minimum tax.) This deduction does not affect the 25% deduction limit otherwise available for contributions to repay principal for C corporations.[6]

Another important point is that the employer can deduct only the dividends it pays to the ESOP trust or passes through to participants. Consequently, the special class of stock created for the ESOP allows the company to declare a deductible dividend payable only to the ESOP, excluding the need to make non-deductible dividend payments to all other common shareholders.

The Risk of Dissolution Sometimes features are included specifically to limit the ESOP's downside risk, such as giving the ESOP stock a preferential position ahead of the common stock to receive distributions in a liquidation of the company's assets and a dissolution of the business. This downside protection, although only having value in a worst-case scenario, provides financial comfort to the ESOP trustee and helps justify the existence of the dividend feature.

The Dilution of the Selling Shareholder's Total Wealth Perhaps the greatest benefit of the dividend-paying stock, from the perspective of the selling shareholder, is that it typically helps mitigate the dilution to the selling shareholder's total wealth (which is assumed here to be comprised only of that shareholder's remaining equity interest in the company plus the proceeds received from the ESOP transaction.) In discussing the valuation of this remaining equity interest (which is 70% in the examples below), we use a control basis, which reflects the additional value attributed to the shareholder's ability to control the company's operations. In contrast, this article's earlier examples, which deal with a 30% to 35% interest sold to an ESOP (tables 1 and 2), use a minority basis with no such additional value.[7]

Assume that our hypothetical "Base Case" company is worth $12,000,000 on a control basis immediately before the ESOP transaction, in which case a 70% ownership interest would be worth $8,400,000 (Control Base Case, table 3). Had the owner sold 30% of the stock to an ESOP for $3,000,000 as in the Base Case,[8] his or her total wealth would be worth approximately $9,800,000 immediately after the sale, which value is 18.3% dilutive compared to the 100% equity value before the transaction (Control Case 2,[9] table 3). However, as a result of using a dividend-paying stock, the dilutive impact of the ESOP transaction is lower. Control Case 3 shows that the incremental dividend value reduces the dilution to the selling shareholder's total wealth to 15.8% (table 3).

Table 3. Value of the Selling Shareholder's Total Wealth

	Control Base Case	Control Case 2	Control Case 3
Control Value of Company Before ESOP	$12,000,000	$12,000,000	$12,000,000
Less Debt Resulting from ESOP		(3,000,000)	(3,500,000)
Add Estimated Tax Benefits Created by ESOP*		750,000	875,000
Control Value of Company After ESOP	$12,000,000	$ 9,750,000	$ 9,375,000
Percentage Remaining After ESOP	70%	70%	70%
Value of Remaining Equity Interest (Rounded)	$ 8,400,000	$ 6,800,000	$ 6,600,000
Reduction in Value from ESOP Transaction	N/A	(1,600,000)	(1,800,000)
Value of Remaining Equity Interest (see above)	8,400,000	6,800,000	6,600,000
Add Proceeds from ESOP Transaction		3,000,000	3,500,000
Total Wealth of Selling Shareholder		$ 9,800,000	$10,100,000
Net Reduction in Shareholder Wealth Due to ESOP		(2,200,000)	(1,900,000)
Percentage of Dilution		(18.3%)	(15.8%)

* Tax benefits are associated with the company's ability to deduct principal repayments on the ESOP loan. The present value of these tax benefits is estimated at 25% of the ESOP loan amount.

Super-Common Stock Versus Convertible Preferred Stock

Tax Problems with Convertible Preferred Stock in ESOP Transactions

In our hypothetical example, the ESOP purchased a super-common stock. Sometimes, a transaction is structured using a convertible preferred stock instead of a super-common stock. A hazard faced when using a convertible preferred stock in an ESOP transaction is that the selling shareholder might be precluded from deferring taxes on the proceeds received. This occurs whenever the stock received by the selling shareholder in the recapitalization and resold to the ESOP is characterized as "Section 306 stock." Preferred stock distributed in a recapitalization will be treated as Section 306 stock if the distribution is substantially similar to a preferred stock dividend. Section 306 of the Internal Revenue Code (the "Code") requires a selling shareholder to treat the gain on the sale of the stock as ordinary income instead of as a capital gain. This difference is significant. Under Section 1042 of the Code, recognition of capital gains upon the sale of stock to an ESOP can be deferred by the seller, whereas it is unclear whether recognition of ordinary income can be deferred.

Stock received in a recapitalization may avoid being characterized as "Section 306 stock" if certain of its features are modified. First, because common stock is, by definition, not Section 306 stock, the receipt of stock characterized as common stock will not constitute the receipt of Section 306 stock. The type of stock that would be characterized as common stock might include stock that is not subject to redemption and that represents an unrestricted right to share in the equity growth of the company. Where the class of stock has the same voting rights as the existing common stock and shares equally with existing common stock in dividends and liquidation distributions after receiving the preferential dividends and liquidation distributions, the Internal Revenue Service has viewed the stock as having an unrestricted right to share in the equity growth of the company for purposes of Section 306.

Avoiding the Problems of Preferred Stock by Using Super-Common Stock

To avoid the tax-related pitfalls of the preferred stock altogether, the ESOP in the above examples was structured so that the company was recapitalized with a new class of common stock that pays a dividend instead of using a convertible preferred class of stock. If super-common stock is used, future sales to the ESOP must be done using super-common and not just common stock, since an ESOP in a closely held company must own either common stock with the greatest dividend and voting rights or preferred stock convertible into such common stock.

Impact of S Election for ESOP Companies

The discussion of value-enhancing alternatives in an ESOP transaction has focused up to this point on those alternatives available in a C corporation. In 1998, corporations that sponsor ESOPs first became eligible to make the election to be treated as S corporations for federal income tax purposes. In S corporations, different classes of stock are not allowed. Stock in the same class can differ with regard to their voting rights, but differences in dividend rights or liquidation rights can not exist. In the context of an S corporation, "dividends" are made in the form of "distributions" to shareholders and are made in a non-discriminatory manner. Because preferred stock is not allowed in an S corporation, the preferred stock alternative discussed earlier is not available. Because distributions in an S corporation take the place of dividends in a C corporation, the concept of a dividend-paying ("super-common") stock is also not relevant in an S corporation setting. However, for reasons discussed below, the conversion of a C corporation to an S corporation provides other opportunities to enhance the value of the stock the ESOP is purchasing in a negotiated transaction.

S corporations are treated differently than C corporations for federal tax purposes. C corporations apply a corporate-level tax on all earnings of the corporation. Distributions of corporate income in the form of dividends from C corporations are also taxed at the individual level. S corporations, on the other hand, eliminate income tax at the corporation level, allocating corporate income to its shareholders, who then pay income tax at the individual level. For this reason, it is often said that "double taxation" applies to C corporation income, whereas S corporation income is only taxed once.

The structure of an ESOP transaction, when it includes converting from a C corporation to an S corporation, can significantly enhance the shareholder value being received by the ESOP. The additional value created by the elimination of the "double taxation" on corporate income accrues to the benefit of the ESOP shareholders. In a negotiated stock transaction, this additional value can offset the purchase price required by a seller for the stock being purchased by the ESOP trustee and helps provide an adequate rate of return on the ESOP's investment.

The appraiser should take care to ascertain the likely use of future cash flow generated by the S corporation tax savings. For example, if the future tax savings are kept inside the company and not distributed to management and other employees (in the form of compensation) or shareholders (in the form of distributions) then equity value can be expected to increase as a result of the tax savings. Tax savings kept inside the company can be used to generate additional equity value by enabling the company to invest in new capital equipment, make strategic acquisitions, hire new personnel that will improve the company's future growth opportunities, or simply accumulate the additional cash in an interest-bearing account as a corporate investment. However, if 100% of the tax savings is disbursed and therefore the company receives no net cash flow benefit from the S election, then equity value will not be affected. The appraiser should receive an indication from management or the board of directors regarding the likely use of any tax savings that may result from the S election. Further, the appraiser should not assume a 100% probability that the tax savings will be kept inside the company, since management and the board of directors will make ongoing decisions regarding the use of cash in the corporation and a risk exists that decisions made today may be overturned in the future.

A common use of the tax savings resulting from the S election for ESOP companies is to prefund the company's ESOP repurchase obligation. Each year, the company can make a tax-deductible contribution to the ESOP trust within the limits imposed by Code Sections 404 and 415, or can make a cash distribution to its shareholders which will create a cash balance inside the ESOP trust. In either case, the tax savings resulting from the S election has been spent by the Company, and the Company may end up in a cash position very similar to where it would have ended up if it were a tax-paying entity. No increase in equity value should be expected under these circumstances, except for the valuation impact that may result from a company's ability to partially or totally prefund its ESOP repurchase obligation. However, the distributions that result in the prefunding of the ESOP repurchase liability creates additional value for ESOP participants, since the cash balances that are accumulating inside the ESOP trust must be allocated to the ESOP participants. When coupled with the value of the company's stock, the cash balance allocated to each participant can create a significantly larger account balance for each participant than if the S corporation tax savings did not exist.

The appraiser can estimate the value of the future tax savings that may result from the S election. For example, suppose that a company is expected to generate $1,000,000 in taxable income as a C corporation next year and that earnings are expected to grow at an annual rate of 5%. Further, suppose that the company's weighted average cost of capital is 15%. If an ESOP transaction were structured to include the conversion from a C corporation to an S corporation, the maximum value of the S election would be $3,570,000 and would be calculated as shown in table 4.

Because a significant risk exists that 100% of all future tax savings resulting from the S election will not remain inside the company, only a portion (perhaps only a small portion) of the total value of the tax savings should be used to justify the price of the stock being purchased by the ESOP trustee in a negotiated transaction. If an ESOP trustee uses too much of the value

Table 4. S Corporation Valuation

Calculation of Annual Tax Savings	
Next Year's Taxable Income as a C Corporation	$1,000,000
Federal Income Tax Rate for C Corporations	34%
Next Year's Federal Income Tax as a C Corporation	$340,000
Calculation of Valuation Multiple	
Annual Growth Rate for Pretax Income (g)	5%
Weighted Average Cost of Capital (WACC)	15%
Valuation multiple to be applied to estimated annual tax savings *[formula = (1+g) / (wacc-g)]*	10.5
Calculation of Estimated Value	
Next Year's Federal Income Tax as a C Corporation	$340,000
Valuation Multiple	10.5
Estimated Value of Federal Income Tax Savings	$3,570,000

of the future tax savings to justify a high purchase price for the stock, an adequate rate of return on the ESOP's investment may not result. Therefore, the appraiser should calculate an expected internal rate of return on the ESOP's investment at the time of the ESOP transaction.

Use of Tax Savings to Repay ESOP Acquisition Debt

In a leveraged ESOP transaction funded by independent third-party debt (the "ESOP acquisition debt"), the use of the tax savings resulting from the S election to repay the ESOP acquisition debt creates additional value that accrues to the benefit of the ESOP participants. Even though the cash resulting from the tax savings does not remain inside the company, the use of the cash to reduce bank indebtedness will increase the company's equity value. If the tax savings were large enough to fully fund all future principal and interest payments for the ESOP acquisition debt, the S election might in fact result in a "free" acquisition of the stock by the ESOP trustee.

The deduction limits imposed by the Code require that principal and interest payments on the ESOP acquisition loan represent no more than 15% of eligible ESOP payroll unless a money purchase pension plan component is added to the ESOP. Distributions made by the company to the ESOP shareholders may be used to repay the ESOP acquisition loan. However, it is currently unclear if distributions on both allocated and unallocated shares may be used for such purposes. A common viewpoint among ESOP practitioners is that distributions on *unallocated ESOP shares only* may be used to repay an ESOP acquisition loan. Under this assumption, a larger proportion of total distributions that occur in the earlier years of indebtedness will be available for repayment of the ESOP acquisition loan, and a much smaller portion of total distributions that occur in the later years of indebtedness will be available for repayment. The distributions that are ineligible to apply to the ESOP acquisition loan will build up as a separate investment inside the ESOP, thereby increasing the total account balance of the ESOP participants, and may be used to fund future ESOP share repurchases.

Conclusion

In negotiated sales of stock to an ESOP, a knowledge of alternative ways to enhance shareholder value is useful in completing the transaction. This article shows how a dividend-paying stock, in particular a super-common stock, can be used to enhance the value of the equity interest purchased by the ESOP in the context of a C corporation. In the context of an S corporation, the value of the future cash flow generated by the company due to the tax savings resulting from the S election can be used to justify a higher purchase price for the stock as long as an adequate rate of return is expected for the ESOP.

Notes

1. A minority basis reflects no value attributable to the ability of the shareholders to control the operations of the company. A marketable basis assumes the existence of a market comprised of willing buyers at whatever time the shareholder desires to sell the stock. In the case of an ESOP, the company becomes this market, because it is required to repurchase the stock of ESOP participants in specific circumstances.
2. The "super-common" stock receives its name from its similarity with the regular class of common stock except for its right to receive preferential dividend payments and liquidating distributions.
3. The recapitalization would occur under the provisions of Section 368(a)(1)(E) of the Internal Revenue Code (the "Code").
4. One of the requirements of an ESOP is that the company must offer to repurchase the shares distributed to participants under certain circumstances at fair market value, as determined annually by an independent appraisal of the shares.
5. The option pricing method is a robust and sophisticated technique for allocating firm value among the various debt and equity claimants, and is preferred over other techniques because it takes into account the conditional probability of each claimant receiving its share of value. The option pricing method goes beyond other allocation techniques by giving consideration to the risk of bankruptcy of an organization and the priority of each claim in the event of bankruptcy. The use of the option pricing methodology is beyond the scope of this article.
6. Under Code Sections 404 and 415, the company can receive a tax deduction only for contributions up to 25% of the company's eligible payroll in a C corporation. If dividends are used first to make principal (not interest) payments on the loan, which does not count against the 25% deduction limit, more of the 25% is available for

deducting loan payments. Deduction limits differ in the context of an S corporation. Generally, the deduction limits in an S corporation apply to both principal and interest payments, and such payments are limited to 15% of eligible payroll.

7. See note 1.
8. The Base Case uses a common stock without any dividends.
9. A control basis is used here because the selling shareholder still owns 70% of the company's stock after the ESOP transaction.

5

An ESOP Valuation Case Study

Sheryl L. Cefali
Sandra M. Wimsatt

The case study presented below illustrates why an owner of a closely held company might be motivated to sell stock to an ESOP, even if presented with other attractive alternatives, including an outright sale of 100% of the company's stock. The article illustrates how fair market value is determined using a discounted cash flow approach and a comparable public company approach, and highlights certain features unique to ESOP transactions, such as the 1042 rollover.

Starting with an idea and very little capital 30 years ago, Doug McCann created a company that today generates over $40 million in sales and employs close to 200 people. The success of his company enabled Doug and his family to enjoy a very comfortable standard of living; moreover, Doug was able to provide careers for his three sons who now capably ran Specialty Products on their own with very little input from him. His sons had families of their own, and it gave Doug great pride to be able to give his children the head start he never had. Now 60 years old and in good health, Doug was at the stage in his life when he was ready to retire and enjoy the fruits of his labor. Doug had one problem, however, that continued to plague him: most of his personal wealth was tied up in Specialty Products.

Background

Specialty Products imports and sells corporate gifts and other specialty advertising products to a wide array of clients. Products often include a company's name or logo and are given as promotional items or gifts and used as a form of advertising. Specialty Products has a wide array of products ranging from personalized mugs, pens, and T-shirts to personalized golf bags and corporate gift baskets. The company has a main office in Los Angeles and 14 regional offices scattered throughout the western United States.

The key to Specialty Products' success is its strong sales force, represented by 90 account executives. The account executives work independently to market to prospective clients and develop marketing solutions for existing clients. Specialty Products' management team includes Doug; his

Sheryl L. Cefali is a managing director in the Los Angeles office of Duff & Phelps, LLC, a a national financial advisory and investment banking firm. Sandra M. Wimsatt was a vice president with Duff & Phelps when this article was written.

three sons, Brian, Stephen and Michael; and Robert Goldstein, the chief financial officer.

Options for Selling the Company

One day, Doug received an unsolicited offer for his company of $14 million in cash from Global Products. Doug read and reread the offer letter and was uncertain what to do. Finally, he decided to hire a professional consultant to help him analyze the alternatives available to him. After much discussion, the consultant determined that there were several viable options available to Doug. The first was to sell Specialty Products outright to Global Products for $14 million. Another option available to Doug was to take his company public. A similar-sized competitor, Multi-Service Corp., had recently gone public. Doug was very familiar with the problems that Multi-Service Corp. had experienced with the final pricing of the issue as well as the significant costs associated with the offering. Based on this information, Doug quickly rejected this option. The third option available to Doug was to sell his stock over time to an employee stock ownership plan (ESOP). To adequately analyze the ESOP option, Doug needed to have a valuation of Specialty Products performed to determine the price the ESOP could pay for his stock. This entailed hiring an independent valuation consultant to determine the "fair market value" of Specialty Products' stock.

Three Levels of Fair Market Value

During the first meeting with the valuation expert, Doug learned there was more to the issue of value than he expected. There are actually three different levels of fair market value: enterprise or controlling interest value, marketable minority interest value, and nonmarketable minority interest value.

Stock in a publicly traded company, where there is adequate trading volume, represents a marketable minority interest level of value. The stock is liquid and can easily be converted to cash, but ownership typically is represented by small blocks of stock that exert little or no control over the company. When a company is acquired or sold, the stock is typically priced at the enterprise or controlling interest value level. This can be illustrated when analyzing the stock price of a public company before and after a tender offer is made. The pre-tender offer price typically represents the marketable minority interest level. After the offer is announced, the stock price appreciates by the "control premium," or the premium paid for the ability to control the company. The offer Doug received from Global Products would be considered to be at a controlling interest value.

In a private company, where there is no ready market for the company's stock, minority blocks of stock are worth a discount to the marketable minority interest value because they lack the inherent liquidity of publicly traded securities. However, shares of ESOP stock in private companies may be subject to little or no discount for lack of marketability. This is because ESOPs offer their participants a "put" option to redeem their stock at fair market value. The ESOP, therefore, effectively creates a market for the ESOP securities provided the company has the financial wherewithal to honor the put obligation.

Doug also learned that in a potential ESOP transaction, the purchase of his stock would be through a leveraged transaction. For this reason, the amount of debt Specialty Products could take on must be considered. If a company does not have a significant amount of hard assets to collateralize and does not have stable, predictable cash flows, it is generally not possible to sell 100% of the stock to an ESOP in a leveraged buyout. Either a smaller percentage of the company's stock would have to be sold to the ESOP, or the deal would have to be structured with blocks of stock purchased by the ESOP over time.

If the seller is interested in using the sale proceeds or replacement securities as collateral for the ESOP loan or is willing to provide seller financing, it is often possible to increase the amount of leverage in the transaction and, therefore, sell a greater percentage of stock to the ESOP if the cash flows are sufficient to service the debt. Unfortunately in either case, the selling shareholder would continue to bear the risk of the company successfully meeting its debt amortization.

Doug was interested in gaining liquidity for at least a portion of his stock, but was unwilling to either pledge sale proceeds as collateral or provide the necessary seller financing. For this reason, Doug was interested only in a transaction in which the debt would be collateralized by the company's assets. The valuation consultant explained that Specialty Products could not be leveraged to the extent required to purchase a controlling interest under these conditions; therefore, if Doug sold to an ESOP, the ESOP would need to purchase a minority interest in the company. This means that the stock would be valued on a marketable minority interest basis. Had Doug sold all or a controlling portion of the stock to the ESOP, the ESOP's stock would have been valued at the highest level of value, the controlling interest level.

Valuing Speciality Products

To determine the fair market value of a company's stock, one must examine the company's size and growth potential; the diversity and stability of the company's customer base; the quality and depth of management; the company's financial condition, and earning and cash flow generating ability; and the overall condition of the economy and the industry in which the company operates. The determination of fair market value is a matter of judgment that factors in all relevant qualitative and quantitative factors and relates them to the company's earning power and cash flow generating ability and the risks associated with them.

One of the first steps to determining the fair market value of Specialty Products on a marketable minority interest basis involved understanding the historical performance of the company. Highlights of the company's performance and selected balance sheet information from fiscal year 1991 through 1994 are shown below (table 1).

Table 1. Specialty Products' Performance from 1991 Through 1994

	1994	1993	1992	1991
Net Sales	$43,500,000	$41,600,000	$41,000,000	$44,000,000
Operating Cash Flow	1,793,000	1,396,000	985,000	1,382,000
Total Assets	8,988,000	8,228,000	7,820,000	8,933,000

Due to the softening in the Southern California economy, Specialty Products experienced a 7% decline in sales and a 29% decline in cash flow from 1991 to 1992. The company recovered in 1993 due to new pricing policies, strong cost-cutting efforts, and a strengthening economy. By 1994, while sales had not returned to the level achieved in 1991, the company's operating margin was at an all-time high.

The fair market value of Specialty Products was determined using the following two valuation methodologies: (1) an analysis of Specialty Products' projected future cash flows discounted to the present at a rate appropriate for the relative risks of the business (the discounted cash flow approach); and (2) an analysis of recent market prices and resulting valuation multiples for publicly traded companies that are engaged in business activities considered similar to those of Specialty Products (the comparable public company approach).

The Discounted Cash Flow Approach

The discounted cash flow analysis is an important valuation methodology because investors are willing to pay only for anticipated future—not historic—cash flows. To perform the discounted cash flow analysis, five-year financial forecasts for Specialty Products were developed. The company's sales were directly correlated with the strength of the economy: in a healthy economy, Specialty Products' sales could be expected to increase and in a weak economy sales would generally fall. In late 1993 and into 1994, the economy was beginning to show signs of improvement. Based on the overall strengthening of the economy, sales were forecasted to grow 5% in fiscal year 1996 and then slow gradually to a rate just above the expected inflation rate. Specialty Products had also just finished a major cost reduction program that would materially affect the ongoing profitability of the company.

The projections for Specialty Products assume that the company would continue to be operated based on the existing policies of management. The assumptions include no changes or improvements a control buyer could implement, such as reducing costs or improving growth. The projections reflect what a minority interest investor could reasonably expect the company's performance and returns to be over the next five years. The projected income statement for Specialty Products from 1995 through 1999 is in appendix 1.

The projections for Specialty Products were developed on a debt-free basis. This means that the projections exclude interest expense in the projected income statement and the amortization of principal in the cash flow statement. Furthermore, the projections ultimately arrive at the company's free cash flow. Free cash flow is operating cash flow adjusted for required changes in working capital and net capital expenditures and taxes. By definition, free cash flow is net of cash needed by the business to meet its projections and is, therefore, theoretically available to shareholders as dividends. Investors are willing to pay only for the present value of future cash flows available to them for distribution, taking into consideration both the timing of the distribution flows and the perceived risk of achieving the projected cash flows.

It is important for the financial advisor to evaluate independently the reasonableness of the projections used in the discounted cash flow analysis. A company often has long-term projections it has prepared for internal use. Although company management may know the business better than the independent advisors, conflicting interests may require an independent check of the financial forecasts. Methods of checking the reasonableness of projections include:

- Analyzing the industry's projected growth in the specific markets served by the company.
- Determining the market share implied by the company projections; rarely do competitors stand still in the face of a major threat to market position.
- Questioning any extraordinarily high growth expectations; it is nearly impossible for a company to keep doubling its size over a long period of time.
- Challenging the expected realization of excessive profits, particularly in a regulatory environment.
- Analyzing the source of projected revenue growth; if growth is to occur through acquisitions, an examination of how the acquisition costs are factored into the projections must be made.

There are two primary components to value in the discounted cash flow: (1) the present value of the interim cash flows and (2) the net present value of the terminal value of the enterprise. Computing the terminal value, or the value of an enterprise years into the future, is more difficult than computing the value of the interim cash flows. The terminal value may be calculated using multiples derived in the market comparable approach (discussed in the next section), a perpetuity approach known as the Gordon Growth Model[1] (which assumes a constant growth beyond the projection period or, in some instances, a series of discrete annual growth rates), or other methods selected as appropriate by the valuation consultant. In the case of Specialty Products, the terminal value was based on the Gordon Growth Model assuming a perpetuity growth rate of 3%.

The discount rate used to calculate the net present value of future expected cash flows is based on the overall risks of the business and the risks to a shareholder inherent in realizing the projected stream of free cash flow. There are no simple formulas for selecting an appropriate discount rate. Analytical techniques are available, such as the Capital Asset Pricing Modes (CAPM)[2] to help the valuation consultant select a reasonable cost of equity and, where required, a blended or weighted average cost of capital (WACC).[3] A blended or weighted average cost of capital considers the cost of debt, the cost of equity, and the proportional amount of each in the company's capital structure.

After considering all relevant risk factors as they pertain to Specialty Products, the perceived risk of achieving the projections, the calculated WACC of Specialty Products of 15%, as well as returns that could be achieved by investors in alternative investments, it was determined that an appropriate discount rate to apply to Specialty Products projected free cash flows ranged from 14.5% to 15.5%. The resulting indication of fair market value for Specialty Products, including the value of both debt and equity, was in the range of $11.4 million to $11.8 million. To determine the fair market value of the company's equity, the market value of debt needed to be deducted. After deducting $550,000 in debt, the resulting indications of fair market value of Specialty Products' equity was in the range of $10.9 million to $11.2 million, as shown in appendix 1.

The Comparable Public Company Approach

The second method used to determine the fair market value of Specialty Products was the comparable public company approach. The comparable public company approach is based on the premise that a company's value is based on investors' perceptions of the risks and rewards from an investment in the subject company relative to other investments. When valuing a company that does not have an active trading market, the valuation consultant cannot directly observe how investors value it. It is often possible, however, to identify publicly traded companies that resemble the subject company from an investor's standpoint. By comparing the subject company to such comparable public companies on the basis of accepted risk and reward measures such as size, liquidity, leverage, profitability, and growth statistics, the valuation consultant can judge its relative financial and operating risk profile.

Other risk factors that should be considered are qualitative. The qualitative information is acquired during the valuation consultant's visits to the company's facilities and during interviews with management. These qualitative factors include key customer or key supplier risk, key employee risk, diversity of operations, reputation, market share, and future growth opportunities. After analyzing the company's financial, operating, and qualitative risk profiles, the valuation consultant will ascertain the subject company's risk and potential reward relative to the selected comparable public companies.

There are two primary components to the comparable public company approach. The first is determining the level of earnings and cash flow that is representative of Specialty Products' earnings and cash flow generating capabilities. The second is determining appropriate capitalization ratios (e.g., P/E multiples) to apply to those representative levels.

To determine a representative level of earnings and cash flow to capitalize, it is important to analyze both historical and projected results for the subject company. Since both the revenue and income of Specialty Products are expected to increase in the next fiscal year, fiscal 1994 results were determined to be the most representative of Specialty Products' current earnings and cash flow generating capacity. Specialty Products' 1994 results were adjusted for nonrecurring items. The nonrecurring expense consisted of the write-off of a new computer that was determined to be useless. The calculations are shown in appendix 2.

The second part of this approach requires identifying public companies with similar investment characteristics to Specialty Products. In the case of Specialty Products, there was only one publicly traded company in the specialty products business, Multi-Service Corp. Since this analysis is more meaningful if a larger group of comparable public companies is used, the comparable company search was expanded to include companies in a related area of business that an investor would view to have a similar investment risk due to either a similar product line, customer base, or other business attribute. After extensive screening, five other companies were identified that fit these criteria.

Market multiples, such as price/earnings (P/E) ratios, are computed by dividing the stock price for the period immediately preceding the valuation date by the earnings per common share. The value derived from multiplying the subject company's earnings by a P/E ratio is the company's aggregate market value of common equity on a marketable minority interest basis.

When the company being valued has a significantly different capital structure than the comparative public companies used to generate market multiples, it is useful to apply debt-free approaches to valuation. Debt-free approaches measure the value that debt and equity holders together ascribe to the respective income and cash flow streams of a company. To calculate debt-free multiples for comparable companies, the total market value of debt is added to the market value of equity to compute total invested capital. The total invested capital is then divided by debt-free earnings or debt-free cash flow levels, such as earnings before interest and taxes (EBIT) or earnings before depreciation, amortization, interest, and taxes (Operating Cash Flow) to arrive at Price/EBIT and Price/Operating Cash Flow ratios.

There are two primary components that comprise a market multiple or capitalization ratio—risk and growth. The greater the company's risk, the lower the multiple; the stronger the company's growth, the higher the multiple. Specialty Product's financial performance was compared to the six publicly traded companies. Based on Specialty Products' slightly weaker financial performance and smaller size, it was determined that Specialty Products represented a greater investment risk with slightly weaker growth potential compared to the comparable public companies taken as a group.

Based on Specialty Products' comparative risk and growth profile, the capitalization multiples selected were at the lower end of the range of valuation multiples. The capitalization ratios for the six public companies, including the selected capitalization multiples selected for Specialty Products, are shown in appendix 4.

Applying the selected capitalization multiples to the previously determined representative earnings and cash flow levels yielded valuation indications ranging from $10.7 million to $11.7 million. The calculations are shown in appendix 3.

The different valuation methodologies yield different ranges of fair market value. In many cases, the valuation ranges for the various approaches overlap, as was the case with Specialty Products. If the valuation ranges for the discounted cash flow analysis and the comparable company analysis do not overlap, the valuation consultant must use his or her professional judgment to determine which valuation methodology is the most meaningful and weigh it accordingly.

The valuation analysis described above yielded ranges of fair market value of the common stock of Specialty Products on an aggregate marketable minority interest basis, as follows:

Discounted Cash Flow Approach: $10.9–$11.2 million
Comparable Public Company Approach: $10.7–$11.7 million

Based on the analysis discussed above, the concluded fair market value of the common stock of Specialty Products on a marketable minority interest basis was determined to be $11 million.

Discussions with lenders indicated that the borrowing capacity of Specialty Products was limited to $4 million. For this reason it was determined that a maximum of 36% ($4 million divided by $11 million) of the company's common stock could be sold to an ESOP.

Valuation Methodologies Not Used Here

Even though the discounted cash flow analysis and the comparable company analysis were determined to be the most appropriate valuation methodologies in the case of Specialty Products, there are other valuation methods that may be appropriate for other types of companies. These methods include the comparative transaction analysis and asset based approaches. The comparative transaction analysis approach is based on reports of actual sales of companies or their assets and is similar to that of the comparable public company method. Valuation multiples such as the sale price to earnings, cash flow, and net worth are analyzed, as are financial measures such as profitability, leverage, and growth. Appropriate valuation multiples are then selected to apply to representative levels of earnings, cash flow, and revenue of the subject company being valued. In the case of Specialty Products, there were no completed or announced sales of companies similar to Specialty Products within a reasonable time period before the valuation date.

The asset approach is another method commonly used to value companies. It is generally applicable to businesses having substantial capital investments in tangible assets and for which the operating earnings are relatively insignificant as an indicator of investment value. Businesses for which the asset approach may be most appropriate include real estate or natural resource holding companies and mutual funds.

In addition, industry rules of thumb are sometimes used to value companies. These rules of thumb, such as valuing a company at one times revenue, can be very misleading. The value of a company is very subjective, and is a function of the quality of its management team, its market position, and its ability to generate profits.

The Section 1042 Rollover

Doug found the most attractive feature of selling stock to an ESOP was the "1042 rollover." The 1042 rollover, which was enacted in the 1984 Tax Reform Act, would allow Doug to postpone indefinitely the payment of capital gains taxes due on that transaction if the sale met the conditions of Section 1042 of the Internal Revenue Code. To qualify for a 1042 transaction, the ESOP must be sponsored by a C corporation (not an S corporation) and own at least 30% of a company's securities after the transaction. Doug must then reinvest the proceeds from the sale in qualified replacement securities. Qualified replacement securities are stocks and bonds of domestic operating corporations actively engaged in trades or businesses that do not receive more than 25% of their income from passive investments. These securities must be acquired within a period of three months before and twelve months after the transaction date. If the qualified replacement securities were carefully selected, it would be possible for Doug to defer paying taxes on the gain throughout his lifetime. Doug also found out that he could avoid paying taxes on the gain altogether if, upon his death, he passed the stock on to his wife with a stepped-up basis.

Section 1042 treatment is available only to private companies. Furthermore, the seller must have held the securities for at least three years before selling to an ESOP. In addition, after a 1042 transaction, the ESOP must hold the stock for three years or the sponsor company will incur an excise tax equal to 10% of the amount realized on the disposition of the stock. The securities sold must be "qualified employer securities" and must be sold by an individual, trust, estate, partnership, or S corporation. Finally, the 1042 rollover is not available if the seller is a C corporation.

Selling to an ESOP and taking advantage of the 1042 rollover offered many unique benefits to Doug and would allow him to achieve several goals simultaneously. If the selling shareholder holds at least 81% of the company's stock before a transaction, selling 30% of the company's stock to an ESOP enables the seller to not only realize liquidity, but continue retaining control (51%) of the company. Careful planning would allow Doug to gradually decrease his ownership in the business by selling his stock to the ESOP in blocks over time, thereby giving him liquidity. Furthermore, in many cases, including that of Specialty Products, the selling shareholder would be able to realize higher returns on the sale to an ESOP than on one to a third-party buyer, even if the third party's price is somewhat higher. This is because the seller will pay capital gains taxes on the proceeds received from the third-party buyer, whereas with an ESOP sale, the seller can roll over the proceeds into qualified replacement securities, paying no taxes. This can result in higher net proceeds even when the ESOP's purchase price is lower.

Weighing the Options

Once the valuation analysis of Specialty Products was completed, Doug sat down with his valuation consultant to analyze his options. Doug's initial impression was that Global Products' offer of $14 million was a better offer from a purely financial point of view. Since Global Products would be buying 100% of Specialty Products' common stock, its offer included a premium for control of approximately 27%. (The 27% figure is derived by dividing the $14 million controlling interest value by the $11 million marketable minority interest value and subtracting 1.)

Doug's valuation consultant pointed out that because Doug's basis in

Specialty Products was very low ($1 million), the resulting federal capital gains taxes in the sale to Global Products would be $3.6 million (28% of the $13 million gain.) Although the ESOP's offer was $3 million lower than the Global Products', in a sale to the ESOP Doug would be able to roll over his proceeds into qualified replacement securities and eliminate the payment of capital gains taxes; thus, the net proceeds under the ESOP scenario were actually higher (table 2)!

Table 2. Comparison of a Sale to an ESOP to a Sale to an Outside Buyer

	ESOP Sale	Global Products
Offer Price	$ 4 million*	$ 14 million
Less Capital Gains Taxes	(0)	(3.6 million)
Value of Remaining Interest	7 million**	0
Net Proceeds to Seller	11 million	10.4 million

* This is the ESOP price based on the total marketable minority interest value of Specialty Products of $11 million. The company is able to borrow only $4 million; therefore, if the ESOP option is chosen, the ESOP is able to purchase only 36% of Doug's stock. If Doug chooses to sell additional shares to the ESOP at a later date, the price paid for those shares will be based upon the appraisal when those shares are ultimately sold.

** Doug retains the remaining 64% interest in the company. Stated on a marketable minority interest basis, the 64% interest is worth $7 million. Because the 64% represents a control block of stock, the fair market value of this block may be higher due to a controlling interest premium that may be appropriate to apply. On the other hand, the value of the remaining interest may be adversely affected due to the new ESOP debt imposed on the company. This potential negative impact can be minimized, however, if the ESOP debt servicing costs merely replace other benefit costs. Further, the effective use of tax advantage financing provided by the ESOP debt is a positive feature.

Doug's primary concern regarding the ESOP transaction was that initially only 36% of the stock could be sold to the ESOP. This means that Doug would receive $4 million in cash and would continue to hold $7 million in stock. The remaining 64% of Doug's stock would have to be sold in increments over time as the company's borrowing capacity increased or the ESOP debt was paid down.

How Will the ESOP Pay for the Stock?

The question foremost in Doug's mind was the ability of the employees to pay for the stock. The financing for an ESOP transaction is typically accomplished through leverage. The ESOP borrows money either directly from a bank or the company borrows the funds from the bank and lends it to the ESOP. If the ESOP borrows the funds from the bank, the company guarantees the loan and provides the assets needed for collateral.

The company is required to make contributions to the ESOP sufficient to cover both the principal payments and interest expense. The company is able to deduct these contributions and the result is that the debt is amortized with pretax dollars. Annual contributions to a leveraged ESOP are limited to 25% of defined covered payroll to repay principal on an ESOP loan. Interest payments are excluded from the limitation. However, dividends paid on stock held by an ESOP used to repay an ESOP loan are tax deductible and are not subject to the annual contribution limits. The ability to deduct principal repayments results in significant corporate tax savings and enhanced cash flow relative to conventional financing.

Based on Specialty Products' projected cash flow, the $4 million loan could easily be paid off in five years. If during the next five years Specialty Products has an especially strong year, the amortization could be accelerated through additional contributions.

The ESOP as a Motivational Tool

The motivational aspect of the ESOP transaction was particularly appealing to Doug. He felt that an ESOP would serve as a very good motivational tool for his account executives. Doug believed that by allowing his employees to become part owners in his company he could enhance productivity and increase employee loyalty. The key to reaping these "intangible" benefits from an ESOP is to create an environment that embraces the concept of employee ownership. This involves a participative environment with increased employee owner involvement and open communications throughout the organization, including the sharing of information regarding the ESOP and the company's performance.

Conclusion

Doug was flattered that a company as highly regarded as Global Products would be interested in paying $14 million for his company. Even on an after-tax basis, the proceeds of $10.4 million seemed appealing. The ESOP transaction, however, offered many other benefits not available with an outright sale. It gave Doug's sons the chance to continue to build successful careers in Specialty Products and to motivate and reward the account executives who were critical to the company's future success. The proposed structure of the ESOP transaction allowed Doug to retain control over the next five years, enabling him to make sure the transition went as smoothly as possible. Finally, by rolling his proceeds over in a 1042 transaction, Doug could maximize the amount he would receive for his stock in the company. In his final analysis, Doug felt confident that the ESOP transaction was the best transaction, not only for him and his family, but for the clients and employees of Specialty Products as well.

APPENDIX 1

Specialty Products: Projected Financial Statement for the Years Ending March 31 (Amounts Are in Thousands of Dollars)

	Actual	Projected				
INCOME STATEMENT	**1994**	**1995**	**1996**	**1997**	**1998**	**1999**
Sales	$43,500	$45,675	$47,730	$49,640	$51,129	$52,663
Cost of Goods Sold	28,275	29,689	31,025	32,266	33,234	34,231
Gross Profit	15,225	15,986	16,705	17,374	17,895	18,432
Commission Expenses	6,820	7,194	7,518	7,818	8,053	8,294
Selling Expenses	2,670	2,750	2,849	2,963	3,046	3,134
General & Administrative	4,062	4,143	4,243	4,395	4,448	4,515
Misc. (Income)/Expenses	(120)	(130)	(160)	(180)	(200)	(210)
Total Operating Expenses	13,432	13,957	14,450	14,996	15,347	15,733
Operating Cash Flow	1,793	2,029	2,255	2,378	2,548	2,699
Depreciation	182	191	238	222	209	198
Other (Income) /Expense	(298)	(200)	(218)	(229)	(241)	(216)
Earnings Before Interest and Taxes (EBIT)	1,909	2,038	2,235	2,385	2,580	2,717
Income Tax Provision (assuming a 40% tax rate)	764	815	894	954	1,032	1,087
Debt-Free Earnings	1,145	1,223	1,341	1,431	1,548	1,630

CASH FLOW STATEMENT Sources/(Uses)	**1995**	**1996**	**1997**	**1998**	**1999**
Debt-Free Earnings	$1,223	$1,341	$1,431	$1,548	$1,630
Depreciation	191	238	222	209	198
Net Change in Working Capital	(145)	(130)	(121)	(94)	(97)
Capital Expenditures	(250)	(180)	(190)	(200)	(210)
Net Cash Flow	$1,019	$1,269	$1,342	$1,463	$1,521

DISCOUNTED CASH FLOW ANALYSIS

Weighted Average Cost of Capital	**14.50%**	**15.00%**	**15.50%**
Continuing Value (1999) (based on perpetuity growth of 3.0%)	$13,625	$13,057	$12,535
Present Value of Continuing Value	7,099	6,961	6,827
Present Value of FYE 1995–1999 Cash Flows	4,682	4,633	4,585
Total Enterprise Value	11,781	11,594	11,412
Less the Market Value of Debt	550	550	550
Total Equity Value	$11,231	$11,044	$10,862

APPENDIX 2

Specialty Products: Determination of Representative Levels for the Fiscal Year Ending March 31 (Amounts Are in Thousands of Dollars)

	1992	1993	1994	
Operating Cash Flow	$985	$1,396	$1,793	
Plus Nonrecurring Computer Expense	0	0	75	
Adjusted Operating Cash Flow	$985	$1,396	$1,868	
Concluded Representative Operating Cash Flow				**$ 1,870**
Representative Operating Cash Flow			$1,870	
Less Depreciation Expense			(180)	
Representative Other Income			200	
Earnings Before Interest and Taxes (EBIT)			$1,890	
Concluded Representative EBIT				**$ 1,890**
Representative EBIT			$1,890	
Less Representative Interest Expense			(50)	
Earnings Before Taxes			1,840	
Less Taxes at 40%			(736)	
Earnings			$1,104	
Concluded Representative Earnings				**$ 1,100**
Projected 1995 EBIT			$2,038	
Less Estimated Taxes			(815)	
1995 Projected Earnings			$1,223	
Representative Projected Earnings				**$ 1,220**
Sales	$41,000	$41,600	$43,500	
Concluded Representative Sales				**$43,500**

APPENDIX 3

Specialty Products: Capitalization of Representative Levels (Amounts Are in Thousands of Dollars)

	Representative Level		Capitalization Multiple	Less: Debt*		EQUITY VALUE
Price to Earnings	$ 1,100	×	10.0		=	$11,000
Price to Projected Earnings	$ 1,220	×	9.0		=	$10,980
Value to Operating Cash Flow	$ 1,870	×	6.0	– $550	=	$10,670
Value to EBIT	$ 1,890	×	6.5	– $550	=	$11,735
Value to Sales	$43,500	×	0.25		=	$10,875
			Mean Equity Value			$11,052
			Median Equity Value			$10,980
			Range	$10,670	–	$11,735

* As discussed earlier, the debt-free approaches arrive at value indications for the total value of the company. Therefore, the value of the debt must be subtracted to derive the value of the equity.

APPENDIX 4

Specialty Products: Valuation Multiples of Publicly Traded Comparable Companies

	Price as a Multiple of Earnings per Share		
	Latest 12 Months	*Projected Fiscal Year*	*3-Year Average*
Comparable companies			
Argosy Promotions	9.8	8.7	DEF
Communication Associates	21.7	17.9	21.0
Kandela Corp.	27.1	21.6	51.9
Margate Corporation	13.1	10.5	22.0
Multi-Service Corp.	10.3	9.2	NA
Prospect Industries	16.9	NA	11.9
Range: High	27.1	21.6	51.9
Low	9.8	8.7	11.9
Mean	16.5	13.6	26.7
Median	15.0	10.5	21.5
Selected Multiple	**10.0**	**9.0**	

	Capitalized Value as a Multiple of:				Price as a Multiple of Book Value
	Operating Cash Flow		Sales	EBIT	
	Latest 12 Months	*3-Year Average*	*Latest 12 Months*	*Latest 12 Months*	
Comparable companies					
Argosy Promotions	5.9	11.1	0.44	6.4	0.9
Communication Associates	6.9	8.7	0.31	8.4	2.8
Kandela Corp.	10.5	19.1	1.38	14.1	2.0
Margate Corporation	5.9	6.3	0.51	8.8	1.3
Multi-Service Corp.	6.4	23.4	0.34	7.0	3.7
Prospect Industries	3.7	5.6	0.22	5.1	1.0
Range: High	10.5	23.4	1.38	14.1	3.7
Low	3.7	5.6	0.22	5.1	0.9
Mean	6.6	12.4	0.53	8.3	2.0
Median	6.2	9.9	0.39	7.7	1.7
Selected Multiple	**6.0**		**0.25**	**6.5**	

Notes

1. The formula for the Gordon Growth Model is:

   $$\frac{D}{V = (K - G)}$$

   Assuming the dividend (D) grows forever at a constant rate G, and G is less than the discount rate K, then V is the present value of the growing annuity stream.

2. The Capital Asset Pricing Model is a framework for analyzing the relationship between risk and rates of return. The relationship between risk and return is known as the Security Market Line and is expressed by the following equation:

   $$E(Ri) = Rf + B \times [E(Rm) - Rf]$$

   where:

E(Ri)	=	the expected returns on stock i
Rf	=	the risk-free rate of return
B	=	the beta coefficient for stock i
E(Rm)	=	the expected return on the market

3. The Cost of Capital is a weighted average of the firm's cost of debt and equity. The Cost of Capital can be determined with the following equation:

   $$Ko = (D \div V)(Ki)(1 - t) + (E \div V)(Ke)$$

   where:

Ko	=	weighted average cost of capital
Ki	=	company's cost of debt
t	=	company's marginal tax rate
V	=	market value of the company's total invested capital
D	=	market value of the company's debt
E	=	market value of the company's equity
D ÷ V	=	proportion of debt to total invested capital
E ÷ V	=	proportion of equity to total invested capital
Ke	=	company's cost of equity

6

The Valuation Implications of the ESOP Repurchase Obligation

Eric G. Hess

The factor that generally distinguishes stock held by an employee stock ownership plan (ESOP) from non-ESOP stock in a closely held company is the put option associated with the ESOP shares. Although this put option can significantly improve the marketability of ESOP shares (and therefore increase their fair market value), it simultaneously creates a contingent financial obligation that can also reduce the company's future growth potential. This article describes how this reduction in growth potential, and the manner by which the shares are repurchased, can affect the value of the company and its stock.

The Internal Revenue Code provides that stock acquired by an employee stock ownership plan (ESOP) after December 31, 1979, must be subject to a put option if the stock is not readily tradable on an established market at the time of distribution to participants.[1] This put option, which requires a closely held company to repurchase its shares at the current fair market value, creates an ability to liquidate ESOP shares that previously did not exist. The improved marketability and liquidity of the ESOP shares relative to non-ESOP shares can significantly enhance value.[2] However, because the put option will enhance value only to the extent that the company has the ability to meet its obligation, the repurchase obligation should be considered when assessing the marketability of ESOP shares.[3]

The repurchase obligation may affect more than the marketability of the shares, however. In many cases, even though the company has the ability to meet the obligation, it will have to sacrifice certain growth opportunities to do so. To the extent that this occurs, the repurchase obligation also may reduce the company's value (before any consideration is given to the marketability of the shares). Consequently, the potential effect that the repurchase obligation can have on the fundamental economics of the business also should be considered.

Companies generally fulfill their repurchase obligations either by repurchasing the ESOP shares directly or by making regular contributions to the ESOP, which are then used to fund the continual repurchase of ESOP shares. From a valuation perspective, these two situations should be viewed

---

Eric G. Hess, CPA, is a vice president with Merrill Lynch's Business Advisory Services division, which provides specialized investment banking services to middle-market companies. He is based in Chicago.

differently. When the company uses a repurchase transaction to reduce the number of outstanding shares, it is participating in a capital market transaction regardless of what party holds the shares. Consequently, if the price paid represents fair market value, there should be no effect on the per-share value of the outstanding shares after the transaction. On the other hand, if the company makes regular cash contributions to the ESOP in order for the ESOP to continually repurchase the shares, the company is essentially funding a component of its overall compensation program. Therefore, share repurchases by the ESOP also may reduce share value if the repurchase obligation results in increased compensation expense.

This article begins by providing some relevant background information on the repurchase obligation, including a discussion of the two key factors affecting its size: employee turnover and share value growth. The article then describes an approach to forecasting future share values, and discusses the valuation differences between a share repurchase by the ESOP and a share repurchase by the company. Finally, the effect that the repurchase obligation can have on the company's growth potential and share valuation is discussed.

Background

Although not reflected on the balance sheet, a closely held company has a legal obligation to repurchase its ESOP stock distributed to former plan participants and their beneficiaries.[4] In general, the put option attached to the ESOP stock requires the company to offer to repurchase its shares at fair market value during two option periods following the date of distribution.[5]

Distribution and Vesting Requirements

There are certain distribution and vesting provisions that an ESOP must provide. Unless the participant elects otherwise, distributions of vested balances must begin following the occurrence of one of the following four events:[6]

- *Retirement:* Distributions must begin within one year after the end of the plan year in which the participant retires. If the stock was acquired with an ESOP loan, however, in some cases distributions can be deferred until the loan is repaid.[7] This distribution can generally be spread over a maximum of five years with six annual installments.[8]
- *Death or Disability:* The distribution rules are generally the same as for retirement, but plans tend to provide that benefits become 100% vested.
- *Termination (Voluntary or Involuntary):* Distributions can be deferred for up to six years for pre-retirees or until an existing ESOP loan is

repaid. Once distributions begin, they can be spread over a five-year period with six annual installments.

- *Diversification:* Participants reaching age 55 with 10 years of participation in the plan have the option of diversifying up to 25% of their stock account. This election period runs for five years, after which they have an option to diversify a total aggregate of 50% of their stock account.[9]

The current vesting requirements provide that benefits must either be (1) 100% vested after five years of participation in the plan, or (2) 20% vested after three years, with an additional 20% for each of the following years so that a participant is 100% vested after seven years of service.[10]

Factors Affecting the Size of the Repurchase Obligation

The overall magnitude of the repurchase obligation is a function of the percentage of equity held by the ESOP as well as the specific distribution and vesting provisions adopted by the plan. Clearly, if the ESOP holds 100% of the equity, the company's repurchase obligation will be greater than if the ESOP holds 10%. Similarly, if the ESOP has distribution and vesting provisions that exceed the minimum requirements, the repurchase obligation will generally be more significant. However, for any particular ESOP, employee turnover and growth in the value of the stock are the factors most likely to affect the size of the repurchase obligation.

Employee Turnover

Employee turnover became a much more significant factor after the Tax Reform Act of 1986 ("TRA '86") for two reasons. First, employees terminating their employment before retirement must now receive their distributions earlier. As noted previously, terminating employees must now begin receiving their distributions after six years. Before TRA '86, the company could generally postpone these distributions until the employees reached retirement age. Second, TRA '86 significantly accelerated the vesting schedule for employees. Before TRA '86, the company could elect a vesting schedule in which employees were 100% vested only after 10 to 15 years of service.

The accelerated distribution and vesting requirements have a considerable effect on the size of the repurchase obligation when the company adopts a recycling process in which it repurchases the shares and contributes them back to the ESOP (or, more commonly, has the ESOP repurchase the shares directly through company contributions). Because the repurchased shares are reallocated to the remaining ESOP participants, employee turnover (either through retirement or termination) means the company must repurchase the same shares more than once.[11]

Because most employees terminate their employment before retirement, pre-retirement employee turnover often represents the largest percentage of the total repurchase obligation.[12] Pre-retirement turnover also increases the repurchase obligation because it creates forfeitures that accelerate the development of account balances of those employees who remain. Therefore, pre-retirement turnover is particularly significant because the company may be required to repurchase a larger number of shares more often.[13]

Value Growth

The other key factor affecting the size of the repurchase obligation is the future value of the ESOP shares. Whereas employee turnover generally affects the number of distributions, share value growth affects the distribution amounts. One way in which the company can reduce the effect of share value growth is to distribute the shares at the earliest distribution date and repurchase them for cash or a note. By immediately distributing the shares and repurchasing them, the company minimizes the participant's account balance because he or she no longer participates in the appreciation of the stock. However, as discussed earlier, when the company recycles ESOP shares, employee turnover means the company (or the ESOP) is purchasing the same shares more than once. Hence, an immediate distribution by the ESOP has the offsetting effect of increasing the number of shares to be repurchased over a period of time. Consequently, employee turnover and share value growth must both be analyzed to determine the overall magnitude of the repurchase obligation.

Projecting Future Share Values

Given the significance of share value growth on the size of the repurchase obligation, future share levels should be analyzed annually to determine the effect of the repurchase obligation on the marketability of the shares and the company's growth potential. One approach to project future share levels is to use a constant rate of share appreciation. For example, a future rate of appreciation could be selected based on the 12.4% annual return that small company common stocks have provided over the last 73 years.[14] However, using a constant rate of appreciation may not provide the best estimate of the company's future share value because it ignores various company-specific factors such as changing cash and debt levels, risk, and the manner by which the company handles its repurchases. For example, when the company is projected to repay a significant amount of debt in the near future, the equity value will likely appreciate at a faster rate than would occur simply based on an increase in the company's overall value.

An alternative approach that attempts to capture the company-specific factors is to project future share levels based on the company's financial forecast. The company's operating value can be estimated throughout the forecast period by using projected operating fundamentals (e.g., operating income, operating cash flow, and revenues) as a basis. By identifying the most relevant price relationships, using the most recent valuation or longer-term pricing benchmarks, one can estimate the company's future value.[15] Then, by deducting the projected level of interest-bearing debt claims from the calculated company value, one can derive a projected equity value. To the extent that the financial projections are reasonable, this methodology should provide a better estimate of future share values than applying a flat share return estimate.

To illustrate this approach, assume that ABC Company has an ESOP that holds 50% of the company's equity. The company's management is concerned about the effect that the ESOP repurchase obligation could have on its growth plans and has retained an actuarial consultant to estimate the amount and timing of employee turnover. Management intends to use the actuary's analysis along with the company's projections to assess the effect of the repurchase obligation.

ABC Company has a current (invested capital) value of $48 million, based on a representative operating cash flow of approximately $8 million and an invested capital multiple of 6.0. The company has $16 million of interest-bearing debt outstanding, so its current equity value is $32 million, or $32.00 per share based on one million shares outstanding. These facts are summarized in table 1.

Table 1 also shows the company's projected operating cash flow and value changes for the next three years. Based on a representative invested capital multiple of 6.0, the value of the company is projected to increase by 12.5% by the end of the first year to $54 million. The company is also projected to repay $2 million of debt in the first year. Because any excess cash will likely be used to repay debt, the company is not expected to have a significant cash position at any time during the forecast period.

Subtracting the projected debt balance of $14 million from the projected company value of $54 million provides a projected equity value of $40 million, or $40.00 per share, at the end of the first year. As a result of the projected debt repayment, the equity value is projected to appreciate by 25% in the first year, which is 12.5% greater than the appreciation in the value of the company. Based on appreciation in the second and third years of 12.5% and 11.1%, respectively, the stock is projected to have a value of $50.00 per share at the end of the third year.

Because the equity value at the end of the explicit forecast period (three years in the example) serves as a base value for all future appreciation, a more precise estimate of equity appreciation during the first few years should improve the estimate of the repurchase obligation in all future periods. Consequently, in many cases it is possible to assess the effect of the repurchase obligation more precisely by using share appreciation rates based on the company-specific forecast in addition to those based on historical averages.

Table 1. Projected Share Appreciation for ABC Company

Operating cash flow	$ 8,000,000
Invested capital multiple	x 6.0
Company value	$ 48,000,000
Less: outstanding debt	(16,000,000)
Equity value	$ 32,000,000
Shares outstanding	÷ 1,000,000
Value per share	$ 32.00

	Projection		
	Year 1	Year 2	Year 3
Operating cash flow (000's)	$ 9,000	$ 9,500	$ 10,000
Invested capital multiple	x 6.0	x 6.0	x 6.0
Company value (000's)	$ 54,000	$ 57,000	$ 60,000
Change in company value	12.5%	5.6%	5.3%
Less: outstanding debt (000's)	(14,000)	(12,000)	(10,000)
Equity value (000's)	$ 40,000	$ 45,000	$ 50,000
Value per share	$ 40.00	$ 45.00	$ 50.00
Change in value per share	25.0%	12.5%	11.1%

Share Repurchase: Company vs. ESOP

Although most companies make contributions to the ESOP so that the ESOP can continually repurchase the ESOP shares, this is not necessarily required.[16] The company also may repurchase the shares directly from the participants and then retire them or place them in treasury. The characteristic that generally distinguishes a company repurchase (figure 1) from an ESOP repurchase (figure 2) is the number of outstanding shares after the transaction. With a company repurchase the number of outstanding shares is reduced after the transaction, whereas with an ESOP repurchase the number of outstanding shares remains the same.

Company Share Repurchase

From a valuation perspective, a repurchase of shares by the company is treated differently than a repurchase by the ESOP. When the company repurchases its shares directly, regardless of what party holds the shares, it is essentially participating in a capital market transaction. Consequently, if the price paid represents fair market value, there should be no effect on the per-share value of the outstanding shares after the transaction. Further

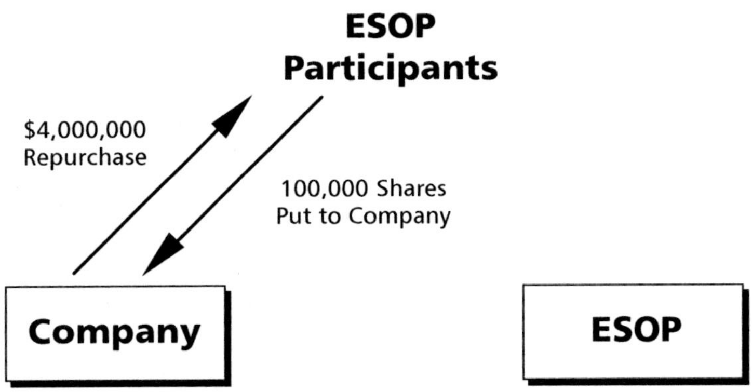

Figure 1. Company share repurchase

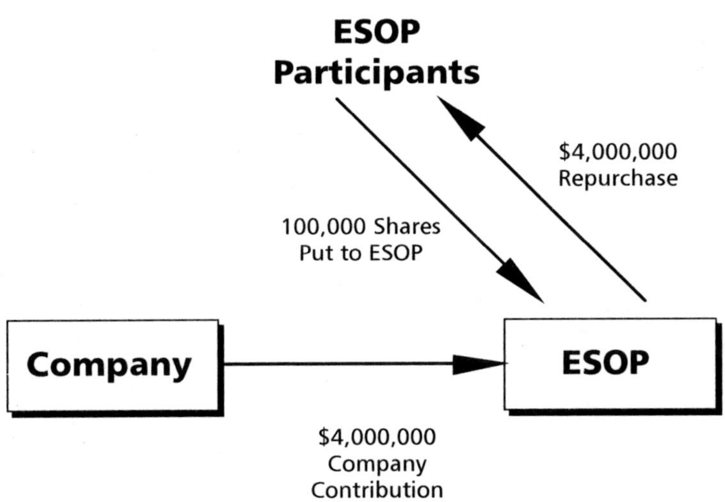

Figure 2. ESOP share repurchase

analysis of our hypothetical ABC Company will illustrate this point. Assume that the actuary projects that 100,000 ESOP shares will be distributed next year. As table 1 indicates, the fair market value of the company's equity is projected to be $40 million, or $40.00 per share, at the end of the first year. Based on these projections, the company will have a $4 million repurchase obligation at the end of next year. If the company repurchases the shares at $40.00 per share, the value of the equity will fall by $4 million, but the value per share will remain unchanged at $40.00. The value per share remains unchanged because the number of outstanding shares also will decline. This analysis is shown in table 2.

Of course, if the company adopts a policy of repurchasing its ESOP stock and does not recontribute any shares to the ESOP, the number of outstanding shares held by the ESOP as well as its percentage of ownership will decline over time (assuming the ESOP does not hold 100% of the equity). As a result, new employees may have limited opportunities to participate in the ESOP.

Table 2. Value Effect of Company Repurchase

Before Repurchase of ESOP Shares:		
Equity value	$40,000,000	
Shares outstanding	÷ 1,000,000	
Value per share	$ 40.00	
After Repurchase of ESOP Shares:		
Equity value (pre-repurchase)	$40,000,000	
Less: cash paid to repurchase shares	(4,000,000)	
Equity value (post-repurchase)	$36,000,000	(1)
Shares outstanding (pre-repurchase)	$ 1,000,000	
Less: treasury shares	(100,000)	
Shares outstanding (post-repurchase)	900,000	(2)
Value per share (post-repurchase)	$ 40.00	(1) ÷ (2)

ESOP Share Repurchase

A repurchase of shares by the ESOP is different than a company repurchase because it essentially represents a component of the company's compensation program. By making annual cash contributions to the ESOP for the ESOP to continually repurchase the shares, the company is contributing to its overall compensation program just as it would to a 401(k) or similar retirement plan. Accordingly, the company receives a tax deduction for its contributions to the ESOP.

The effect of an ESOP repurchase on share value depends on whether the company's contributions to the ESOP represent increased compensation expense. The level of compensation expense reflected in the share value depends on whether the ESOP shares represent a control position.[17] If the ESOP shares represent a control block, the benefit expense reflected in the share value should generally be based on the market level for similar-sized firms in the industry.[18] On the other hand, if the ESOP holds a minority interest, the value of the shares should generally be based on the existing level of ESOP benefits.[19] In either situation, if the level of company contributions to the ESOP exceeds the level of compensation expense reflected in the share value, an ESOP repurchase will result in share value dilution.

To illustrate, consider the previous example, except that instead of having the company repurchase the shares directly, the ESOP will repurchase 100,000 shares at $40.00 per share. Also assume that the entire amount of the repurchase represents increased compensation expense. In this case, the ESOP will also have to pay $4 million to repurchase the shares but the company will receive a tax benefit of $1.6 million ($4 million × 40% tax rate) for its contribution, so the net cost will be $2.4 million. At the same time, however, the number of outstanding shares will not be reduced, so the value per share is projected to decline by $2.40, as shown in table 3.

Table 3. Value Effect of ESOP Repurchase (Additional Benefit Case)

Before Repurchase of ESOP Shares:		
Equity value	$40,000,000	
Shares outstanding	÷ 1,000,000	
Value per share	$ 40.00	
After Repurchase of ESOP Shares:		
Equity value (pre-repurchase)	$40,000,000	
Less: cash paid to repurchase shares	(4,000,000)	
Add: tax benefit of repurchase	1,600,000	
Equity value (post-repurchase)	$37,600,000	(1)
Shares outstanding (pre-repurchase)	1,000,000	
Less: treasury shares	- 0 -	
Shares outstanding (post-repurchase)	1,000,000	(2)
Value per share (post-repurchase)	$ 37.60	(1) ÷ (2)

As figure 2 indicates, a repurchase by the ESOP is essentially equivalent to a company repurchase with a recontribution of shares. In the previously described company share repurchase (table 2), if the company had recontributed the 100,000 shares it had purchased for $4 million to the ESOP, the value per share would have declined by $2.40 as well. This understanding is important because it highlights the effect of the various components of a repurchase transaction. In the repurchase phase of the transaction, the equity value falls by $4 million but the value per share remains unchanged. In the recontribution phase, the equity value remains unchanged, but the value per share falls by $2.40. As this analysis indicates, if the recontribution of shares represents increased compensation, the transaction will transfer wealth from non-ESOP shareholders to the ESOP participants. Consequently, when the shares are repurchased by the ESOP, any increased benefits provided come at the expense of the non-ESOP shareholders.

The effect of an ESOP repurchase on share value will be reduced, however, if the ESOP contributions replace or reduce existing wages or benefits. To illustrate, assume that when ABC Company's ESOP was formed, the company discontinued contributions to its profit sharing plan, which had historically represented approximately 10% of payroll. Also assume that instead the company has been contributing 10% of its payroll to the ESOP and that the company's payroll is projected to be $20 million next year. As with the previous example, the projection indicates that the ESOP will repurchase 100,000 shares at $40.00 per share for a total of $4 million. In this case, however, the value of the equity already reflects a normal level of retirement benefits based on 10% of payroll, or $2 million. As table 4 indicates, because the company has to contribute only an additional $2 million to repurchase the shares, the value per share is projected to decline by $1.20 rather than $2.40.

The company can eliminate any effect on share value by having the company repurchase and retire the shares that represent benefits above the normal level.[20] Consequently, even though the ESOP repurchases will vary from year to year, the company can maintain a target level of benefits by contributing a certain benefit percentage to the ESOP each year. In years when the repurchase amount is less than the target benefit level, the company can contribute cash to the plan to be allocated to accounts, which may be used to fund future repurchases. In the last example, if ABC Company wished to have retirement benefits represent 10% of payroll, the ESOP and the company could both repurchase $2 million of stock. Because the level of employee benefits is limited in this manner, the value per share remains unchanged.

The Repurchase Obligation's Effect on Value

The effect of the repurchase obligation on share value is largely a function of the percentage of equity held by the ESOP and the funding options avail-

Table 4. Value Effect of ESOP Repurchase (Replacement Benefit Case)

Share value	$ 40.00	
Shares repurchased	x 100,000	
Cash paid to repurchase shares	$ 4,000,000	
Less: amount of repurchase reflected in current share value	(2,000,000)	
Additional cash paid to repurchase shares	$ 2,000,000	
After Repurchase of ESOP Shares:		
Equity value (pre-repurchase)	$40,000,000	
Less: additional cash paid to repurchase shares (see above)	(2,000,000)	
Add: net tax benefit of repurchase	800,000	
Equity value (post-repurchase)	$38,800,000	(1)
Shares outstanding (pre-repurchase)	1,000,000	
Less: treasury shares	- 0 -	
Shares outstanding (post-repurchase)	1,000,000	(2)
Value per share (post-repurchase)	$ 38.80	(1) ÷ (2)

able. If the ESOP holds a very small percentage of the stock or if the company could easily fund the obligation through alternative means, the repurchase obligation is likely to have little effect on value. However, because most closely held companies are faced with funding their own repurchases, the repurchase obligation can affect both the marketability of the ESOP shares and the company's growth opportunities. Consequently, ESOP companies should generally integrate their analysis of the repurchase obligation with their overall business plan.

The repurchase obligation will probably have an effect on the company's growth potential before it affects the marketability of its shares. Even if the company is able to honor the put option, the repurchase obligation may still have an effect on the fundamental economics of the business. This occurs because the repurchase obligation must be met before cash flow can be diverted to projects that add value to the company. Moreover, because any effect on the fundamental economics of the business affects non-ESOP shares as well, non-ESOP shareholders can suffer a detriment in wealth at the same time that the value of ESOP shares is enhanced through improved marketability.

The Corporate Life Cycle

Although closely held companies are obliged to offer to repurchase their ESOP shares, public companies generally are not. In fact, public companies that are growing rapidly often do not repurchase shares or pay dividends until their growth slows.[21] In the meantime, they can reinvest their free cash flow in projects that provide a rate of return that exceeds their cost of capital.

The history of IBM provides an excellent example of the typical corporate life cycle. Although IBM has paid dividends since the 1930s, most investors historically bought the stock for its growth opportunities. Throughout the 1950s and 1960s the dividend yield was generally between 1% and 2% at a time when its sales, earnings, and dividends were growing at compound annual rates of roughly 20%. By the mid-1970s, however, IBM lacked investment opportunities attractive enough to justify continued growth at that rate. Still, the business remained healthy and profitable and the company accumulated cash at a very high rate. At the end of 1976 and 1977, the company had cash and marketable securities of $6.2 billion and $5.4 billion, respectively. As a result, IBM began paying more and more generous dividends. In 1978, it paid $2.88 per share on earnings per share of $5.32, a 54% payout ratio. At the same time, the company spent about $2.1 billion to repurchase its shares during 1977 and 1978. This pattern continued until 1991, when IBM's sales, earnings, and operating cash flow began to decline. Since then, the company has significantly reduced its expenses, and its cash flow has improved significantly. As a result, IBM's board authorized additional share repurchases.

The closely held ESOP company may not have the luxury of being able to follow the typical corporate life cycle, however. Consequently, closely held ESOP companies that are growing rapidly may have to forgo certain growth opportunities to fund the repurchase obligation. Therefore, the repurchase obligation can depress the value of the company and its stock.

Forgone Growth Opportunities

The value of a company is ultimately based on its future cash flows. In other words, the value of a company is based on its current cash flow generating ability plus any investments made to increase its future cash flows. The following equation summarizes this relationship:

$$\text{Value of Company} = \frac{\text{Free Cash Flow}_1}{r} + \text{PVGO}$$

The first term represents a perpetuity of the company's current free cash flow (revenues minus costs minus base level investment) based on the company's cost of capital (r) in a no-growth state. The second component represents the present value of growth opportunities (PVGO) resulting from investment projects that will increase future cash flows. This equation indicates that a company can be generating very little free cash flow at the present time, but may still have significant value as a result of its investments for future growth. For companies in the early stages of their life cycle, the present value of growth opportunities is generally the more significant component.

Because the value of the company's equity is simply the value of the company less any interest-bearing debt outstanding, the value of the equity is also determined by the company's future cash flows. The following equation summarizes the value of the company's equity:

$$\text{Value of Equity} = \text{Value of Company} - \text{Debt}$$

By substituting the equation for the value of the company in the above equation, one can see that incremental equity value is also based on the company's future growth opportunities. If the company has no investment opportunities that increase shareholder value, the shareholders are better off if the company uses available cash to pay a dividend or repurchase shares. From the company's perspective, the best return it can achieve in this case is to invest in itself.

Assessing the Effect

To assess the likely effect of the repurchase obligation, consideration should be given to where the company is in its life cycle. The company's financial leverage and cash flow variability should also be examined, because the repurchase obligation is likely to have the largest effect on a company's growth opportunities when the company has high financial leverage and highly variable cash flows. If the company is highly leveraged, particularly with non-ESOP debt, the company will have little additional borrowing capacity and therefore less flexibility to fund the obligation. As a result, the repurchase obligation is more likely to create a situation where the company must forgo investments that would create additional shareholder value.

Similarly, companies that have highly variable cash flows are more likely to be affected by the repurchase obligation. Companies generally have more variable cash flows if they are in industries that are capital intensive, cyclical or otherwise volatile, characterized by high operating leverage, or given to short product life cycles. If the company's free cash flow is reduced at a time when it needs to fund its repurchase obligation, the company will have fewer resources to fund projects that will increase future cash flows. Figure 3 summarizes the risk relationship between the company's characteristics and the repurchase obligation's effect on growth opportunities.

		Financial Leverage: High	Financial Leverage: Low
Cash Flow Variability	High	Highest Risk Level	Moderate Risk Level
	Low	Moderate Risk Level	Lowest Risk Level

Figure 3. Degree of risk that the repurchase obligation will affect the company's growth opportunities

Conclusion

The repurchase obligation can affect the company's growth prospects, employee compensation, and, ultimately, shareholder value. Thus, to minimize any effect on share value, the repurchase obligation should be considered during the initial plan design as well as in subsequent years as part of the annual business planning process.

Notes

1. Internal Revenue Code ("Code") § 409(h)(1)(B). In addition, employer securities acquired with the proceeds of an ESOP loan after September 30, 1976, must be subject to a put option if the shares are not readily tradable upon distribution.
2. Several empirical studies have shown that the value of shares with restricted marketability is substantially less than the value of actively traded shares in the same company. For example, one of the most recent studies examined private placements of unregistered stock between 1981 and 1988 and found the average discount was 33.75% relative to the publicly traded price. William L. Silber, "Discounts on Restricted Stock: The Impact of Illiquidity on Stock Prices," *Financial Analysts Journal* 47 (July-August 1991): 60-64.
3. The U.S. Department of Labor stated this position in its Proposed Regulation Relating to the Definition of Adequate Consideration, 29 C.F.R. Part 2510.
4. Once the stock has been put to the company, the amount that has not been paid should be reflected as a liability on the company's balance sheet, however.
5. In most cases, the put option requires the company to repurchase its ESOP stock at the current fair market value during the 60-day period following the date of the distribution. If the person or entity receiving the distribution fails to exercise the put during this initial time frame, the distributee receives a second opportunity in the form of another 60-day period after a new stock valuation has been completed and communicated to the distributee during the next plan year. Code § 409(h)(4).
6. These distribution requirements need only apply to employer stock acquired by the ESOP after December 31, 1986. As a practical matter, however, many ESOPs

apply these accelerated distribution requirements to all stock regardless of acquisition date. See Code Section 409(o)(1), the minimum distribution requirements of Code Section 401(a)(9), and the general distribution rules of Code Section 401(a)(14).

7. Code § 409(o)(1)(B).
8. If the balance credited to a participant's account exceeds $500,000, the distribution period may be extended an additional year for each $100,000 or fraction thereof by which the participant's account exceeds $500,000. (These amounts are adjusted annually by the IRS to reflect cost-of-living increases, and for 1999 are respectively $735,000 and $145,000.) However, the distribution period cannot be extended for more than an additional five years, regardless of the amount of the participant's account balance, unless the participant elects to receive his or her benefits over a longer period of time.
9. This feature was added as part of the Tax Reform Act of 1986 and is effective for stock acquired by an ESOP after December 31, 1986. Code § 401(a)(28).
10. Code § 411(a). These vesting schedules apply for plan years beginning after December 31, 1988.
11. The reallocation process can be delayed by using additional ESOP loans.
12. Pre-retirement turnover may have little effect on a company's repurchase obligation if employee turnover largely occurs during the first few years of employment and the company adopts a five-year "cliff vesting" schedule. If these conditions exist, very few shares will be vested when most employees terminate their employment.
13. Because pre-retirement employee turnover is often most difficult for the company to predict, it is also most likely to create unexpected constraints on the company's cash flows.
14. See *Stocks, Bonds, Bills, and Inflation: 1999 Yearbook* (Chicago: Ibbotson Associates, 1999), which examines various rates of return and inflation from 1926 to 1998.
15. Any reference to the company value is based on its invested capital. Invested capital represents the company's interest-bearing debt and equity. It is generally easier to compare a closely held company with publicly traded companies based on invested capital than equity, because equity multiples are more likely to be influenced by leverage, making comparisons across companies more difficult.
16. A 1991 study conducted by the National Center for Employee Ownership found that 56% of ESOP companies had the ESOP repurchase the shares and 23% had the company repurchase the shares. See Corey Rosen, "How ESOP Companies are Handling Repurchase Obligations," *Journal of Employee Ownership Law and Finance* 4, no. 1 (winter 1992): 39-56.
17. The determination of whether the block of stock held by the ESOP represents a control position depends on the facts and circumstances of each case and should not be based simply on the ESOP's percentage of ownership. The U.S. Department of Labor's position is that the payment of a control premium is unwarranted unless the plan obtains both voting control and control in fact. For additional discussion on the issue of control see "Valuation Issues—The Premium for Control," chap. 6 of *Valuing ESOP Shares* (Washington, D.C.: The ESOP Association, 1994).
18. When the ESOP shares represent a control position, a hypothetical third-party buyer would most likely adjust the company's benefit expense to the level neces-

sary to retain and motivate employees in a particular industry. Therefore, when valuing ESOP shares representing a control block, ESOP expense levels should be adjusted to reflect a market level of retirement benefits.

Surveys have shown that larger companies generally provide higher levels of benefits than smaller companies and certain industries have a higher benefit level than others. See, e.g., Chamber of Commerce of the United States, *Employee Benefits: Survey Data from Benefit Year 1993* (Washington, D.C., 1994).

19. When the ESOP holds a minority interest, the buyer would most likely have little influence over the determination of employee benefits. Consequently, the value of minority interest shares should be based on the existing level of ESOP benefits.

20. The use of a company repurchase is also appropriate when the total contribution to the ESOP exceeds the maximum allowable for tax purposes.

21. A company share repurchase and a cash dividend are essentially equivalent although a company repurchase is generally tax-advantaged to the shareholder. For additional discussion, see Richard A. Brealey and Stewart C. Myers, "The Dividend Controversy," chap. 16 in *Principles of Corporate Finance* (New York: McGraw-Hill, 1996).

7

Repurchase Economics and Valuation Effects

E.W. (Sandy) Purcell

It is generally accepted appraisal practice to make an adjustment to the expense structure of a company for the ongoing ESOP contribution expenses. The allocation should incorporate both the normal level of benefit expense and the expected level of ESOP expense for repurchase into the future. The difficulty is predicting the amount of future ESOP contributions. These contributions are dependent on future prices of the ESOP stock. The future prices of the ESOP stock are dependent on the expected future ESOP expense. This issue can be dealt with by setting up a spreadsheet with a circular argument and allowing the iteration calculation to solve the circular argument. This article discusses the issue of benefit compensation related to expected future ESOP expense and what factors may have an impact on the magnitude of the cash required to fund repurchases.

Over the past few years, an evolution in thinking about the effects and implications of the repurchase obligation in closely held employee stock ownership plan (ESOP) companies has taken place. Contributions to an ESOP represent compensation to the employee participants. In some instances, these contributions exceed the level of "normal compensation" for the industry. Can this excess level of compensation have an impact on the value of the company sponsoring the ESOP, and does the decision to redeem shares versus recycle shares have any impact on this conclusion? In this article I propose a framework for quantifying the repurchase obligation and further suggest there is a valuation implication to a company from the repurchase obligation.

Valuation

The value of a company is typically determined by using a market approach or an income approach. The market approach compares the performance measures of the subject company to the observable measures of companies traded publicly. This methodology relies on historical cash flows and may

E.W. (Sandy) Purcell is a director in the Chicago office of Houlihan Lokey Howard & Zukin, a national business valuation consulting firm. He holds an MBA from the University of Chicago and has more than 18 years of experience in the financial services and advisory industry. Mr. Purcell manages business valuation and financial advisory projects; works on capital assignments involving the sale of businesses, mergers, and raising debt and equity for client companies; has been involved in financial restructurings; has significant experience with implementation of ESOPs; and has worked at structuring, negotiating, and closing complex financial and capital transactions.

not include the impact of ESOP contributions unless an explicit adjustment for the appropriate amount of expected ESOP contribution is made. The income approach looks to the performance measures of earnings and cash flows projected into the future. Performance measures typically include compensation and benefit expenses but generally exclude the cash flows required to redeem shares in the future since it is difficult to predict the amount of future ESOP contributions that are dependent on future ESOP stock prices.

Where an ESOP is the buyer of a company and the purchase is accomplished with debt, the post-transaction value of the company's equity is reduced by an amount that is represented by the face value of the debt since the debt is related to a distribution of cash to selling shareholders and the number of shares outstanding remains the same. Contributions to the ESOP during the loan amortization period frequently exceed the level of benefits considered normal for the industry. After the loan is amortized, the ESOP company will have continuing contributions to meet the repurchase obligation. There is an underlying assumption that the ESOP contributions represent normal levels of benefit expense. Generally, value is affected for debt in the valuation context, but not for the continuing contributions made by an ESOP company for the repurchase of shares. Unfortunately, once the debt is repaid, the impact of the continuing contributions is frequently ignored. To the extent that the continuing contributions are not reflected in the compensation expense of the company, the effect is to miss an element of the cost structure of the company and to potentially overvalue the company (figure 1) (i.e., if ongoing ESOP expense is not considered or adequately qualified, then the company may be overvalued). Again, the difficulty is estimating the amount of future ESOP contributions that are dependent on future ESOP stock prices.

A question most closely held ESOP companies deal with is whether the contributions, including those required to retire debt and the subsequent contributions that will be made for repurchase obligations, exceed the level of market-related compensation. Compensation cost includes the total compensation package. The first step is to get a sense of the benefit levels for the company's industry. What are the normal or standard compensation costs in that industry? What is the benefit cost of the ESOP as measured against this standard?

As an example, my firm recently looked at benefit costs as a percentage of total compensation for one client. The standard industry benefits as a percentage of compensation were compared to the benefits paid by the client, including its ESOP contributions. Table 1 depicts the result of the comparison.

The cost structure of the company reflects higher levels of benefits over the industry level for each of the last three years. Compensation amounts up to the normal industry level are considered normal compensation. Com-

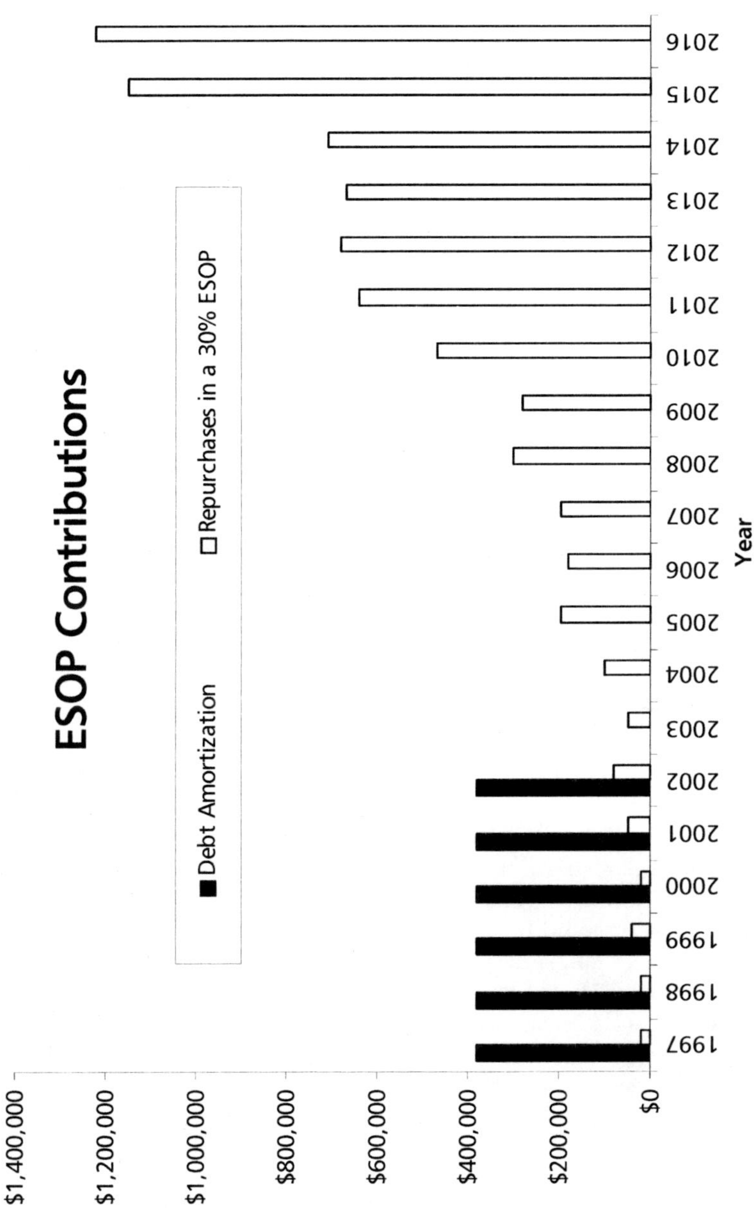

Figure 1. Debt amortization occurs for five years and contributions for ESOP share repurchases go on indefinitely

Table 1. Benefits as a Percentage of Compensation

Benefits as a percentage of compensation:	1995	1996	1997
Industry standard	7.8	7.9	8.1
ABC ESOP Company's benefits	10.2	8.6	12.3

pensation amounts in excess of the normal industry levels are considered excess compensation. For the company with employee ownership as a strategy and the ESOP as a long-term benefit, the cost structure differential (normal versus excess compensation) should be taken into consideration for valuation purposes.

Redemption Versus Recirculation

The repurchase obligation results from the requirement that the sponsoring employer repurchase shares of stock distributed to ESOP participants. In essence, the ESOP creates an ownership transition issue. Most ownership transitions are decided by company shareholders. In an ESOP company, the demographics of the employee population and the provisions of the plan document determine the timing of the ownership transition. When a participant "puts" stock, the company must make a strategic decision to "redeem" shares or "recirculate" them (the latter is sometimes referred to as "recycling").

In redeeming the shares directly from the participant, the company uses its assets to buy the shares. The impact is to reduce the value of the company by the amount of the purchase. However, the redemption also lowers the number of shares outstanding. There is no dilutive impact on the per-share value as a result of the redemption to the remaining shareholders as long as the transaction occurs at fair market value.

The other repurchase option available to the company is to repurchase the shares from the participant and then contribute those shares to the ESOP for redistribution to remaining employees as part of a continuing benefit. (A variation would be to make contributions directly to the ESOP trust and have the redemptions take place in the trust.) Whether the shares are contributed or purchased by the ESOP trust, they are reallocated to the remaining participants. In this manner, the remaining participants receive compensation. The end result is to provide the company with an opportunity to make tax-deductible contributions to a qualified plan and to maintain the relative size of the ESOP.

Where recirculation occurs, the continuing contributions for recirculation of shares has the potential for diluting the per-share value to the remaining shareholders. Since the same number of shares remain outstanding, the appearance of the redemption is that the company has made a distribution to all shareholders. To the extent that the contributions represent a higher amount of compensation expense and the operating "cost" structure of the company has changed, then there can also be an impact on the value of the company.

A side-by-side example shows the dilutive result of a recirculation when compared to redemption (table 2). Assume the market equity value is $10 million, there are 1 million shares outstanding, and the per-share price is $10. Now assume participants put 100,000 shares to the company at a fair market value. What is the post-redemption fair market value price per share?

In those ESOP companies that intend to perpetuate their ESOPs, it is important to recognize that making the contributions to the ESOP necessary to recycle shares is like paying a dividend, since the number of shares that remain outstanding is unchanged. In this respect, the ESOP can be viewed as a perpetual transition program. Ownership transition occurs between the departing participant and the remaining participants. Recycled shares that are reallocated represent compensation to the participants. A recycling decision is also a compensation decision. The impact of this decision on the cost structure of the company relates to the issue of whether the company is paying normal versus excess compensation levels.

Factors Affecting the Repurchase Amount

There are several factors that affect the dollar magnitude of the repurchase obligation. Plan provisions are very important. The decisions made at the time of the inception of the ESOP have potential timing effects on when distributions will occur. Ultimately, the provisions only defer the obligation. However, there are three factors having an obvious effect on the amount of the repurchase obligation. These factors are (1) the size of the ESOP, (2) the rate of turnover in the employee population (included here is the diversification requirement), and (3) the growth of the underlying stock value.

The size of the ESOP is measured as the percentage of ownership of the company. The magnitude of the repurchase obligation would be smaller for a 30% ESOP-owned company than for a 100% ESOP-owned company. All other things being equal, each participant would hold a greater number of shares as the ESOP ownership percentage increases.

The level of turnover of the employee population is an important factor in the determination of the ESOP repurchase obligation. The higher the level of turnover, the higher the expected level of repurchase obligation. The company with a 20-year turnover of the employee population could expect to have a much smaller annual compensation contribution to the ESOP than the company with a 10-year employee population turnover.

The growth in the value of a company is reflected in the share value. The higher the growth level of the value of the company, the higher the per-share price of the ESOP shares distributed to participants. If the growth rate in the company value is zero, we would expect no increase in the magnitude of the

Table 2. Comparison of the Relative Effect of Recycling and Redemption on Per-Share Value

Recycling of Shares		Redemption	
Equity value	$10,000,000	Equity value	$10,000,000
less cash for repurchases	– $1,000,000	less cash for redemption	– $1,000,000
plus tax savings of contributions	400,000	Post-redemption equity value	$9,000,000
Post-repurchase equity value	$9,400,000		
Shares outstanding	1,000,000	Shares outstanding (pre-redemption)	1,000,000
		Shares redeemed	100,000
		Shares outstanding (post-redemption)	900,000
Per-share value	$9.40	Per-share value	$10

underlying repurchase obligation. However, when one considers the implications over time of a 3%, 5%, or 10% growth rate on the value of the stock of a company, the impact on the dollar amount of the repurchase obligation is dramatic.

Figure 2 demonstrates the relationships of size, turnover, and growth to the cash requirements to fund the repurchase obligation. The amount of cash required to fund repurchases is reflected on the left. The magnitude of cash required grows with increased growth, increased turnover, and increased size.

In all of these cases, the compensation benefit is unrelated to total compensation but has become related to other factors. More importantly, the repurchase obligation is both a compensation transaction (when recycling shares) and a capital transaction (when purchasing shares). Theoretically, the ESOP benefit in the form of an equity stake in the company can be expected to increase in value at an equity appreciation rate over time, currently in the 12% to 15% range. Normal compensation levels in a company would rise at the 3% to 5% rate under most circumstances. The widely different appreciation expectations indicate that an ESOP company could experience compensation benefit costs that are rising significantly faster than overall compensation rates for the industry.

Are those continuing contributions reflected in the cost structure of the business and has the overall compensation expense been recognized in the valuation approaches discussed earlier? Has the company increased its cost structure through the implementation of the ESOP? To recognize the appropriate level of compensation expense, one must know the expected level of contributions in the future.

Quantifying the Repurchase Obligation

The issue here is how we quantify the repurchase obligation and its impact on value.[1] There has been a problem with quantifying the amount of the repurchase obligation, except for those who can follow some circular reasoning. The value of the repurchase obligation is dependent on the future per-share value of the company. The future per-share value is based on the future value of the company. A component of the future value of the company is the amount of expected contributions required to meet the repurchase obligation. The expected contributions are dependent on the future per-share value of the company. This leads to a circular argument that can be resolved by using an "iterative"[2] process.

One methodology used to analyze the impact of the repurchase obligation on the value of a company is the discounted cash flow (DCF). With the DCF method, the objective is to determine the available free cash flow after considering the company's working capital and capital expenditure requirements. The future contributions to the ESOP for repurchases either are not

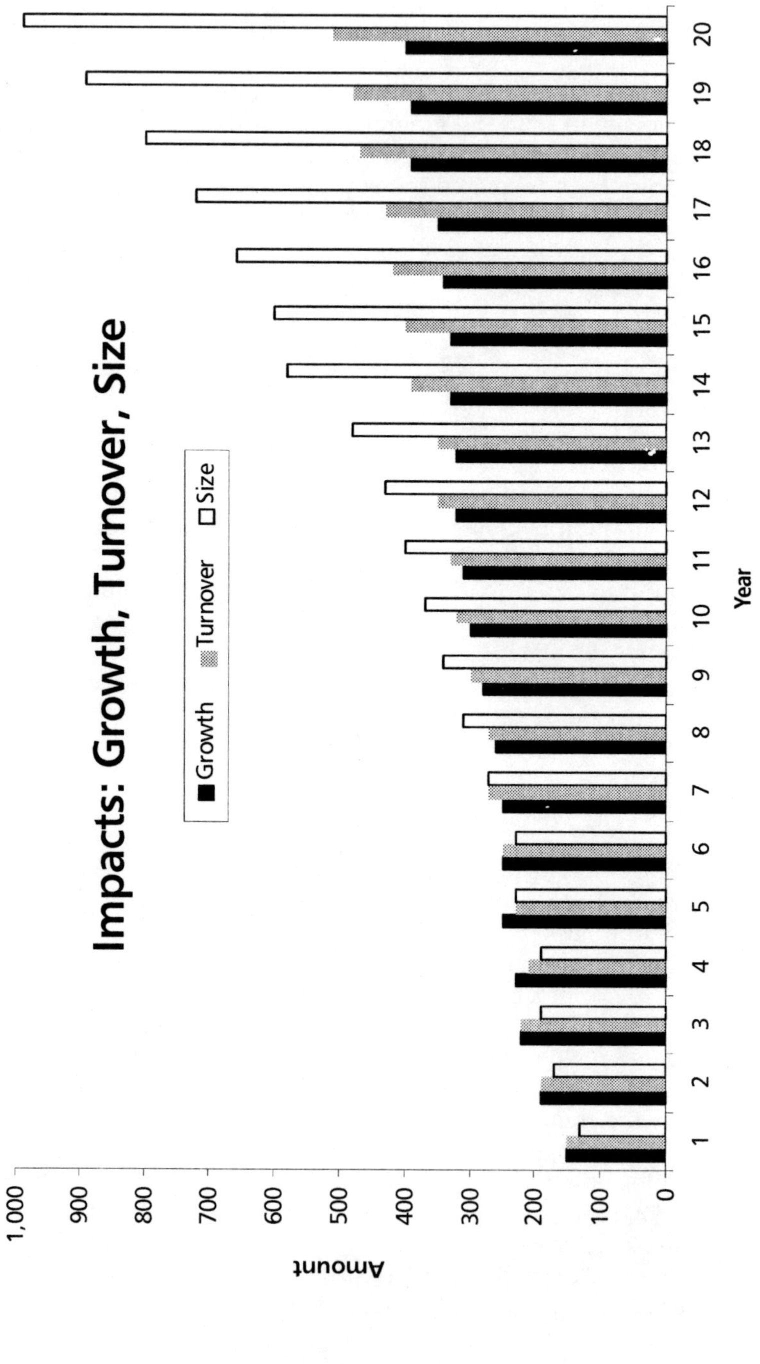

Figure 2. Relationships of growth, turnover, and size to the cash requirements to fund the repurchase obligation

included in the projected income statement or are stripped out separately so that we may analyze the potential repurchase impact on the company value on a going-forward basis.

Separately, the present value of the future contributions for the repurchase obligation is calculated. A spreadsheet is set up with a circular argument that is solved using an iteration calculation; it calculates the values of the company and the repurchase obligation simultaneously. In this manner, one can test the changes to the magnitude of the repurchase obligation based on changes to the factors affecting the repurchase obligation. The spreadsheet uses literally hundreds of estimates to solve the problem in just a few seconds. The value of the company, taking into consideration the impact of the repurchase obligation based on the future value of the company, can be determined.

If one applies the strict definition of the "willing buyer" in the fair market value test, the company would be analyzed on the basis of normal levels of compensation. The excess level of compensation would be ignored. This is practical when planning to sell a company. However, it makes little sense for the company with a strategy of maintaining employee ownership as a long-term benefit. The cost structure of the business is different. By ignoring the total compensation picture, the company can be overvalued.

Scenario Analysis

Once one has a model from which to analyze the potential magnitude of the repurchase obligation and its impact on the value of the company, one can formulate several scenarios where different assumptions are used to assess the best strategy for the company. The decision on redeeming or recycling can be quantified based on all the considerations, including the tax benefit of ESOP contributions and the cost of other replacement benefits if the company elects to redeem all shares over time. The fact is, based on the factors that impact the magnitude of the repurchase obligation, there may be no disadvantage to recycling versus redeeming.

Table 3 compares the effects of redeeming versus recycling on the present value of the expected repurchase obligation for a company, based on similar scenarios over a 20-year projected period.

One can determine the optimal level for meeting repurchases from available cash flows when analyzing the financial dynamics of an ESOP company. One should consider the financial impact of one's objectives on the repurchase obligation and the value of the company and then decide on redeeming versus recycling.

Conclusion

The repurchase obligation of an ESOP company is a compensation decision and should be viewed in relation to the compensation levels that are preva-

Table 3. Present Value of Repurchase Obligation

	Scenario 1 Redeem	Scenario 2 Recycle	Scenario 3 Recycle	Scenario 4 Recycle	Scenario 5 Redeem	Scenario 6 Recycle	Scenario 7 Redeem	Scenario 8 Recycle
Residual growth rate	2.5%	2.5%	7%	7%	0%	0%	3%	3%
ESOP size (% of ownership)	100%	100%	60%	60%	60%	60%	49%	49%
Ending ESOP ownership	100%	100%	39.2%	60%	39.4%	60%	36%	49%
Ratio of repurchase obligation to covered compensation*	13.63%	11.72%	13.2%	12.07%	11.86%	11.09%	11.42%	10.92%
Present value of repurchase obligation (in millions)	$5.345	$5.219	$5.178	$5.399	$3.094	$3.137	$4.264	$4.693

*Company had a target benefit cost of 10%.

lent in the company's industry. An understanding of the differences in the methods of redeeming ESOP shares and a recognition of the impact of the repurchase obligation on the value of the company is essential. Quantifying the repurchase obligation is now possible and requires only projections of the number of shares expected to be eligible to be put to the company in the future. The effort to understand and plan strategies for dealing with repurchases is needed early in the life of an ESOP company.

The wrong thing to do is to wait until the repurchase obligation becomes a major problem. Companies should use available resources to estimate the shares that will be eligible for the put option over the next 10 to 20 years. A company should further talk to its valuation advisor and ESOP trustee to determine how the repurchases are being dealt with in their valuation. Armed with the knowledge of how the repurchase obligation affects the business, the management of the company can set about to control the growth of the obligation, recognize the timing of the requirement for cash flows, and develop plans for funding the repurchases.

Notes

1. To estimate the repurchase obligation, it is necessary to have an estimate of the number of shares that will be distributed to ESOP participants that are eligible to be "put" to the company. This can usually be accomplished by having a repurchase study conducted or through using software designed to provide the same information.
2. Years ago, one would not attempt to do this type of calculation by hand. Nowadays, computer programs allow one to calculate a circular problem to a "steady state," providing a workable solution to the problem.

8

ESOP Valuation and Financial Advisory Analysis Due Diligence Checklist

Robert F. Reilly
Steven D. Garber

This article presents a checklist enumerating the most common procedures that are performed during an ESOP valuation or a financial advisory analysis due diligence leading to a fairness opinion in an ESOP securities purchase transaction. The checklist can serve as a useful reminder to ESOP valuation practitioners, ESOP fiduciaries, and other ESOP advisors. It may be useful in conducting an ESOP valuation or a financial advisory analysis. It may also be helpful in the review and assessment of an ESOP valuation report or a financial advisor's analysis and opinion. However, the checklist should not be used as a substitute for the experience and judgment of the valuation practitioner or the financial advisor.

The Employee Retirement Income Security Act (ERISA) requires employee stock ownership plans (ESOPs) to pay no more than adequate consideration when investing in employer securities. These employer securities include both common stock and convertible preferred stock.

The adequate consideration requirement has two general components: (1) a fair market value determination and (2) a good-faith process. This means that the ESOP trustees and fiduciaries must determine in good faith the fair market value of the employer securities. This determination must be made in compliance with certain regulations issued by the Internal Revenue Service and the United States Department of Labor (DOL).

This article presents a checklist that may be considered by ESOP valuation practitioners in conducting an ESOP securities valuation or in performing a financial advisory due diligence analysis, such as that performed before issuing a fairness opinion in an ESOP securities purchase transaction. This checklist may also be used by ESOP trustees and fiduciaries in their good-faith assessment of an ESOP securities valuation or of an ESOP transaction financial advisory opinion. Finally, this checklist may be consulted by ESOP administrators and other ESOP advisors (attorneys, accountants, etc.) who rely on ESOP valuations or other financial advisory opinions.

Robert Reilly, ASA, CFA, is a managing director of Willamette Management Associates, a valuation consulting, economic analysis, and financial advisory firm headquartered in Chicago. Steven Garber, CFA, was the director of Willamette's San Francisco office when this article was written and presently is a senior vice president in the San Francisco office of investment bank Houlihan Lokey Howard & Zukin.

There are many caveats associated with this checklist, as discussed below. These caveats should be carefully considered before this checklist is applied in an actual ESOP valuation or financial advisory due diligence analysis.

Transactions Involving an Opinion of Adequate Consideration

The following types of transactions involving employer securities require the assessment of adequate consideration:

- A contribution of employer stock to the ESOP.
- A contribution of cash to the ESOP, where the cash is then used to buy employer stock (either directly from the employer corporation or from other shareholders).
- The purchase of employer stock from the ESOP trustee.
- The distribution of cash to former ESOP participants in place of the distribution of employer stock.
- The purchase of employer stock by the trustee from ESOP participants.

In each of these types of transactions, the ESOP trustee or fiduciary must address the issue of adequate consideration. The checklist presented in this article is intended to be useful in assessing adequate consideration.

Valuation Opinions and Fairness Opinions

As part of the adequate consideration assessment, the fair market value of the employer securities must be estimated. This estimation is typically documented and reported in a valuation opinion. Some transactions involving ESOP-owned securities also involve an assessment of the fairness, from a financial perspective, of the proposed securities purchase transaction. This is particularly true in the case of multi-investor ESOP transactions. In these cases, an independent financial advisor typically will perform a financial advisory due diligence analysis and issue a fairness opinion. The checklist presented in this article is also intended to be useful in the assessment of transactional fairness.

Caveats Regarding the Checklist

It is important to consider several caveats regarding the use of any checklist of standardized valuation or financial advisory due diligence procedures.

First, the checklist should never substitute for the financial advisor's (or for the trustee's) independent judgment. Second, the following checklist is not intended to be comprehensive and all-inclusive. For example, it does not discuss every available ESOP valuation method, but only the more common ESOP valuation methods. Third, the terminology used in the checklist may have several interpretations. For example, the checklist refers only to "premiums and discounts"; the informed reader will understand that this term includes consideration of all related valuation factors, such as the discount for lack of marketability, the effects of the repurchase obligation, the discount for lack of control/premium for control, and the effects of leverage. Fourth, this checklist does not include a complete consideration of all of the aspects of a leveraged ESOP transaction or a leveraged ESOP valuation. Finally, this checklist assumes that the valuation subject is a security of an employer corporation for which there is no generally recognized secondary market.

This checklist should not be used to derive a quantitative score to evaluate the quality of an ESOP valuation or financial advisory analysis. That is, the fact that an individual analysis did not receive a "score" of 100 does not indicate that the analysis is not in compliance with promulgated regulations and recognized professional standards. Such an analysis may still be professional and competent, and it may be the appropriate basis upon which to assess adequate consideration.

Likewise, the fact that an individual analysis received a very high "score" does not necessarily indicate that the analysis was prepared in compliance with all promulgated regulations and recognized professional standards. Such an analysis may still be lacking in professional competence and may be an inadequate basis on which to assess adequate consideration.

The checklist is just that—a handy tool that valuation practitioners and ESOP fiduciaries can use as a procedural reminder in conducting and assessing ESOP valuations and financial advisory opinions. The checklist may be used to document whether the requisite procedures were or were not performed. But the checklist will not evaluate the analytical quality and the professional judgment involved in the performance of the actual procedures. The checklist should not substitute for the good faith, due diligence, prudence, and professional care of the ESOP trustee or ESOP fiduciary.

Finally, the experienced ESOP valuation practitioner or financial advisor will understand that not all of the listed procedures are applicable (or even possible) for each analysis. The professional judgment of the experienced ESOP practitioner (and the practical realities of data constraints, industry-specific practices, and so on) will determine which procedures are appropriate for each analysis.

Procedural Checklist for the ESOP Valuation and Financial Advisory Analysis Due Diligence Process

I. Engagement Letter and/or Engagement Work Product

A. State the purpose and objective of the engagement

1. Identify the purpose of the analysis, or the reason to conduct the analysis (to issue a transactional fairness opinion, an annual valuation update, etc.)

2. Identify the objective of the analysis, i.e., what the analysis is intended to do (to estimate the fair market value of a specified ESOP ownership interest, etc.)

B. Define the analysis assignment

3. Identify the retaining party (i.e., the client)

4. Identify the business entity and specific security interest being appraised

5. Identify the form of the subject business (C corporation, S corporation, limited liability company, etc.)

   a. Indicate the state of incorporation

   b. Indicate the date of incorporation

6. Identify the specific ownership business or security interest subject to analysis

7. Identify the valuation date (i.e., the "as of" date of the analysis)

C. Document the standard of value and premise of value

8. Identify and define the appropriate standard, or definition, of value (e.g., fair market value or fair value)

9. Identify and define the appropriate premise of value—based on an analysis of the highest and best use of the subject business or security interest (its value as a going concern, its value in exchange, etc.)

II. Due Diligence/Collection of Data

A. Collect and review company documents and information

10. Request historical financial information (typically, last five fiscal years and latest interim statements), including:

    a. Income statements

  b. Balance sheets
  c. Statements of cash flows
  d. Capital statements or statements of retained earnings
  e. Explanatory footnotes and supplemental disclosures to the financial statements

11. Request a list of subsidiaries and/or financial ownership interests in other related companies
  a. Obtain relevant historical financial information (the same as listed in II.A.10 above)
  b. Obtain a description of the business entities and interests, including the type of organization, the percentage of ownership, the original cost investment, and so on

12. Request other financial information, including:
  a. All current financial budgets and/or projections and/or forecasts (prepared for any reason)
  b. Other financial schedules, prepared as of the valuation date (fixed asset balances, accumulated depreciation, inventory, accounts receivable, accounts payable, open orders, production backlog, etc.)
  c. Copies of all material existing contracts/leases (employment agreements, non-compete agreements, labor agreements, customer contracts, real estate leases, etc.)
  d. Amounts and description of insurance in force (key person, property/casualty, business interruption, etc.)
  e. Compensation schedule for senior management and employee/owners (salary, options, commissions, etc.)
  f. Prior business valuation and/or asset appraisal reports (prepared for any purpose during the past five years)
  g. Schedule of dividends declared and paid during the past five years

13. Request company legal documents, including:
  a. Articles of incorporation, bylaws, amendments to articles and bylaws, etc.
  b. Any existing stock buy/sell agreements, options, rights of first refusal, etc.
  c. Minutes from recent shareholders' meetings, typically covering the past two years

d. List of all stockholders
   (1) Number of shares owned by each,
   (2) Number of shares owned by senior management, and
   (3) Number of shares owned by employee/owners
e. Descriptions of all recent prior transactions of the subject stock and any recent bona fide offers to purchase the company and/or subject securities
f. ESOP transaction documents, including:
   (1) ESOP-related loan agreements
   (2) Stock purchase agreements
   (3) ESOP plan and trust documents
   (4) ESOP plan summary
   (5) Any other documents that may affect the rights appurtenant to the ESOP-owned securities

14. Request other relevant operational information, including:
   a. History (since inception) and current description of the business
   b. Copies of all current sales/marketing materials, brochures, advertisements, etc.
   c. List of locations (owned or leased) in which the company operates
   d. List of major customers by annual dollar volume
   e. List of major suppliers by annual dollar volume
   f. List of major competitors (including their size and/or market share, if available)
   g. Breakdown of personnel (by department or function) and résumés of senior management
   h. Descriptions of all patents, trademarks, copyrights, and other owned or licensed intellectual properties
   i. Description of any contingent and/or off-balance sheet assets and liabilities
   j. List of related industry or trade associations, related industry or trade publications, and corporate memberships of the subject business

k. Description and current appraisals (if available) of all non-operating assets of the subject business

l. Operational budgets (for production, sales, purchases, inventory, etc.) and/or projections and/or forecasts

B. Conduct management interviews

15. Speak with senior management in all relevant functional areas, regarding:

a. Historical operations and results

b. Prospective operations and results

c. Responsibility for functional areas

16. Discuss with senior management and/or outside legal counsel any pending or potential litigation or claims, including:

a. Commercial litigation

b. Employment disputes

c. Occupational and safety issues

d. Environmental issues

e. Tax disputes

f. Other matters

C. Conduct plant/site inspections

17. Inspect representative plants and sites; consider:

a. Capacity limits and physical condition of existing plants, facilities, and equipment

b. Functional and technological adequacy (and/or obsolescence)

18. Discuss plants and sites with management representatives; consider:

a. Future facilities expansion and capital investment plans

b. Competitive effects of planned plant and facility changes

c. Expected operating cost effects of planned plant and facility changes

III. Economic Environment (As of Valuation Date)

A. Consider the national and international (if relevant) economic environment

19. Research and analyze the national and international economic environment and outlook (as relevant)

B. Consider the regional and local (if relevant) economic environment

   20. Research and analyze the regional and local economic environments and outlook (as relevant)

C. Consider the historical and expected relationship of the relevant economic environment to the performance of the company

   21. Identify and quantify (if possible) significant relationships of the performance of the relevant economic environment with the performance of the company

IV. Industry Environment (As of Valuation Date)

A. Consider the industry in which the company operates

   22. Research and analyze the nature and history of the industry

B. Consider the current outlook for the industry

   23. Research and analyze the current outlook for the industry

V. Fundamental Position of the Company (As of Valuation Date)

A. Consider the subject company's capitalization and ownership

   24. Analyze all classes of outstanding stock, including:

      a. Rights, seniority, voting, etc. of each class

      b. Total number of outstanding shares and percentage distribution of ownership of each class

B. Consider the subject company history and operations:

   25. Review company history

   26. Review and analyze current business operations, including:

      a. Locations and markets served

      b. Product lines, service lines, and customer base

      c. Competition

         (1) Current and projected market size

         (2) Position of the subject company within the industry

         (3) The subject company's competitive strengths and weaknesses, both on an absolute basis and relative to competitors

d. Management and work force

e. Overall positive and negative aspects of the subject company's operations

f. Strengths, weaknesses, opportunities, and threats of the subject company, compared to the industry in general and compared to direct competitors in particular

C. Consider the outlook for the subject company

27. Review current strategic plans, business projections, and the current business outlook

VI. Financial Statement Adjustments and Analysis

A. Make appropriate financial statement adjustments, including:

28. Adjust inventory, as appropriate

a. LIFO vs. FIFO basis of inventory cost accounting

b. Inventory write-offs and/or write-downs, including assessment of reasons for shrinkage, obsolescence, etc.

29. Adjust for excessive/insufficient management compensation, as appropriate

30. Adjust for nonrecurring financial statement items as appropriate, including:

a. Nonrecurring gains/losses, insurance proceeds, nonrecurring revenues, and/or expenses, etc.

b. Results of the effects of changes in accounting principles or methods

B. Perform historical financial statement analysis

31. Calculate and analyze common-size financial statements

32. Compute and analyze financial and operating ratios, including:

a. Size ratios

b. Growth ratios

c. Liquidity ratios

d. Profitability ratios

e. Turnover/activity ratios

f. Leverage ratios

33. Identify and explain any significant financial trends

C. Perform prospective financial statement analysis

34. Identify key financial variables (capacity constraints, cost/volume/profit relationships, etc.) for prospective results of operations
35. Obtain (if available) and analyze projections/budgets/forecasts for prospective results of operations
36. Assess reasonableness of projections relative to historical company results
37. Assess reasonableness of projections relative to industry data

VII. Valuation Analysis

A. Consider and select appropriate valuation approaches

38. Identify and select appropriate valuation approaches (i.e., market approach, income approach, or asset-based approach)

B. Perform a market approach—guideline company method, if appropriate

39. Identify guideline publicly traded companies; consider:
    a. Same or a similar line of business
    b. Size
    c. Trading activity/pricing evidence
    d. Financial condition
40. Adjust financial statements of the guideline publicly traded companies (i.e., adjust guideline companies to make them more comparable to the subject company, that is, "apples to apples")
41. Identify appropriate financial and operating fundamentals
42. Calculate market-derived pricing multiples for the selected guideline publicly traded companies
43. Analyze the range of market-derived guideline company pricing multiples
    a. Statistical analysis of range of pricing multiples
    b. Correlation of pricing multiples with performance factors (e.g., growth rates, ratios of return, etc.)
44. Compute and analyze financial and operating ratios for the selected guideline publicly traded companies, including:

a. Size ratios

b. Growth ratios

c. Liquidity ratios

d. Profitability ratios

e. Turnover/activity ratios

f. Leverage ratios

45. Compare the subject company to the selected guideline publicly traded companies

46. Select the appropriate market-derived pricing multiples for the subject company

47. Apply the selected pricing multiples to the appropriate subject company financial and operating fundamentals

48. Synthesize an estimate of value

    a. Subtract the market value of subject company outstanding long-term debt if "invested capital" valuation approaches are used

    b. Estimate a value of the subject company equity

49. Identify appropriate valuation premiums/discounts (for the specific level of business ownership interest subject to appraisal)

50. Quantify appropriate valuation premiums/discounts (for the specific level of business ownership interest subject to appraisal)

51. Apply appropriate valuation premiums/discounts (for the specific level of business ownership interest subject to appraisal)

C. Perform a market approach–guideline merged and acquired company method, if appropriate

52. Identify guideline merged or acquired companies/transactions, consider:

    a. Same or a similar line of business

    b. Size

    c. Financial condition

    d. Relevant time frame

    e. Availability of pricing information

53. Adjust financial statements of the selected guideline merged and acquired companies (that is, adjust guideline companies to make them more comparable to the subject company, that is, "apples to apples")
54. Identify appropriate financial and operating fundamentals
55. Calculate transaction pricing multiples for the selected guideline merged and acquired companies
56. Analyze the range of market-derived guideline company transaction pricing multiples
    a. Statistical analysis of range of pricing multiples
    b. Correlation of pricing multiples with performance factors (growth rates, rates of return, etc.)
57. Compute and analyze financial and operating ratios for the selected guideline merged and acquired companies, including:
    a. Size ratios
    b. Growth ratios
    c. Liquidity ratios
    d. Profitability ratios
    e. Turnover/activity ratios
    f. Leverage ratios
58. Compare the subject company to the guideline merged and acquired companies
59. Select the appropriate market-derived, transaction-based pricing multiples for the subject company
60. Apply the selected multiples to the appropriate subject company earnings and operating fundamentals
61. Synthesize an estimate of value
    a. Subtract the market value of subject company debt in debt-free valuation approaches
62. Identify appropriate valuation premiums/discounts (for the specific level of business interest subject to appraisal)
63. Quantify appropriate valuation premiums/discounts (for the specific level of business interest subject to appraisal)
64. Apply appropriate valuation premiums/discounts (for the specific level of business interest subject to appraisal)

D. Perform an income approach—discounted economic income method, if appropriate

65. Review and analyze financial projections related to prospective results of company operations for a relevant (e.g., five-year) discrete projection period

66. Develop the appropriate economic income fundamentals for analysis, for example, net cash flow, which consider:

    a. Earnings

    b. Noncash expenditures (depreciation expense, amortization expense, etc.)

    c. Capital expenditures

    d. Net working capital requirements

67. Develop the appropriate yield capitalization discount rate for the present value calculation, with consideration to:

    a. Current capital market investment and rate of return environment, including:

        (1) Risk-free rates of return

        (2) Equity rates of return (and/or equity risk premiums)

        (3) Company-specific risks/required rates of return, with consideration to:

            (a) Expected attainability of subject company financial projections

            (b) Degree of subject company financial/operating leverage

            (c) Degree of diversification of the subject company business base

    b. Capital structure

        (1) Capital structure (i.e., mix of debt and equity components of "invested capital") of the subject company

        (2) Typical capital structure in the subject industry

68. Develop an estimate of the terminal/residual value, with consideration to:

    a. Terminal/residual year financial fundamentals (e.g., net cash flow projection for terminal/residual year)

b. Terminal/residual year direct capitalization rate (e.g., as derived from the Gordon dividend growth model)

69. Apply the derived yield capitalization discount rate to the discrete period estimated economic income projection (e.g., net cash flow); include:

   a. The discrete projection period of periodic economic income

   b. The terminal/residual value estimate

70. Calculate an estimate of value

   a. Subtract the market value of subject company outstanding long-term if "invested capital" valuation approaches are used

71. Identify appropriate valuation premiums/discounts (for the specific level of business ownership interest subject to appraisal)

72. Quantify appropriate valuation premiums/discounts (for the specific level of business ownership interest subject to appraisal)

73. Apply appropriate valuation premiums/discounts (for the specific level of business ownership interest subject to appraisal)

E. Perform an asset-based approach—adjusted net asset method, if appropriate

74. Adjust all on-balance sheet assets to current market value (including all current asset accounts, fixed asset accounts, investment accounts, etc.)

75. Identify all off-balance sheet intangible assets

76. Estimate the fair market value of all off-balance sheet intangible assets

77. Estimate the fair market value of the total of all of the on-balance sheets and off-balance sheet tangible and intangible assets

78. Adjust all liability accounts to current market value (including consideration of any off-balance sheet and contingent liabilities)

79. Calculate an estimate of the overall subject company equity value as the total current market value of all assets, tangible and intangible, less the total market value of all liabilities

80. Identify appropriate valuation premiums/discounts (for the specific level of business ownership interests subject to appraisal)

81. Quantify appropriate valuation premiums/discounts (for the specific level of business ownership interests subject to appraisal)

82. Apply appropriate valuation premiums/discounts (for the specific level of business ownership interests subject to appraisal)

F. Consider other relevant business valuation and security analysis approaches

83. Consider the application of any alternative valuation approaches

84. Perform the appropriate alternative valuation approach methods or document why such alternative approaches are not applicable

G. Prepare a synthesis of value

85. Determine the relevance of each of the respective valuation approaches used in the analysis

86. Weight the alternative estimates of value

H. Reach a conclusion of value

87. Conclude the appropriate fair market value estimate for the business ownership interest appraisal subject

VIII. Reporting the Results of the Valuation Analysis and Financial Advisory Analysis Due Diligence

A. Prepare a transactional fairness opinion, as requested

88. Describe the proposed securities purchase transaction

89. Analyze the proposed securities purchase transaction in order to conclude whether the ESOP is paying no more for the business ownership interest appraisal subject than any other typical willing buyer would pay

90. Opine on the fairness of the proposed securities purchase transaction from a financial point of view, with consideration of the concluded fair market value for the business ownership interest appraisal subject

IX. Documentation of the Valuation Analysis and Financial Advisory Analysis Due Diligence

A. Prepare engagement analytical work papers

91. Prepare and maintain work papers and files that document the valuation analysis and the financial advisory analysis due diligence

B. Prepare a valuation opinion and narrative valuation report

92. Opine on the adequate consideration with regard to the business ownership interest appraisal subject consistent with the DOL proposed regulations

93. Opine on the fair market value of the business ownership interest appraisal subject consistent with the DOL proposed regulations

94. Prepare a narrative valuation report in compliance with the fair market value requirement of the DOL proposed regulations, containing the following information:

    a. A summary of the qualifications of the analyst performing the valuation to appraise assets of the type being valued

    b. A statement of the subject asset's value, a statement of the methods used in estimating that value, and the reasons for the valuation conclusion in light of those methods

    c. A full description of the subject asset being valued

    d. The factors taken into account in making the valuation, including any restrictions, understandings, agreements or obligations limiting the use or disposition of the subject asset

    e. The purpose for which the valuation was made

    f. The relevance or significance accorded to the valuation methods taken into account

    g. The effective date of the valuation

    h. In cases where a valuation report has been prepared, the signature of the person making the valuation and the date the report was signed

95. Include in any written valuation report an assessment of the following factors, consistent with the DOL proposed regulations:

a. The nature of the business and the history of the enterprise from its inception

b. The economic outlook in general and the condition and outlook of the specific industry in particular

c. The book value of the securities and the financial condition of the business

d. The earnings capacity of the company

e. The dividend-paying capacity of the company

f. Whether the enterprise has goodwill or other intangible value

g. The market price of securities of corporations engaged in the same or a similar line of business, which are actively traded in a free and open market

h. The marketability, or lack thereof, of the securities

i. Whether the seller would be able to obtain a control premium with regard to the appraisal subject; in cases where a control premium is added, confirm that:

    (1) Actual control (both in form and in substance) is passed to the purchaser with the sale (or will pass to the purchaser within a reasonable time)

    (2) It is reasonable to assume that the buyer's control will not be dissipated within a short period of time after the securities purchase

9

ESOP Valuation for Banks and Bank Holding Companies

Terry S. Brown

Appraisals of banks and bank holding companies for ESOP purposes differ in a number of ways from ESOP appraisals for other types of companies. While some of the issues overlap, others do not and are a function of the way banks and bank holding companies operate, how they are structured, the composition of the shareholder base, and the public market's perception of the stock. This article broadly focuses on a few of these issues, including a basic overview of financial performance and position, data available on public guideline companies, generally accepted valuation methodologies, and marketability considerations. It originally appeared in the fall 1997 issue of our journal.

Valuations of the stock of closely held financial institutions, whether for employee stock ownership plan (ESOP) or other purposes, tend to be different from other valuations because of the nature of the industry. This difference results from the way a financial institution is structured, the manner in which it operates and generates earnings, the size of the industry, and the fact that it is considered to hold funds in public trust and is an entity regulated by federal and state authorities. A financial institution is different from other companies in very distinct ways, and the differences require specific knowledge and experience to avoid errors in the appraisal process. This article will focus on the appraisal of closely held banks and bank holding companies (BHCs) rather than thrifts; however, some of the valuation techniques discussed are applicable to thrifts as well.

The issues for any company in which an ESOP holds an interest tend to overlap those of a bank; however, there are a few aspects of ESOP valuation in banks that present special considerations. This article covers two of these areas: (1) general valuation considerations and concepts unique to financial institutions that an ESOP appraiser, practitioner, or company should be aware of, and (2) special ESOP issues that are unique to banks. The focus is on closely held banks because publicly held institutions are actively traded and the value of their stock is determined by the public equity markets daily. There are about 9,500 commercial banks and BHCs in the U.S. that

---

At the time this article was written, Terry S. Brown, ASA, was a senior vice president at Mercer Capital Management, where she directed the development and organization of the corporate ESOP valuation department. She has extensive experience in the area of ESOP valuations for financial institutions, as well as a variety of other types of businesses.

are insured (by the Federal Deposit Insurance Corporation [FDIC]); 1,062 of these are publicly traded BHCs, leaving about 8,400 that are thinly traded or closely held. ESOPs became popular with banks in the 1980s as a vehicle to provide liquidity and create a market for the bank or holding company stock, provide or augment an existing employee benefit plan, raise capital, and improve productivity. This popularity resulted in a significant number of BHCs with ESOP ownership. The National Center for Employee Ownership (NCEO) estimates that about one in 10 of the 10,000 or so ESOPs in the U.S. is in a bank or thrift.

Valuation Theory and Bank Holding Company (BHC) or Bank ESOPs

Although banks and BHCs (the difference will be discussed below) differ from manufacturing, distribution, service, or other entities, many of the same general valuation theories and concepts apply to them, and in some respects, the features that are unique to banking can result in less complicated valuation issues. On the other hand, to the appraiser inexperienced and unfamiliar with banking, an attempt to appraise a bank can be a road to nowhere but confusion. An understanding of the basics of bank financial statements and their analysis is critical to understand how earnings are generated. With some basic knowledge, the ESOP appraiser can begin to apply generally accepted valuation principles and concepts.

Overview of a Bank or BHC's Position and Performance

Available Information All banks insured by the FDIC are required to file quarterly "Consolidated Report of Condition and Income" reports ("call reports"). These reports, which are public information, compile and detail the components of an institution's balance sheet and income statement and provide other required regulatory analysis. As a result, access to any of a number of databases that compile call report information (SNL Securities, Compustat, and so on) or a request for call reports from the institution will provide sufficient information to begin an analysis of the institution for valuation purposes. In addition, most financial institutions have an annual audit, review, or compilation. One of the unique aspects of preparing a financial institution valuation is the availability of thorough, detailed financial information on publicly and privately held companies. As an example of the information that can be derived from the call report data mentioned above, the appraiser can review and analyze historical balance sheet and income statements; a breakdown by type of the loan and securities portfolios; charge-offs and recoveries and the bad debt reserve; a breakdown of the deposit base by type; key earnings ratios; a detailed analysis of other income and expenses; and asset/liability management. The availability and accessibility of information can give the knowledgeable appraiser a head start on valuation, but to the untrained appraiser help may be in order. The following will provide some guidance.

The Bank Balance Sheet One of the key differences in the balance sheet of a bank and any other type of company is the classification and composition of assets and liabilities. Whereas a non-bank entity classifies assets and liabilities as either current or non-current, a bank balance sheet reflects earning and non-earning assets. A bank's earning assets are composed of interest- or dividend-earning assets, including loans, investment securities, repurchase agreements with other institutions, and federal funds sold. A bank's balance sheet is assessed by the percentage of earning assets it has relative to total assets. This is measured as a percentage (e.g., 93%), and all other things being equal, the higher the percentage the better. A high percentage indicates that a substantial portion of the bank's income is derived from interest income. Remaining assets are considered non-earning because they do not generate revenue, but are typically needed for the ongoing operation of the bank. These items include other fixed assets or the bank's property, cash for depositor liquidity needs or reserve requirements, intangibles, or subsidiary investments.

Liabilities are typically classified as deposits, either interest bearing or non-interest bearing. These deposits are also typically measured as a percentage of total assets because they reflect a measurement of the interest expense of the bank. All other things being equal, the higher the percentage of non-interest bearing deposits, the higher the bank's earnings. However, since these non-interest-bearing deposits require account maintenance such as transaction costs and customer service costs, some of this increased income is offset by the costs of maintaining these dollars. Remaining liabilities are typically considered other liabilities, and these, along with the institution's total deposits, comprise a measure of the bank's leverage, which, when compared with other types of companies, tends to be significantly higher. Interest-bearing liabilities can amount to as much as 70% to 80% of a bank's total assets. Other types of companies, unless financially distressed or in a high-growth situation, are not generally this leveraged.

The final major component of the balance sheet is the bank's shareholders' equity account, which comprises assets minus liabilities (as in any other non-bank entity). The subject of the equity or capital account (capital is an industry term that also includes other types of equity and a loan loss reserve) is a complex one, and the degree to which capital is required is affected by regulatory requirements, unrealized gains or losses on marketable securities, marketplace perceptions, earnings, dividends, and management's plans for the institution's growth.

The Income Statement The method in which banks generate income is the business of borrowing and selling (or lending) money. Therefore, the accounting for revenues and expenses differs somewhat from the income statement of a manufacturing or service firm. The following explanation is helpful to understand the differences and how to analyze them for ESOP valuation purposes.

Income statements are comprised of and categorized by interest income (received from earning assets), interest expense (paid on interest-bearing funds), fee income (income other than interest income such as fees on deposit accounts), and non-interest operating expense (or general administrative expenses). Interest is the amount earned or paid for the use of money. The difference in the amount earned and the amount paid is called "the spread" and comprises about 80% of the net sales (interest income and fee income) of a bank. A bank's income statement is very much driven by the composition of the balance sheet or the level of earning assets relative to total assets and the level of interest-bearing funds to total assets. The difference in the yields obtained on earning assets (interest income) and the cost (interest expense) of interest-bearing funds is net interest income or net interest margin, when it is measured as a percentage of assets. The best indicator of a bank's ability to sustain its net interest margin is its historical net interest margin and the composition of the balance sheet. Other factors affect this ratio, such as competition; economic and market conditions; interest rates; and management's asset/liability, lending, and investing policies.

Fee income (sometimes referred to as non-interest income) is generated from charges assessed bank customers for services rendered or provided, such as service charges on deposit accounts, fees from sale of insurance, loan origination fees, and fees for other ancillary services.

Operating expense (sometimes referred to as non-interest operating expense) is typically divided into three categories, including personnel expense (including compensation and employee benefit expenses), fixed asset expense or occupancy (including rent, depreciation, and maintenance), and other expenses, which is a catch-all category for professional fees, FDIC insurance premiums, losses on sales of assets, and any other expenses not classified under personnel and occupancy.

A complete explanation of the analysis of bank income statements is beyond the scope of this article, but an ESOP appraiser can use the above information to develop a basic understanding of the income statement and to develop an estimate of ongoing earning power.[1] It is important to remember that the ESOP appraiser must consider the earnings stream of a bank just as it would any other type of company appraisal. Earnings should be examined in detail to identify any non-recurring gains or losses or potential changes in the bank's cost structure, such as the initiation or paydown of ESOP debt and the impact of contributions going forward, trading activity in securities or the sale of foreclosed real estate that generates non-recurring gains or losses, historical and planned capital expenditure needs that will affect expenses, non-recurring litigation settlements, or professional fees.

Bank or BHC Stock—Which Does the ESOP Own?

The majority of stock in a bank is commonly held by a BHC that was formed to acquire the stock of one or more banks. BHCs have unique features. They are allowed to acquire their own stock (which banks are legally prohibited from doing), incur leverage (which can then be downstreamed to the bank as capital), receive certain tax benefits, and own other types of financial subsidiaries that the bank may be prohibited from owning. These features are typically why a holding company is formed.

A common misconception (sometimes even among bank management) is that the ESOP always holds stock in the bank. The ESOP does own an interest in the bank if there is no holding company, but this is not generally the case. It is more likely that the holding company owns most or all of the stock of the bank and shareholders, including the ESOP, in turn own shares of the holding company. This is one of the reasons ESOPs became so popular in financial institutions in the early 1980s. A holding company with an ESOP has two vehicles, the ESOP and the holding company, to generate a market and provide liquidity for the participants and other shareholders.

The financial statements filed by a holding company must also be analyzed to determine whether there are any subsidiary investments, other assets, or leverage at the holding company level. This may be frequently encountered in the case of an ESOP. The ESOP may borrow funds and record the debt at the holding company (particularly if it is guaranteed by the company) and then use the funds to inject capital into the bank. If the company's only subsidiary is the bank and there is no leverage at the company level, then its earnings will closely mirror those of the bank since the company's earnings are dividend income received from the bank and the equity in the undistributed income of the bank. If the company has ESOP debt, interest expense may be recorded, resulting in different income for the leveraged company.

The following discussion applies to BHCs, but keep in mind that the same issues or principles apply to a bank if there is no holding company.

Guideline Company Approaches for BHC ESOP Appraisals

The requirements of Revenue Ruling 59-60 include an assessment of the market price of securities of corporations engaged in the same or a similar line of business that is openly traded in a free and active market, either on an exchange or over the counter. As noted above, the proliferation of information about publicly traded BHCs and the availability and accessibility of public information about them is one of the advantages of preparing ESOP valuations (minority or controlling interest) for banks. Closely held banks and BHCs are valued based on their publicly traded counterparts. A number of guideline company methods can be used to develop a range of value, validate methodologies, or make relative value comparisons, since data are readily available. Typically, the strongest valuations and those that produce a reasonable value use a combination of guideline company approaches and weight them based on the appraiser's judgment about a market proxy for the particular institution's ESOP shares.

Publicly Available Data The appendix to this article represents the data that is widely available for bank valuation purposes.[2] As noted above, there are currently 1,062 publicly traded BHCs in the U.S. Public transaction data are based on minority interest transactions in the stock of these companies. This factor tends to be favorable to the valuation expert when valuing bank ESOPs, since most ESOP interests in financial institutions are minority interests.[3] Since call reports are filed quarterly, reasonably current earnings data are always available either from the institution or other data sources. The first section of the appendix (the first facing pages) presents a sample public company group and the ratios most commonly used to analyze and make comparisons with publicly traded institutions and those that would most likely serve as a market proxy for the stock of a privately held institution. In addition, the third and fourth sections of the appendix present historical data and other comparative ratios on the public companies being used for valuation purposes.

Guideline Company Capitalized Earnings Method Capitalized earnings is a common guideline method used to develop an indication of value for a financial institution. This method requires two components: an estimate of ongoing earning power and a multiple with which to capitalize earnings. To the inexperienced or untrained eye, an estimate of a BHC's ongoing earning power may be one of the most difficult factors to determine in the assessment of value for ESOP purposes. However, as in other ESOP appraisals, this determination is one of the most critical components in the valuation. The ability of the institution to sustain a given level of earning power is dependent upon a variety of external, internal, and philosophical factors. Earning power is driven by the mix of assets and liabilities; management's' philosophy about composition, maturity, yield, and costs; the bank's competitive environment; its customer base; its products and services and the resulting ability to generate fee income; management's philosophy about managing and controlling expenses; and the risk inherent in the loan portfolio. In addition, earnings can be significantly affected by external factors such as fluctuations in interest rates, general economic conditions, and market conditions.

An element of complexity is added to this determination when an ESOP is planned or currently owns an interest in the institution. Consideration must be given to the impact on earnings of:

- The amortization schedule of the ESOP debt, if present.
- The ongoing contribution to the ESOP, whether it is leveraged or not.
- The company's normalized level of retirement plan expense, and whether the additional ESOP benefit requires an "adjustment" to earnings.
- Improved performance as a result of the company's and the employee's perception of the new employee benefit plan and of the company's status as an employee-owned business.
- The favorable tax treatment of the principal and interest payments in a leveraged ESOP.
- The underlying performance of the institution that is related to earnings growth or improved margins.

Once an estimate of pre- and/or post-ESOP earning power has been determined, the next issue the appraiser has to grapple with is the capitalization factor and how it relates to the institution being appraised. As noted earlier, while the public information available on price/earnings multiples is helpful, it also requires the appraisal be approached with caution. It is difficult for someone without a knowledge of the business to assess the factors that should be considered and those that the industry considers benchmark indications. A heavy dose of uninformed or inexperienced "appraiser judgment" could result in an unreasonable appraisal. Capitalization rates for public BHCs can have a wide range at a point in time and can also vary widely over a period of time. Sometimes it is necessary to make fundamental adjustments to market derived capitalization ratios for differences in return on equity, implicit growth assumptions, over-capitalization, dividend yields, access to capital markets, lack of market diversification, and management depth.

Guideline Company Capitalized Book Value Method A second method commonly used in bank ESOP appraisals is capitalized book value. The ratio of price to book value is a commonly used benchmark in the banking industry, and is a valid one in the context of other methodologies. However, it should not be used as a "rule of thumb" appraisal, and certain factors should be considered when it is used for ESOP appraisals.

One factor to consider when using the capitalized book value method is excess capital. In favorable economic periods, as have been experienced in recent years, community BHCs tend to generate favorable returns, which sometimes result in higher than normal equity/asset ratios relative to a guideline group of companies. This may occur for a number of reasons (e.g., a desire not to pay or increase dividends, to engage in stock buybacks, or to acquire other institutions or new branches). Typical median equity-to-asset ratios for larger publicly held institutions are in the range of 8% to 9%, but for smaller community BHCs this ratio can be significantly higher.[4] In these cases the BHC is considered to have "excess equity or capital." An investor is not willing to capitalize excess equity, but is willing to pay dollar-for-dollar for it. Thus, for ESOP purposes, reported equity or book value needs to be adjusted to reflect a normalized level of equity (currently, 8% to 9% of total assets on average). The difference in normalized equity and excess equity is then added dollar-for-dollar to the capitalized book value. Table 1 below presents an example of the determination of value using capitalized book value in the case of excess equity. The price to book value multiple and the normalized equity asset ratio used is presented in the appendix.

Table 1. Determination of Value Using Capitalized Book Value

Guideline Company Method Applied to a Sample BHC

Price/Book Valuation Analysis:

Mid-South Group Median Price/Book Ratio as of 12/31/96 (from appendix)	$ 1.98
Fundamental Discount of 20.0% (appraiser's estimate)	0.40
Adjusted Price/Book Ratio	1.59
Normalized Book Value Estimated at 8.91% of Total Assets (value as of 12-31-96)	$ 8,900,000
Adjusted Price/Book Ratio (rounded from above)	1.60
Capitalized Book Value	$14,240,000
Add Back Excess Equity Above 8.91%	$ 2,000,000
Indicated Value: Guideline Company Value (Price/Book Approach)	$16,240,000

As noted earlier, capitalized book value for ESOP purposes should be used in the context of other determinants of value and not as a sole indicator. Price-to-book multiples are a function of a company's earning power and leverage, and the value should be considered in the context of these factors also. Reliance on the price-to-book ratio may result in a value that is too high or too low.

BHC ESOPs and Marketability

Many of the issues that differ between BHCs and their counterparts for ESOP appraisal purposes surround the issue of marketability. BHCs often have special features that may affect the liquidity and the valuation of the shares.

Put Option on ESOP Shares

Although the arguments about the significance of the put option applicable to ESOP shares and its impact on marketability tend not to differ for BHCs, it should be noted that strong support for mitigation of the discount lies in a couple of factors prevalent in only a few other industries. Some of these factors are the acquisition market for BHC stocks, shares of closely held BHCs that may be traded on regional exchanges, and sometimes larger than normal shareholder bases.

Readily Tradable Securities

Many BHCs have what might be referred to as "quasi-public" markets, (e.g. with perhaps several hundred shareholders, very thin trading, a regular or irregular quotation by a local brokerage firm, or a listing in the "pink sheets"), and management and the ESOP trustee mistakenly assume that this means their shares are "readily tradable" for ESOP appraisal purposes. This is a very risky assertion for ESOP trustees.

The proposed guidelines relating to the definition of adequate consideration issued by the Department of Labor in 1988 state that the question of whether there is a recognized market for a security must be determined in light of the security's trading characteristics. Isolated trading activity is generally not sufficient to show the existence of a recognized market.

Two private letter rulings (PLRs) by the IRS help clarify the "tradability" issue (PLR 89100667, dated December 14, 1988, and PLR 9036039, dated September 11, 1990). The first PLR involved two shareholders who wanted to sell stock held in a corporation to a newly established ESOP, which had made an offer to purchase the shares held by these shareholders. The stock had not been traded on a national or regional securities exchange or the NASDAQ system. However, a local brokerage firm published a "bid" price for the stock on a daily basis. The taxpayer requested a ruling that the stock was "not readily tradable on an established securities market" within the meaning of Sections 409(1) and 1042(c)(1) of the Internal Revenue Service Code. These sections define "qualified employer securities" as those that are readily tradable on an established securities market. Since the stock in question was quoted by a local brokerage firm rather than an established exchange, the IRS ruled the stock as "not readily tradable" for ESOP purposes despite the daily price quotations.

The second PLR involved a similar ESOP situation. Two shareholders wishing to sell their shares to a newly established ESOP requested a ruling as to whether the company's securities were considered "readily tradable" under Section 409(1) of the Code. In this case, just before the establishment of the ESOP the stock was traded on NASDAQ. After approval of the ESOP, the shares were delisted but continued to appear in the "pink sheets" under two market makers. The IRS ruled in this instance that the company's stock ceased to be considered "readily tradable" on an established securities market when it ceased to be traded on NASDAQ.

In summary, the PLRs state that stock, in order to be considered "readily tradable," must be traded on national or regional exchanges or quoted on a system that is sponsored by a national securities association such as the National Association of Securities Dealers. While these letter rulings are not considered definitive, they do support the view that BHC stock is not readily tradable for ESOP purposes if daily price quotations by a local brokerage firm or a listing in the "pink sheets" is the stated reason for marketability. An appraiser may rely on public price quotations or pink sheet trades as an indication of value, but it should be considered as merely a component of value in the context of an independent assessment of the value of the shares held by an ESOP.

Transactions in the Subject BHC's Marketplace

Because a BHC is an entity that provides a service to the community, the ESOP appraiser will typically find that citizens of the community who transact business with the bank own stock in the company. This sometimes results in a larger shareholder base than one typically finds in other types of institutions. Another factor that tends to create large shareholder bases is the age of many financial institutions. Many banks that were predecessors of BHCs have been in existence since the turn of the century, and dispersion of the stock has occurred through inheritance by children and grandchildren over the course of several generations. Large shareholder bases sometimes tend to result in a significant number of transactions in the stock. The ESOP appraiser should discuss each transaction with management in detail to determine the parties involved, the number of shares traded, and the basis for pricing. It is not uncommon in small and mid-sized community BHCs to obtain some indication of value based on limited transactions. But it is also not uncommon to discover transactions in which pricing may be based on any number of circumstances totally unrelated to the stock's fair market value. A thorough investigation of the events and situations involving each transaction is necessary.

At issue is what discount for lack of marketability is implied when transactions of an arms' length nature occur outside an ESOP, and how this reconciles with the discount related to the ESOP shares. Since this is a measure that is difficult to quantify, if the appraiser deems the transactions significant from a valuation standpoint, he or she might weight the transaction value to some modest degree in the context of the overall appraisal. For example, if a number of arms' length transactions have occurred or if transactions have occurred that represent a significant portion of the ownership (10% or more), a transaction value could be determined by averaging the price at which transactions occurred and assigning this transaction value a weight of 10%, while the remainder (or the heavier weight) is applied to guideline company methods.

The Public Acquisition Market

In recent years, the market for controlling transactions or acquisitions of financial institutions has been very active. In other words, the generally more liquid nature of the market for BHC stocks has some impact on the value of ESOP shares, even on a minority basis. Increased multiples as a result of a "hot" merger and acquisition market tend to inflate the overall market valuation of BHC stock even though the particular institution being analyzed may not be a takeover candidate. Median price to earnings multiples and price to book multiples in control transactions increased from 14.8× to 16.6× and 147× to 195×, respectively, nationwide from 1991 to 1996.[5] This factor, as well as strong fundamental performance during the current strong economic cycle, has tended to have a favorable impact on freely tradable minority interest values. This market phenomenon also creates the perception (or reality) that liquidity in the stock of a closely held institution could result in a short period of time, thus further mitigating the marketability discount.

Conclusion

The issues surrounding ESOPs in other types of companies—including the impact of ESOP contributions, dilution, repurchase obligation, the impact of leverage, minority versus control value, trustees, and adequate consideration rules—also affect ESOPs in banks and BHCs. The differences in ESOP appraisals for banks and BHCs and ESOP appraisals for other types of companies lie primarily in understanding how a bank operates, the structure of BHCs and their subsidiary banks, a knowledge of generally accepted methodologies, access to public information, and liquidity. Particular attention to the estimate of ongoing earnings, appraisal methodology, and the factors that affect marketability should result in a soundly reasoned, well documented, defensible ESOP appraisal.

Notes

1. For a complete analysis of financial institution economics and how to analyze bank financial statements, see Z. Christopher Mercer, *Valuing Financial Institutions* (Homewood, IL: Business One Irwin, 1992): 97-168.
2. Note that this is a representative sample. There is much additional information or ratios that could be added to this analysis. This analysis is also limited to banks located in the Mid South, simply to illustrate that public guideline groups can be limited to geographic areas.

3. ESOPs generally own less than 25% of a bank or BHC. This is usually related to regulatory capital requirements that constrain or restrict initial or gradual ESOP ownership. In addition, there is a regulatory hurdle to cross when the ESOP owns 25% or more of a bank holding company's stock. When that occurs, the ESOP itself is required to file as a bank holding company, which subjects it to additional regulatory compliance and filing requirements, an additional layer of reporting most bankers prefer not to deal with.
4. The highest one the author has encountered recently had equity/asset and capital ratios in the range of 14% to 14.5%.
5. Source: SNL Securities database.

Appendix (beginning on next page): Regional BHC Public Market Pricing Analysis for Southeast U.S.

- Source: SNL Securities Data Corporation
- 49 banks were considered; 25 of the 49 were excluded
- Thinly traded banks are those with average annual trading volume less than 0.15%
- Quarter 4 is the most recent quarter available; the respective previous quarters follow
- NA = Not Available
- NM = Not Meaningful (insufficient data)

CURRENT PUBLIC

Short Name	State	Ticker	52 Week High	52 Week Low	Current Pricing Date
Alabama National BanCorp	AL	ALAB	$19.750	$12.250	12/31/96
Colonial BancGroup, Inc.	AL	CNB	24.000	15.625	12/31/96
Compass Bancshares, Inc.	AL	CBSS	32.167	21.000	12/31/96
Average of Alabama BHCs					
Simmons First National Corp.	AR	SFNCA	28.250	21.833	12/31/96
First Commercial Corporation	AR	FCLR	42.000	27.857	12/31/96
Average of Arkansas BHCs					
Farmers Capital Bank Corp.	KY	FFKT	41.500	33.500	12/31/96
CBT Corporation	KY	CBTC	27.500	20.063	12/31/96
Mid-America Bancorp	KY	MAB	21.000	15.170	12/31/96
Community Trust Bancorp.	KY	CTBI	26.000	18.409	12/31/96
Average of Kentucky BHCs					
ArgentBank	LA	AGB	20.750	17.250	12/31/96
Whitney Holding Corp.	LA	WTNY	40.500	29.500	12/31/96
First Commerce Corp.	LA	FCOM	45.625	32.250	12/31/96
Hibernia Corp.	LA	HIB	14.750	10.000	12/31/96
Average of Louisiana BHCs					
Mississippi Valley Bcshs, Inc.	MO	MVBI	47.000	28.000	12/31/96
Magna Group, Inc.	MO	MGR	35.000	21.750	12/31/96
UMB Financial Corporation	MO	UMBF	42.500	33.333	12/31/96
Commerce Bancshares, Inc.	MO	CBSH	49.875	31.786	12/31/96
Average of Missouri BHCs					
Hancock Holding Company	MS	HBHC	42.500	31.087	12/31/96
BancorpSouth, Inc.	MS	BOMS	30.000	21.500	12/31/96
Trustmark Corporation	MS	TRMK	28.000	20.500	12/31/96
Deposit Guaranty Corp.	MS	DEP	33.375	22.000	12/31/96
Average of Mississippi BHCs					
National Commerce Bancorp.	TN	NCBC	46.000	29.750	12/31/96
First American Corporation	TN	FATN	68.750	41.125	12/31/96
First Tennessee National Corp.	TN	FTEN	49.000	29.000	12/31/96
Average of Tennessee BHCs					

MARKET PRICING SUMMARY

Stock Price ($)	Market Cap ($M)	YTD Price Chng (%)	P/E LTM (x)	P/E FY 97 (x)	P/E FY 98 (x)	Price/ Book (%)	Price/ Tn Book (%)	Dividend Yield (%)
17.750	116	2.11	12.2	10.8	9.6	1.7	2.0	2.6
20.000	655	15.63	12.5	10.6	9.8	1.9	2.1	3.0
26.500	1,611	11.79	12.4	11.3	10.3	2.0	2.4	3.6
....			*12.39*	*10.91*	*9.87*	*1.89*	*2.14*	*3.05*
27.000	154	1.85	14.9	13.3	12.3	1.5	1.5	1.9
37.125	1,070	3.70	15.7	14.3	13.2	2.3	2.5	2.6
....			*15.29*	*13.79*	*12.72*	*1.87*	*2.00*	*2.26*
40.750	155	(1.84)	12.4	12.7	NM	1.4	1.4	4.0
27.500	216	(19.55)	18.6	15.3	NM	2.0	2.0	1.9
19.000	179	4.61	12.1	NM	NM	1.3	1.3	4.0
22.273	224	14.49	11.9	10.9	NM	1.5	1.8	3.3
....			*13.74*	*12.96*	*NM*	*1.55*	*1.63*	*3.30*
17.875	105	11.89	13.6	NM	NM	1.5	1.5	3.1
35.375	676	9.19	14.4	13.2	12.2	1.6	1.7	3.2
38.875	1,512	3.22	13.5	11.4	10.3	2.1	2.1	4.1
13.250	1,708	(0.94)	15.6	13.4	11.9	2.0	2.5	2.4
....			*14.28*	*12.67*	*11.49*	*1.80*	*1.96*	*3.21*
42.500	192	(1.76)	14.6	13.1	11.6	2.5	2.5	1.3
29.500	984	0.85	13.5	12.3	NM	1.7	1.8	3.4
40.500	799	(3.09)	14.0	13.2	12.2	1.4	1.6	2.0
46.250	1,729	(4.86)	14.9	13.4	12.3	1.9	2.1	1.8
....			*14.24*	*13.01*	*12.04*	*1.87*	*1.99*	*2.11*
40.500	434	(0.62)	13.1	12.5	11.7	1.7	1.8	2.5
27.750	583	(3.60)	13.7	12.3	11.1	1.8	1.9	2.7
25.500	890	(4.65)	13.6	12.3	11.3	1.7	1.8	2.2
30.875	1,210	(2.83)	14.3	13.3	NM	2.1	2.5	2.6
....			*13.70*	*12.59*	*11.37*	*1.82*	*1.98*	*2.50*
38.250	933	7.84	16.7	14.5	12.8	3.0	3.0	2.3
57.625	1,708	7.59	14.0	12.1	11.0	2.0	2.3	2.2
37.500	2,413	16.00	14.0	12.1	10.9	2.6	3.0	3.2
....			*14.91*	*12.92*	*11.60*	*2.52*	*2.76*	*2.55*
		Average	**14.02**	**12.65**	**11.44**	**1.88**	**2.04**	**2.74**
		Median	**13.87**	**12.62**	**11.64**	**1.86**	**1.98**	**2.59**
		Maximum	**18.58**	**15.28**	**13.16**	**2.98**	**3.02**	**4.12**
		Minimum	**11.91**	**10.64**	**9.59**	**1.27**	**1.27**	**1.32**

CURRENT PUBLIC

Short Name	State	Ticker	52 Week High	52 Week Low	Current Pricing Date
ALSO CONSIDERED, BUT EXCLUDED:					
BHCs with Assets over $15 Billion					
AmSouth Bancorp.	AL	ASO	54.625	34.875	12/31/96
Regions Financial Corp.	AL	RGBK	61.875	42.250	12/31/96
SouthTrust Corp.	AL	SOTR	41.625	26.500	12/31/96
Mercantile Bancorporation, Inc.	MO	MTL	59.375	43.750	12/31/96
Union Planters Corporation	TN	UPC	47.750	28.625	12/31/96
Average					
Median					
BHCs with ROAE Under 10.00%					
First Southern Bancshares	AL	FSTH	18.500	11.500	12/31/96
Trans Financial, Inc.	KY	TRFI	26.375	15.125	12/31/96
Cardinal Bancshares, Inc.	KY	CARD	86.500	38.000	12/31/96
Average					
Median					
Thinly Traded BHCs					
Peoples BancTrust Co.	AL	PBTC	38.000	21.500	12/31/96
Auburn National Bancorp.	AL	AUBN	27.500	19.000	12/31/96
South Alabama Bancorp.	AL	SABC	15.500	12.250	12/31/96
First United Bancshares, Inc.	AR	UNTD	40.625	26.667	12/31/96
Area Bancshares Corporation	KY	AREA	23.500	15.667	12/31/96
Peoples First Corporation	KY	PFKY	26.500	20.000	12/31/96
S.Y. Bancorp, Inc.	KY	SYBA	35.250	24.625	12/31/96
Premier Financial Bancorp, Inc.	KY	PFBI	15.625	12.250	12/31/96
New Iberia Bancorp, Inc.	LA	NIB	22.000	13.000	12/31/96
Southside Bancshares Corp.	MO	SBCO	27.750	19.000	12/31/96
Cass Commercial Corporation	MO	CASS	22.750	17.000	12/31/96
Peoples Holding Company	MS	PHCO	38.000	34.000	12/31/96
Britton & Koontz Capital Corp.	MS	BKBK	75.000	45.000	12/31/96
Average					
Median					
BHCs with Assets Under $500 Million					
MidSouth Bancorp, Inc.	LA	MSL	11.625	10.250	12/31/96
Allegiant Bancorp, Inc.	MO	ALLE	13.636	9.773	12/31/96
Community Financial Group	TN	CFGI	12.750	9.750	12/31/96
Average					
Median					
M&A Target					
Mark Twain Bancshares, Inc.	MO	MTB	56.375	35.250	12/31/96

MARKET PRICING SUMMARY

Stock Price ($)	Market Cap ($M)	YTD Price Chng (%)	P/E LTM (x)	P/E FY 97 (x)	P/E FY 98 (x)	Price/ Book (%)	Price/ Tn Book (%)	Dividend Yield (%)
48.375	2,710	0.26	15.0	12.5	11.0	1.9	2.4	3.5
51.688	3,434	7.62	14.0	11.9	10.7	2.0	2.3	3.1
34.875	3,353	5.56	13.0	11.6	10.4	1.9	2.2	2.9
51.375	3,165	5.60	16.6	12.2	11.0	1.9	2.2	3.3
39.000	2,558	8.01	20.3	11.0	10.0	2.0	2.1	3.3
....			*16.62*	*11.60*	*10.50*	*1.95*	*2.14*	*3.17*
....			*14.98*	*11.86*	*10.75*	*1.94*	*2.17*	*3.28*
12.250	24	4.08	43.8	NM	NM	1.1	1.1	4.1
23.000	262	1.09	39.0	12.1	11.0	2.0	2.1	3.0
46.000	73	2.17	17.9	NM	NM	1.5	1.6	1.7
....			*33.54*	*12.11*	*10.95*	*1.51*	*1.62*	*2.93*
....			*38.98*	*12.11*	*10.95*	*1.46*	*1.63*	*2.96*
31.000	53	19.35	14.8	NM	NM	1.5	1.6	1.9
23.500	31	6.38	11.1	NM	NM	1.3	1.3	2.0
13.500	57	(2.78)	12.9	NM	NM	1.2	1.3	3.0
33.000	272	19.70	14.9	13.5	NM	1.8	2.0	2.1
20.500	233	9.76	15.0	NM	NM	1.9	2.1	0.6
24.286	243	(2.21)	14.2	12.0	NM	1.7	1.8	3.1
29.000	95	6.90	18.8	17.8	NM	3.0	3.0	1.7
14.000	59	8.93	13.3	12.2	10.8	1.5	1.8	3.6
18.875	57	5.96	16.3	NM	NM	2.2	2.2	3.2
27.750	79	(2.70)	12.2	NM	NM	1.4	1.5	2.3
19.375	75	16.13	11.6	10.5	NM	1.6	1.6	2.7
38.000	148	(2.63)	15.6	15.7	NM	1.6	1.7	2.1
56.000	25	28.57	12.2	NM	NM	1.5	NM	4.3
....			*14.07*	*13.60*	*10.77*	*1.71*	*1.83*	*2.50*
....			*14.20*	*12.82*	*10.77*	*1.56*	*1.78*	*2.31*
11.000	15	2.27	14.5	NM	NM	1.7	1.7	2.2
12.250	35	2.04	16.3	NM	NM	1.7	NM	1.0
10.750	24	4.44	9.6	NM	NM	1.1	1.1	1.9
....			*13.47*	*NM*	*NM*	*1.49*	*1.42*	*1.67*
....			*14.47*	*NM*	*NM*	*1.67*	*1.42*	*1.86*
48.750	813	5.90	15.3	13.8	12.7	2.6	2.7	3.4

PER-SHARE

Short Name	Financial Date Mst RctQ	LTM EPS Bef Ext ($)	FY 97 EPS(E) ($)	FY 98 EPS(E) ($)	BVPS ($)
Alabama National BanCorp	12/31/96	1.45	1.65	1.85	10.15
Colonial BancGroup, Inc.	12/31/96	1.60	1.88	2.05	10.48
Compass Bancshares, Inc.	12/31/96	2.13	2.34	2.58	13.21
Simmons First National Corp.	12/31/96	1.81	2.03	2.20	18.02
First Commercial Corporation	12/31/96	2.37	2.60	2.82	16.49
Farmers Capital Bank Corp.	12/31/96	3.29	3.20	NA	28.86
CBT Corporation	12/31/96	1.48	1.80	NA	14.02
Mid-America Bancorp	12/31/96	1.57	NA	NA	14.92
Community Trust Bancorp.	12/31/96	1.87	2.05	NA	14.42
ArgentBank	12/31/96	1.31	NA	NA	11.54
Whitney Holding Corp.	12/31/96	2.45	2.67	2.89	22.53
First Commerce Corp.	12/31/96	2.89	3.42	3.78	18.66
Hibernia Corp.	12/31/96	0.85	0.99	1.11	6.58
Mississippi Valley Bcshs, Inc.	12/31/96	2.92	3.25	3.65	16.90
Magna Group, Inc.	12/31/96	2.18	2.39	NA	17.15
UMB Financial Corporation	12/31/96	2.89	3.07	3.33	29.54
Commerce Bancshares, Inc.	12/31/96	3.11	3.44	3.76	24.73
Hancock Holding Company	12/31/96	3.08	3.24	3.45	24.42
BancorpSouth, Inc.	12/31/96	2.02	2.26	2.50	15.01
Trustmark Corporation	12/31/96	1.87	2.08	2.26	15.01
Deposit Guaranty Corp.	12/31/96	2.16	2.32	NA	14.83
National Commerce Bancorp.	12/31/96	2.29	2.63	2.98	12.85
First American Corporation	12/31/96	4.11	4.77	5.22	29.32
First Tennessee National Corp.	12/31/96	2.68	3.09	3.43	14.28

DATA

TBVPS ($)	Annualized Dividend ($)	Wk Vol Shares Out (%)	Institut'l Ownership (%)	Insider Ownership (%)	Merger Target? (Y/N)
9.03	0.4600	0.86	7.24	22.60	N
9.56	0.6000	0.38	19.75	11.01	N
11.17	0.9468	1.03	28.27	5.70	N
17.47	0.5200	0.30	15.31	7.32	N
15.13	0.9600	0.33	18.04	18.44	N
28.23	1.6400	0.19	3.68	8.30	N
13.75	0.5200	0.16	3.06	15.90	N
14.92	0.7600	0.23	13.28	30.80	N
12.45	0.7272	0.33	6.55	9.50	N
11.54	0.5600	0.17	1.69	12.41	N
21.34	1.1200	0.43	20.00	12.70	N
18.20	1.6000	1.51	34.70	17.19	N
5.34	0.3200	0.95	30.11	7.96	N
16.90	0.5600	0.23	8.41	33.80	N
16.12	1.0000	1.06	35.58	6.41	N
26.12	0.8000	0.23	29.17	26.09	N
22.38	0.8200	0.71	38.08	11.00	N
22.13	1.0000	0.25	11.13	17.50	N
14.72	0.7600	0.26	8.94	6.96	N
14.56	0.5600	0.32	15.94	22.31	N
12.55	0.8000	0.48	21.42	8.42	N
12.68	0.8800	0.63	27.00	22.30	N
25.54	1.2400	2.57	30.78	7.00	N
12.49	1.2000	1.91	36.70	2.76	N

PER-SHARE

Short Name	Financial Date Mst RctQ	LTM EPS Bef Ext ($)	FY 97 EPS(E) ($)	FY 98 EPS(E) ($)	BVPS ($)
ALSO CONSIDERED, BUT EXCLUDED:					
BHCs with Assets over $15 Billion					
AmSouth Bancorp.	12/31/96	3.23	3.88	4.39	24.91
Regions Financial Corp.	12/31/96	3.70	4.36	4.81	25.52
SouthTrust Corp.	12/31/96	2.69	3.00	3.34	18.05
Mercantile Bancorporation, Inc.	12/31/96	3.10	4.22	4.66	26.52
Union Planters Corporation	12/31/96	1.92	3.55	3.89	19.55
BHCs with ROAE Under 10.00%					
First Southern Bancshares	12/31/96	0.28	NA	NA	11.33
Trans Financial, Inc.	12/31/96	0.59	1.90	2.10	11.55
Cardinal Bancshares, Inc.	12/31/96	2.57	NA	NA	31.58
Thinly Traded BHCs					
Peoples BancTrust Co.	12/31/96	2.10	NA	NA	20.18
Auburn National Bancorp.	12/31/96	2.11	NA	NA	17.71
South Alabama Bancorp.	12/31/96	1.05	NA	NA	11.14
First United Bancshares, Inc.	12/31/96	2.21	2.45	NA	18.14
Area Bancshares Corporation	12/31/96	1.37	NA	NA	10.79
Peoples First Corporation	12/31/96	1.71	2.03	NA	14.46
S.Y. Bancorp, Inc.	12/31/96	1.54	1.63	NA	9.66
Premier Financial Bancorp, Inc.	12/31/96	1.05	1.15	1.30	9.47
New Iberia Bancorp, Inc.	12/31/96	1.16	NA	NA	8.61
Southside Bancshares Corp.	12/31/96	2.27	NA	NA	19.28
Cass Commercial Corporation	12/31/96	1.67	1.85	NA	12.39
Peoples Holding Company	12/31/96	2.44	2.42	NA	23.18
Britton & Koontz Capital Corp.	12/31/96	4.59	NA	NA	37.46
BHCs with Assets Under $500 Million					
MidSouth Bancorp, Inc.	12/31/96	0.76	NA	NA	6.59
Allegiant Bancorp, Inc.	12/31/96	0.75	NA	NA	7.22
Community Financial Group	09/30/96	1.12	NA	NA	9.68
M&A Target					
Mark Twain Bancshares, Inc.	12/31/96	3.18	3.54	3.85	18.68

DATA

TBVPS ($)	Annualized Dividend ($)	Wk Vol Shares Out (%)	Institut'l Ownership (%)	Insider Ownership (%)	Merger Target? (Y/N)
20.12	1.6800	1.00	39.93	1.40	N
22.75	1.6000	0.92	22.85	3.95	N
16.05	1.0000	1.37	38.46	3.32	N
23.68	1.7200	0.96	33.38	10.10	N
18.68	1.2800	1.07	31.40	3.74	N
11.28	0.5000	1.04	4.38	13.84	N
10.77	0.6800	1.80	12.48	9.95	N
28.21	0.8000	1.55	6.79	20.91	N
19.76	0.6000	0.05	1.87	39.03	N
17.71	0.4800	0.07	0.01	34.86	N
10.16	0.4000	0.10	2.87	27.76	N
16.75	0.6800	0.09	6.29	15.19	N
9.72	0.1200	0.03	0.61	47.39	N
13.33	0.7620	0.12	2.38	11.20	N
9.66	0.4800	0.14	15.20	11.13	N
7.57	0.5000	NA	11.67	20.50	N
8.57	0.6000	0.09	0.00	10.12	N
19.03	0.6400	0.03	3.27	39.29	N
12.15	0.5200	0.13	0.00	28.55	N
21.98	0.8000	0.06	1.51	5.19	N
NA	2.4000	NA	NA	38.87	N
6.39	0.2400	0.23	0.10	41.11	N
NA	0.1200	0.17	0.55	50.40	N
9.68	0.2000	0.60	1.73	24.22	N
18.02	1.6400	0.57	19.43	21.10	Y

CURRENT BALANCE SHEET SUMMARY

Short Name	Total Assets*	Equity/ Assets	Loan/ Deposit	Borrow/ Assets	NPAs/ Assets	LLR/ NPL
Alabama National BanCorp	887,712	7.45	90.63	15.34	0.25	543.24
Colonial BancGroup, Inc.	4,870,332	7.05	102.70	17.87	0.64	204.20
Compass Bancshares, Inc.	11,814,212	6.80	80.65	14.49	0.25	542.14
Average of Alabama BHCs		*7.10*	*91.33*	*15.90*	*0.38*	*429.86*
Simmons First National Corp.	881,332	11.67	69.37	3.59	0.40	315.46
First Commercial Corporation	5,530,783	8.59	68.09	3.32	0.34	319.12
Average of Arkansas BHCs		*10.13*	*68.73*	*3.46*	*0.37*	*317.29*
Farmers Capital Bank Corp.	925,319	11.84	70.92	2.18	0.51	183.94
CBT Corporation	960,552	11.47	96.77	13.40	0.54	159.81
Mid-America Bancorp	1,420,933	9.90	97.45	25.26	0.91	267.73
Community Trust Bancorp.	1,815,660	7.97	83.14	9.62	0.65	174.53
Average of Kentucky BHCs		*10.30*	*87.07*	*12.62*	*0.65*	*196.50*
ArgentBank	589,954	11.47	66.94	0.00	0.04	NM
Whitney Holding Corp.	3,774,501	10.72	72.15	12.68	0.33	411.28
First Commerce Corp.	9,190,110	7.87	84.61	11.16	0.35	299.42
Hibernia Corp.	9,306,796	10.06	77.26	4.12	0.27	796.41
Average of Louisiana BHCs		*10.03*	*75.24*	*6.99*	*0.25*	*502.37*
Mississippi Valley Bcshs, Inc.	1,065,777	7.13	79.63	6.13	0.67	193.23
Magna Group, Inc.	5,458,709	8.87	81.36	NA	0.37	264.88
UMB Financial Corporation	6,511,986	8.94	49.20	10.24	0.20	291.16
Commerce Bancshares, Inc.	9,698,186	9.53	66.80	5.58	0.16	704.36
Average of Missouri BHCs		*8.62*	*69.25*	*7.32*	*0.35*	*363.41*
Hancock Holding Company	2,289,582	11.44	60.94	3.87	0.21	681.58
BancorpSouth, Inc.	3,617,239	8.72	78.11	2.48	0.16	927.86
Trustmark Corporation	5,193,684	10.09	73.23	18.62	0.21	750.89
Deposit Guaranty Corp.	6,382,897	9.11	73.32	10.06	0.35	364.22
Average of Mississippi BHCs		*9.84*	*71.40*	*8.76*	*0.23*	*681.14*
National Commerce Bancorp.	4,200,409	7.46	78.89	20.25	0.00	NM
First American Corporation	10,399,468	8.35	85.44	14.28	0.23	754.79
First Tennessee National Corp.	13,058,902	7.31	85.55	19.09	0.21	622.15
Average of Tennessee BHCs		*7.71*	*83.29*	*17.87*	*0.15*	*688.47*
	Average	**9.16**	**78.05**	**10.59**	**0.34**	**444.20**
	Median	**8.91**	**78.50**	**10.24**	**0.30**	**341.67**
	Maximum	**11.84**	**102.70**	**25.26**	**0.91**	**927.86**
	Minimum	**6.80**	**49.20**	**0.00**	**0.00**	**159.81**

*Assets are in thousands of dollars.

LTM INCOME STATEMENT SUMMARY

ROAE	ROAA	Net Int Margin	Fee Inc Avg Ast	Op Exp Avg Ast	Efficiency Ratio	LLP/ Net COs
15.58	1.17	4.63	1.78	3.65	68.61	NM
16.80	1.19	4.17	1.46	3.97	57.86	147.61
17.13	1.18	4.01	1.33	3.82	58.04	100.37
16.50	*1.18*	*4.27*	*1.52*	*3.81*	*61.50*	*123.99*
10.31	1.22	4.65	2.94	3.26	65.77	97.83
15.09	1.30	4.66	1.96	3.01	63.46	NA
12.70	*1.26*	*4.66*	*2.45*	*3.14*	*64.62*	*97.83*
11.80	1.41	4.96	1.31	3.19	59.77	106.91
10.78	1.26	4.91	0.94	3.94	58.82	51.08
11.13	1.14	4.39	0.96	3.65	66.57	73.27
13.53	1.07	4.76	0.81	3.92	58.19	160.39
11.81	*1.22*	*4.76*	*1.01*	*3.68*	*60.84*	*97.91*
11.77	1.35	4.58	0.49	2.94	59.31	NM
10.45	1.14	4.81	1.04	2.51	65.99	NM
16.34	1.39	4.79	2.02	3.18	57.20	117.88
13.49	1.34	4.89	1.39	3.16	62.23	(80.24)
13.01	*1.31*	*4.77*	*1.24*	*2.95*	*61.18*	*18.82*
19.07	1.40	4.01	0.46	4.04	41.57	189.95
13.75	1.20	4.01	0.94	3.67	54.43	122.22
10.02	0.94	4.16	2.06	2.68	70.03	107.41
13.40	1.28	4.40	1.66	3.01	57.53	98.74
14.06	*1.21*	*4.15*	*1.28*	*3.35*	*55.89*	*129.58*
13.74	1.38	5.21	1.16	2.83	57.53	139.93
14.31	1.24	4.81	1.17	3.66	59.22	142.74
13.12	1.27	4.33	1.31	3.16	55.88	120.91
15.15	1.39	4.77	1.90	3.03	62.12	136.40
14.08	*1.32*	*4.78*	*1.39*	*3.17*	*58.69*	*135.00*
18.86	1.51	3.89	1.78	3.96	50.42	188.08
14.64	1.25	3.94	1.83	3.67	60.44	0.00
20.05	1.43	4.13	4.56	3.54	66.35	116.99
17.85	*1.40*	*3.99*	*2.72*	*3.72*	*59.07*	*101.69*
14.18	**1.27**	**4.49**	**1.55**	**3.39**	**59.89**	**106.92**
13.75	**1.27**	**4.61**	**1.36**	**3.40**	**59.27**	**117.44**
20.05	**1.51**	**5.21**	**4.56**	**4.04**	**70.03**	**189.95**
10.02	**0.94**	**3.89**	**0.46**	**2.51**	**41.57**	**(80.24)**

CURRENT BALANCE SHEET SUMMARY

Short Name	Total Assets*	Equity/ Assets	Loan/ Deposit	Borrow/ Assets	NPAs/ Assets	LLR/ NPL
ALSO CONSIDERED, BUT EXCLUDED:						
BHCs with Assets over $15 Billion						
AmSouth Bancorp.	18,407,264	7.58	96.89	21.30	0.51	229.41
Regions Financial Corp.	18,930,175	8.45	88.46	10.88	0.39	274.93
SouthTrust Corp.	26,223,193	6.62	111.71	25.93	0.53	317.68
Mercantile Bancorporation, Inc.	18,986,959	8.61	85.74	11.93	0.40	313.02
Union Planters Corporation	15,222,563	8.89	90.30	13.93	0.54	253.22
Average		*8.04*	*95.92*	*17.26*	*0.49*	*294.64*
Median		*8.45*	*90.30*	*13.93*	*0.51*	*274.93*
BHCs with ROAE Under 10.00%						
First Southern Bancshares	184,484	11.41	121.34	16.06	0.12	NM
Trans Financial, Inc.	2,003,952	6.55	91.88	13.36	0.33	382.65
Cardinal Bancshares, Inc.	629,061	8.00	85.06	3.73	0.10	NM
Average		*8.65*	*99.43*	*11.05*	*0.18*	*382.65*
Median		*8.00*	*91.88*	*13.36*	*0.12*	*382.65*
Thinly Traded BHCs						
Peoples BancTrust Co.	343,301	9.96	79.19	5.34	0.62	125.90
Auburn National Bancorp.	258,055	8.94	73.02	6.50	0.04	NM
South Alabama Bancorp.	350,084	13.45	64.02	1.47	0.32	236.79
First United Bancshares, Inc.	1,531,039	9.77	55.59	4.73	0.22	395.95
Area Bancshares Corporation	1,170,838	10.47	80.44	16.27	0.28	579.67
Peoples First Corporation	1,417,764	10.20	92.93	10.31	0.53	200.28
S.Y. Bancorp, Inc.	415,365	7.61	84.88	6.04	0.27	603.63
Premier Financial Bancorp, Inc.	292,612	13.62	93.21	3.20	0.28	596.45
New Iberia Bancorp, Inc.	299,423	8.63	67.08	1.19	0.25	475.34
Southside Bancshares Corp.	527,907	10.01	63.02	0.64	0.36	540.21
Cass Commercial Corporation	438,322	10.90	111.42	0.56	NA	NA
Peoples Holding Company	893,089	10.14	72.82	1.96	NA	NA
Britton & Koontz Capital Corp.	151,303	10.92	75.88	2.42	0.21	266.24
Average		*10.36*	*77.96*	*4.66*	*0.31*	*402.05*
Median		*10.14*	*75.88*	*3.20*	*0.28*	*435.65*
BHCs with Assets Under $500 Million						
MidSouth Bancorp, Inc.	185,228	6.18	55.26	0.82	0.39	207.63
Allegiant Bancorp, Inc.	377,564	4.34	94.58	13.45	0.11	775.00
Community Financial Group	160,106	13.32	81.94	5.93	0.54	346.67
Average		*7.95*	*77.26*	*6.73*	*0.35*	*443.10*
Median		*6.18*	*81.94*	*5.93*	*0.39*	*346.67*
M&A Target						
Mark Twain Bancshares, Inc.	3,133,265	9.95	83.93	6.24	0.41	361.68

*Assets are in thousands of dollars.

LTM INCOME STATEMENT SUMMARY

ROAE	ROAA	Net Int Margin	Fee Inc Avg Ast	Op Exp Avg Ast	Efficiency Ratio	LLP/ Net COs
13.23	1.02	3.93	1.26	3.90	55.32	100.93
15.19	1.29	4.27	1.22	3.85	53.54	151.94
15.92	1.09	4.03	1.05	4.03	54.18	188.89
11.90	1.06	4.30	1.49	3.44	57.03	85.00
10.42	0.88	4.41	1.45	3.76	63.56	110.84
12.75	*1.01*	*4.25*	*1.33*	*3.74*	*58.26*	*128.24*
13.23	*1.06*	*4.27*	*1.26*	*3.85*	*55.32*	*110.84*
2.04	0.29	4.41	0.29	4.13	56.86	225.00
5.32	0.37	4.52	1.60	3.93	66.19	119.67
9.17	0.67	4.65	0.52	4.03	79.00	222.93
5.51	*0.44*	*4.53*	*0.80*	*4.03*	*67.35*	*189.20*
5.32	*0.37*	*4.52*	*0.52*	*4.03*	*66.19*	*222.93*
11.01	1.12	4.93	1.14	3.49	60.57	135.32
12.58	1.18	3.69	0.97	4.13	57.79	NM
10.36	1.29	5.12	0.95	3.12	61.87	70.95
13.08	1.22	4.34	0.68	3.40	58.09	72.66
13.72	1.44	4.71	1.24	3.54	58.78	123.89
12.75	1.29	4.41	0.64	4.01	52.35	154.79
17.45	1.47	5.05	1.58	3.57	61.52	526.32
12.20	1.53	5.33	0.78	3.95	54.54	47.20
14.33	1.28	4.63	0.82	3.32	56.99	138.86
12.27	1.20	4.42	0.57	3.40	59.63	64.52
14.31	1.50	5.82	5.10	1.07	78.91	0.00
10.84	1.10	4.84	1.26	3.26	66.37	NA
12.53	1.33	4.39	0.67	3.37	64.80	33.11
12.88	*1.30*	*4.74*	*1.26*	*3.36*	*60.94*	*124.33*
12.58	*1.29*	*4.71*	*0.95*	*3.40*	*59.63*	*72.66*
11.36	0.74	5.32	1.27	2.72	76.85	105.97
12.17	0.59	3.50	0.33	4.85	61.56	302.93
12.12	1.59	4.12	0.46	4.12	65.05	NM
11.88	*0.97*	*4.31*	*0.69*	*3.90*	*67.82*	*204.45*
12.12	*0.74*	*4.12*	*0.46*	*4.12*	*65.05*	*204.45*
18.84	1.79	4.63	1.33	3.43	47.88	168.38

QUARTERLY

Short Name	FD EPS Qtr. 4	FD EPS Qtr. 3	FD EPS Qtr. 2	FD EPS Qtr. 1
Alabama National BanCorp	0.39	0.30	0.35	NA
Colonial BancGroup, Inc.	0.37	0.48	0.40	0.38
Compass Bancshares, Inc.	0.43	0.53	0.62	0.49
Average of Alabama BHCs				
Simmons First National Corp.	0.45	0.47	0.39	0.47
First Commercial Corporation	0.60	0.58	0.55	0.56
Average of Arkansas BHCs				
Farmers Capital Bank Corp.	0.82	1.08	0.64	0.77
CBT Corporation	0.31	0.41	0.37	0.43
Mid-America Bancorp	0.37	0.39	0.46	0.37
Community Trust Bancorp.	0.49	0.47	0.42	0.23
Average of Kentucky BHCs				
ArgentBank	0.27	0.35	0.36	0.31
Whitney Holding Corp.	0.61	0.59	0.47	0.64
First Commerce Corp.	0.66	0.76	0.75	0.15
Hibernia Corp.	0.19	0.22	0.21	0.27
Average of Louisiana BHCs				
Mississippi Valley Bcshs, Inc.	0.76	0.73	0.68	0.57
Magna Group, Inc.	0.56	0.54	0.50	0.49
UMB Financial Corporation	0.71	0.72	0.89	0.70
Commerce Bancshares, Inc.	0.81	0.75	0.70	0.71
Average of Missouri BHCs				
Hancock Holding Company	0.79	0.79	0.76	0.69
BancorpSouth, Inc.	0.50	0.53	0.45	0.43
Trustmark Corporation	0.50	0.46	0.44	0.43
Deposit Guaranty Corp.	0.57	0.54	0.56	0.43
Average of Mississippi BHCs				
National Commerce Bancorp.	0.59	0.55	0.52	0.52
First American Corporation	0.93	1.04	1.01	0.86
First Tennessee National Corp.	0.68	0.62	0.54	0.67
Average of Tennessee BHCs				

PROFITABILITY SUMMARY

	ROAE Qtr. 4	ROAE Qtr. 3	ROAE Qtr. 2	ROAE Qtr. 1
	16.76	13.02	15.99	NA
	15.08	19.11	16.85	16.63
	13.87	17.31	19.97	16.58
....	*15.24*	*16.48*	*17.60*	*16.61*
	10.16	10.79	9.14	11.37
	15.09	14.84	14.39	15.38
....	*12.63*	*12.82*	*11.77*	*13.38*
	11.67	15.64	9.33	11.49
	9.25	11.94	11.14	13.22
	10.33	11.16	12.92	10.86
	14.00	13.95	12.42	6.78
....	*11.31*	*13.17*	*11.45*	*10.59*
	10.14	12.31	12.85	11.60
	10.93	10.78	8.74	11.44
	14.95	17.14	17.04	3.81
	12.48	14.44	13.35	18.52
....	*12.13*	*13.67*	*13.00*	*11.34*
	19.80	19.81	18.17	16.33
	14.12	13.82	12.62	12.97
	9.92	10.23	12.39	9.50
	14.03	13.11	12.10	12.65
....	*14.47*	*14.24*	*13.82*	*12.86*
	13.95	14.15	13.70	12.41
	13.93	15.17	13.04	12.99
	13.86	13.16	12.79	12.82
	15.82	15.66	15.88	12.58
....	*14.39*	*14.54*	*13.85*	*12.70*
	20.11	18.89	17.87	18.57
	13.04	14.97	15.00	13.22
	20.82	19.37	17.17	20.75
....	*17.99*	*17.74*	*16.68*	*17.51*
Average	**13.92**	**14.62**	**13.95**	**13.15**
Median	**13.94**	**14.30**	**13.20**	**12.82**
Maximum	**20.82**	**19.81**	**19.97**	**20.75**
Minimum	**9.25**	**10.23**	**8.74**	**3.81**

QUARTERLY

Short Name	FD EPS Qtr. 4	FD EPS Qtr. 3	FD EPS Qtr. 2	FD EPS Qtr. 1
ALSO CONSIDERED, BUT EXCLUDED:				
BHCs with Assets over $15 Billion				
AmSouth Bancorp.	0.62	0.86	0.83	0.82
Regions Financial Corp.	0.82	0.99	0.85	0.71
SouthTrust Corp.	0.68	0.66	0.64	0.61
Mercantile Bancorporation, Inc.	0.92	1.04	0.07	0.89
Union Planters Corporation	0.67	0.80	0.78	0.53
Average				
Median				
BHCs with ROAE Under 10.00%				
First Southern Bancshares	(0.04)	0.00	0.23	0.27
Trans Financial, Inc.	0.26	(0.45)	0.33	0.25
Cardinal Bancshares, Inc.	0.26	2.56	(0.06)	(0.05)
Average				
Median				
Thinly Traded BHCs				
Peoples BancTrust Co.	0.52	0.48	0.54	0.51
Auburn National Bancorp.	0.49	0.55	0.49	0.50
South Alabama Bancorp.	0.27	0.26	0.25	0.25
First United Bancshares, Inc.	0.57	0.52	0.56	0.49
Area Bancshares Corporation	0.33	0.30	0.29	0.26
Peoples First Corporation	0.38	0.44	0.42	0.42
S.Y. Bancorp, Inc.	0.43	0.40	0.32	0.29
Premier Financial Bancorp, Inc.	0.25	0.27	0.26	NA
New Iberia Bancorp, Inc.	0.30	0.29	0.29	0.33
Southside Bancshares Corp.	0.68	0.50	0.58	0.52
Cass Commercial Corporation	0.44	0.38	0.38	0.43
Peoples Holding Company	0.58	0.58	0.59	0.55
Britton & Koontz Capital Corp.	0.73	1.23	1.14	1.17
Average				
Median				
BHCs with Assets Under $500 Million				
MidSouth Bancorp, Inc.	0.15	0.20	0.18	0.20
Allegiant Bancorp, Inc.	0.22	0.18	0.20	0.11
Community Financial Group	0.26	0.29	0.33	0.24
Average				
Median				
M&A Target				
Mark Twain Bancshares, Inc.	0.82	0.79	0.75	0.74

PROFITABILITY SUMMARY

ROAE Qtr. 4	ROAE Qtr. 3	ROAE Qtr. 2	ROAE Qtr. 1
10.14	14.18	13.70	13.85
13.55	16.44	14.43	12.33
15.98	15.93	15.65	15.26
14.28	16.15	1.09	13.91
13.42	16.48	16.37	12.21
14.56	*16.19*	*11.04*	*13.79*
13.55	*16.15*	*14.43*	*13.85*
(1.20)	(0.14)	5.40	6.47
9.58	(15.70)	11.42	8.80
3.49	36.40	(1.02)	(0.81)
3.96	*6.85*	*5.27*	*4.82*
3.49	*(0.14)*	*5.40*	*6.47*
10.85	10.25	11.44	11.06
11.75	13.24	11.93	12.71
11.28	10.81	10.47	11.18
13.58	12.16	13.26	11.74
12.86	12.21	12.38	11.15
11.12	13.32	12.88	13.33
19.22	18.68	15.22	14.21
10.78	11.96	17.64	NA
14.57	14.72	14.86	16.87
14.51	10.93	12.89	11.95
15.00	13.28	13.53	15.42
10.46	10.53	11.19	10.20
7.93	13.70	12.93	13.46
12.61	*12.75*	*13.12*	*12.77*
11.75	*12.21*	*12.89*	*12.33*
9.32	12.53	11.09	9.95
13.55	11.70	13.26	7.74
10.82	12.57	14.40	10.67
11.23	*12.27*	*12.92*	*9.45*
10.82	*12.53*	*13.26*	*9.95*
19.33	18.92	17.94	18.51

10

Valuing S Corporation ESOP Companies

Kathryn F. Aschwald
Donna J. Walker

Recent tax law changes allowing ESOPs in S corporations can result in substantial cash savings to a company. This article explores how these cash savings enhance value from an ESOP perspective. Appropriate appraisal methodologies within the ESOP context also are discussed. Finally, the authors consider fairness issues in S corporation ESOPs.

On January 1, 1998, corporations with employee stock ownership plans (ESOPs) became eligible to elect S corporation status, and existing S corporations became eligible to form ESOPs, without nullifying the S corporation election. For 100% ESOP-owned companies, this change in the tax laws effectively eliminates federal income taxation. For companies that are less than 100% ESOP-owned, that portion of the income attributable to the ESOP's ownership is not taxable. For example, if an ESOP owns 35% of a company, then 35% of the company's income would not be taxable. The remaining 65% of the company's income would be taxable to the other shareholders at the shareholder level.[1]

The elimination of taxes (completely for 100% ESOP-owned companies and partially for less than 100% ESOP-owned companies) presents some interesting valuation questions. Within the appraisal community, there long have been heated discussions regarding the appropriate methodologies to employ in valuing S corporations relative to C corporations due to their unique tax status. Thus, to a certain degree, the question of appropriate methodologies to employ in valuing S corporation ESOPs is not a new one. However, the ESOP's ability to completely eliminate taxes in some instances introduces a new factor to be considered.

Kathryn F. Aschwald, CFA, ASA, and Donna J. Walker, CFA, ASA, are principals of Columbia Financial Advisors, Inc., a business appraisal and financial advisory firm with headquarters in Portland, Oregon, with an office in Seattle, Washington. Ms. Aschwald is a member of the ESOP Association's Valuation Advisory Committee and is the immediate past chair of the Committee. She also is on the editorial board of this journal. Ms. Walker is the course developer for the American Society of Appraiser's ESOP Valuation Course. Both Ms. Walker and Ms. Aschwald are frequent speakers, lecturers, and teachers on the subject of ESOP appraisal and financial advice.

Impact of S Corporation Election on ESOP Company Cash Flows

Less Than 100% ESOP

In this case, the cash savings to the company are limited because cash payments are generally made to all shareholders so that the non-ESOP shareholders have cash available to pay taxes on the S corporation income attributable to the non-ESOP shareholders at the shareholder level. The distributions made to meet these personal tax obligations go, in the case of the non-ESOP shareholders, directly to the shareholder, and, in the case of the ESOP, to the ESOP trust. In either case, the cash is no longer available to the company to reinvest into productive assets. To the extent that these distributions can be used by the ESOP to pay principal and interest (in the case of a leveraged ESOP) or to pay ESOP benefit distributions, then there is a cash savings to the extent that distributions result in lower company contributions to the ESOP.

100% ESOP

In the case of the S corporation that is 100% owned by an ESOP, there are no corporate federal income taxes paid. Therefore, the company realizes, on an annual basis, a cash savings equal to the dollar amount of the taxes the company would have to pay were it a C corporation.

Appraisal Methodologies

The Internal Revenue Service (IRS) and the U.S. Department of Labor (DOL) generally govern appraisals for ESOP purposes. In this article, we will not discuss appraisal methodologies as they apply to ESOPs in general, but rather how they apply to ESOP S corporations specifically.

Value Enhancement Associated with S Corporation Election

There is no question that the absence of taxes represents true cash savings to a company. It follows, then, that the cash savings should translate into some form of enhanced value.

From the most global perspective, value is enhanced via the increase in cash flows available to the company. The source of these cash flows is the cash that would otherwise have gone to pay corporate federal income taxes. As discussed above, the magnitude of the savings depends on the percentage of the company owned by the ESOP. This value enhancement is realized in one of two ways: either through reinvestment of cash flows or through the payment of regular dividends. The reinvestment of the added cash flows into productive assets earning a return in excess of the company's cost of capital enhances value over time as those assets become productive and generate additional cash flows and higher levels of growth than would otherwise be the case. When the cash flows are paid out in the form of dividends, the owner of the ESOP common stock earns a portion of its total return in the form of dividends. In this case, the value is captured either in a capitalization of dividends approach or in the increased marketability (or conversely lower marketability discount) of the security due to its higher income return. The capital gains portion of the value is less than if the company reinvested the added cash flows, but the income portion is higher.

If the company merely retains the added cash flows in the form of cash and marketable securities, which do not earn a return in excess of the company's cost of capital, the S corporation election may not be value-enhancing. *The mere avoidance of taxes does not enhance value. The cash savings associated with the S corporation status must be put to productive use.*

Initial Transactions and Updates

Standard of Value. A significant governing factor in considering the most appropriate appraisal methodologies is the standard of value for ESOP appraisals. IRS regulations, proposed regulations by the DOL, and general case law dictate that the appropriate standard of value is fair market value. Fair market value is defined as follows:

> Fair market value is considered to represent a value at which a willing seller and willing buyer, both being informed of the relevant facts about the business, could reasonably conduct a transaction, neither person acting under compulsion to do so.

Appropriate Methodologies Within the Context of Fair Market Value. The appropriate standard of value and the definition of fair market value require an appraisal incorporating the concept of "any willing buyer" and "any willing seller." For the ESOP company to retain its S election (and the associated tax savings), it must be purchased by an S corporation. The presumption of an S corporation buyer violates the fair market value standard because another S corporation is a specific buyer. It follows, then, that for annual update and transaction purposes, the S corporation is appropriately valued as if it were a C corporation.

Given that valuing the S corporation ESOP company as a C corporation is appropriate, *it is not appropriate to do the following:*

- Apply after-tax multiples to pretax numbers.
- Add the present value of the tax savings associated with the S corporation election.
- Apply after-tax discount rates to pretax cash flows.

It is extremely important to recognize, however, that this does not mean that there will not be added value associated with the S corporation status. The value of the S corporation election is realized over time as the cash flows are reinvested and the company's earnings are higher and/or growing faster than if the company were a C corporation. Intuitively this makes sense. "Any willing buyer" would naturally pay for value enhancements resulting from the reinvestment of cash flows into income-producing assets that were already in place earning a return. Those value enhancements or assets are transferable to "any willing buyer." It also follows, then, that there is no immediate "value pick-up" associated with the S corporation.

As a result, in an initial transaction, the ESOP should generally not pay for value enhancements that are not already in place. Nor should an ESOP pay for benefits that it brings to the table (such as the S election). As discussed above, when the added cash flows are paid out in the form of dividends, the enhanced value is captured in the increased liquidity (and thus the application of a lower discount for lack of marketability) associated with closely held paying securities.

To the extent large cash balances are developed over time, value may even be enhanced from an acquisition standpoint for those ESOP S corporations that simply hold their added cash flows. It is not likely that this value transfers to a minority shareholder, and to the extent it does transfer, it certainly is less than dollar-for-dollar.

Some argue that there is a significant amount of economic value associated with the S corporation election for ESOP companies, and that this economic value is equal to the present value of (or a multiple of) the future tax savings as a result of the S corporation election. Again, however, one must recognize that to retain this economic value, another S corporation must purchase the company and maintain the ESOP to keep the tax savings. Because there are far fewer S corporations than C corporations, the likelihood of an available S corporation buyer is much less. Therefore, within the context of fair market value, the presumption of an S corporation buyer requires the assumption of severely reduced liquidity resulting from a reduced number of "willing buyers." This reduced liquidity and resulting higher discount for lack of marketability would offset the added value implied by the present value of the tax savings to a large (if not total) extent. In addition, many other taxes (such as the LIFO recapture tax, and the built-in capital gains tax, which will be discussed later) may in fact be due from an S corporation upon sale of the company and/or upon conversion to an S corporation. These taxes would offset any value attributable to the tax savings calculated in this way.

Taking this concept one step further, one merely needs to consider the theory from a market perspective. Valuing the tax savings implicitly as described above presumes that a buyer of the S corporation would apply a multiple to pretax income. Assuming a 40% tax rate, a multiple of 5, and

$100 pretax income, this implies a significantly higher price for the S corporation, as shown below:

	S Corporation	C Corporation
Pretax Income	$100	$100
Corporate Taxes	0	40
Net Income	$100	$ 60
Times 5.0 Multiple	× 5	× 5
Value	$500	$300

The question is, would any "willing buyer" (or any buyer) pay 67% more ($500 versus $300) for an S corporation relative to a C corporation? We believe the answer to this question is no. To a C corporation buyer, the S status of the selling company would be of no value. If the buyer were an individual, it would be more economical for that buyer to buy a C corporation and convert it to an S corporation. The cost of doing so would be much less that 67% greater price for the S corporation. Such an individual may be willing to pay a premium for an S corporation but no more than the cost of converting a C corporation to an S corporation. If the buyer were an existing S corporation, it would not pay for tax benefits it already had.

Sale of Company and/or ESOP Termination

We stated above that in an initial transaction, the ESOP should not pay for value enhancements that are not already in place, nor should it pay for benefits that it brings to the table such as the tax-free status in a S election. However, when the ESOP is selling its position, it may be appropriate for the ESOP trustee to consider the favorable S corporation tax treatment.

When an ESOP is selling its position or being terminated, the standard of value is still fair market value. However, the financial advisor to the ESOP trustee is often asked to determine whether the transaction is fair to the ESOP from a financial point of view. This is generally interpreted to mean that the transaction must be fair to the ESOP in both absolute terms (not less than fair market value) and relative terms when compared to numerous financial factors that are not necessarily part of fair market value. For example, is the consideration being received by the ESOP the same as other transaction participants? If the ESOP is leveraged with debt outstanding, we look to see whether or not the ESOP's return on investment would be higher if it did not sell and simply held its investment until the debt was paid down. When the ESOP is considering a sale of its interest, then the trustee must determine that the sale is in the best interests of the ESOP participants. Therefore, a careful analysis of financial factors in addition to fair market value may include an analysis of the enhanced cash flow enjoyed by an S corporation ESOP. This is referred to by some as the ESOP's "economic value." It is typically defined as the present value of the ESOP's pro rata portion of expected corporate income tax savings under an S election discounted at an equity-required rate of return. Many assume that fair market value will be below economic value.

The question is then whether the ESOP can sell at fair market value and thus below economic value. Arguably, an ESOP trustee would have difficulty accepting a fair market value buyout price if the economic value was considerably higher and no compelling reasons for a sale existed. This is most likely with a 100% ESOP-owned S corporation. In other words, an ESOP owning 100% of an S corporation may have a hold position, due to cash flows that are 100% free of corporate income taxes, that is more valuable than the price that a financial buyer or even a strategic buyer may be willing to pay. Absent compelling factors such as poor or deteriorating industry conditions or a repurchase obligation outstripping the liquidity abilities of the company, there may be no reason for the ESOP to forego its enhanced expected future cash flows if its return on investment is higher under a hold position than if it sells its ownership position. In terms of financial fairness, this seems entirely appropriate. It would be unfair to the ESOP to sell if it resulted in a return on investment below the return available to participants if the company continued on a stand-alone basis.

However, the discrepancy between fair market value and economic value as described above may be greatly overstated. First, the calculation of economic value must include all tax impacts. There are costs to converting to an S corporation as well as tax savings. These include LIFO recapture taxes and costs relating to the write-off of deferred tax assets and liabilities. Based on the experience of some of our ESOP clients who have converted from C to S corporate status, the break-even period may be two to three years. In addition, S corporations may be taxed on excessive passive income (over 25% of revenues) carried over from prior C corporation status. Finally, S corporations are subject for 10 years to a built-in gains tax on disposition of appreciated property carried over from the prior C corporation. This tax can be significant, particularly in the case where the value of the company experiences rapid growth from the time of conversion from C to S status. Also, some consideration must be given to possible changes in tax laws that eliminate the tax advantages of S corporations.

These costs may (most likely in the first years after the conversion), when factored in with the tax savings, reduce "economic value" and the relative difference to fair market value. Assuming over time the productive deployment of enhanced cash flows, the value of the S corporation will increase. As stated above, a third party should be willing to pay for this value because it is reflective of productive assets, not a tax status, and because it is transferable to a third party. Thus, over time, fair market value and economic value should converge, and "economic value" should be reflected in the price offered by a prospective buyer.

In conclusion, we urge caution in analyzing the concept of "economic value" as it pertains to S corporation ESOPs. While there may be some intuitive appeal to the concept, economic value is difficult to determine because it is affected by many variables:

- The level of distributions
- Subsequent investment returns
- Expected tax rates in the future
- Expected holding period of investment
- Expected sale price of investments at the end of the hold period

At a minimum, it must be considered within the context of the factors discussed above that offset economic value, such as the built-in capital gains tax.

Conclusion

No increase in value is appropriate in the appraisal of S corporation ESOPs only as a result of a change in tax status. It is not appropriate to add the present value of the tax benefits. The appropriate standard of value and the definition of fair market value require an appraisal incorporating the concept of "any willing buyer" and "any willing seller." In order for the ESOP company to retain its S election (and the associated tax savings), it must be purchased by an S corporation or individuals eligible to elect S corporate status. The presumption of an S corporation buyer violates the fair market value standard because another S corporation is a specific buyer. It follows, then, that for annual update and transaction purposes, the S corporation is appropriately valued as if it were a C corporation. The ESOP generally should not pay for the S corporation status at an initial transaction or for update purposes. However, consideration of the enhanced cash flows resulting from the S corporation status that have not yet been invested into productive assets may be appropriate as a part of the consideration of overall fairness when the ESOP is selling its ownership position or being terminated.

Notes

1. As of this writing, a legislative proposal has been introduced that would repeal the provision of the Taxpayer Relief Act of 1997 that permitted the ESOP's share of an S corporation's taxable income to be exempt from the unrelated business income tax (UBIT). Instead, the proposal would impose a corporate-like tax on the ESOP's share of its S corporation sponsor's income and provide for a complex tax deduc-

tion upon distribution to ESOP participants in order to maintain, technically, the single tax on S corporation taxable income for federal tax purposes. ESOP advocates are fighting this proposal vigorously and hope for a positive outcome.

11

Marketability Discounts and ESOP Acquisitions of Minority Share Interests

Andrew S. Kubersky

An employee stock ownership plan (ESOP) should not pay more for a minority interest in the same security at the same point of time than would a hypothetical buyer in any other situation. To assure that it does not and to help protect the ESOP fiduciary from engaging in a possible prohibited transaction, the independent appraiser must determine and include a marketability discount as part of the valuation process. This discount should take into account the full definition of fair market value, including the assumption of a hypothetical investor, before the opinion should be relied upon by the ESOP fiduciary.

The philosophy behind and quantification of marketability discounts are garnering increasing scrutiny and becoming ever more crucial in the valuation of closely held stock for purposes of employee stock ownership plan (ESOP) acquisitions of minority interests. Marketability discounts are intended to reflect hypothetical buyers' concerns regarding the absence of a ready and available market when they decide, in turn, to sell. The word "hypothetical" is key to this discussion, as the Internal Revenue Service (IRS) and the courts have repeatedly required that the willing buyer and seller mentioned in the long-standing definition of "fair market value" be hypothetical.

Extending this thought, the independent appraiser properly must think in terms of a hypothetical investor rather than a specific investor. This implies that one should not consider the special attributes the ESOP brings to the table when applying an appropriate marketability discount. Any other approach may result in the ESOP paying more for the shares than a hypothetical buyer would pay, which would constitute a prohibited transaction under the Employee Retirement Income Security Act of 1974, as amended (ERISA).

The "Put Option" Argument Is Fallacious

The all-too-common practice by some appraisers of using the ESOP's put option as the justification to lower or eliminate a discount for marketability

Andrew Kubersky, ASA, of San Francisco, has been active in valuing closely held securities since 1972. Providing adequate consideration, fairness and fair market value opinions, he has specialized in ESOP transactions since 1975. He wishes to thank Ronald L. Ludwig of the San Francisco law firm of Ludwig Goldberg & Krenzel for his comments and advice over the years.

in appraisals made in connection with the acquisition of shares by the plan is inappropriate.

First, the put option is not an attribute of the shares but rather of the ESOP itself. There is a fundamental difference between the terminated ESOP participant having the right to sell his or her shares after receiving a distribution of stock and a put option that is part and parcel of the security itself. A put is "a contractual right that entitles the holder, at his option, to sell the stock to a specified party at some time or under some specified circumstances, at the price or mechanism for determining the price specified in the contract."[1]

The seller of stock to the ESOP typically has no put on his or her shares (although securities can be designed so as to contain a put provision). Accordingly, the shares are subject to a put only after the ESOP buys them and then, at some unspecified future dates, distributes them to participants. The ESOP cannot turn around and sell the shares to a third party at a price that includes a value for the put, because the next buyer would not have that contractual right and would not pay for it. Hence, the ESOP should not be forced to pay for the put as though it were an asset of the seller when, in fact, it is an attribute of the ESOP, which should not pay for what it already owns. Again, the issue here is one of what the hypothetical investor would pay without regard to the special nature of a specific buyer (e.g., an ESOP).

Second, the ESOP's eventual put option does not apply to the block of stock as a whole, but only to shares that are distributed to terminated participants. Undoubtedly, in any given year this would be a small portion of the total shares owned by the ESOP. Unless the put applies to the ESOP's entire holding of stock (because of the particular financial and legal design of the securities), at no time does the ESOP have the right to put its entire holding back to the issuing company or to any other entity or individual.

If the contractual put right is attached to the security and could thereby be resold to a third party, then it would be appropriate to argue that the existence of the put could reduce the discount for limited marketability that would otherwise be applied. However, it would be necessary in this instance to show that the party to whom the ESOP could put the shares has the financial ability to fund the put. Absent the necessary liquidity, it would be inappropriate to significantly decrease the discount for limited marketability.

Marketable Minority Interest

Despite the erroneous put option arguments, it has been commonly accepted that the ESOP provides a higher degree of marketability than would otherwise exist in closely held shares. Referring to this oft-cited common wisdom, all too frequently appraisers apply marketability discounts that are lower for ESOP valuation purposes than for other purposes.

The contention is that ESOPs in closely held companies usually are designed to provide a cash benefit to distributees (either by a repurchase by the company or a distribution of cash from the ESOP). It generally has been assumed, therefore, that the ESOP provides a higher degree of liquidity than would otherwise exist and thereby justifies a lower (or zero) discount. Where there is no discount taken for the limited marketability of closely held minority interest shares, appraisers sometimes state that they are valuing the interest on a "marketable minority interest" basis.

Many of the ESOP-related valuations that I have had the opportunity to review have tended to automatically place discounts of between zero and 10% on the value of ESOP shares. Comparable discounts for limited marketability of closely held shares in non-ESOP-related situations typically range from 25% to 40% and can be significantly higher.

The concept of a marketable minority interest has been used for many years. But why should the ESOP pay more for the shares than would a hypothetical third party? Clearly, it should not. Because the ESOP does not have the right to put its entire holding back to the employer, the concept of a marketable minority interest is fallacious and indefensible and unfair to the employee participants in the plan. The U.S. Court of Appeals for the Seventh Circuit found this to be the case in *Eyler v Commissioner of Internal Revenue*, 88 F.3d 445 (7th Cir. 1996). In this case the court found that even with the presence of a put option, the valuation in question was in error because a discount for marketability had not been applied. The IRS recently has been applying *Eyler* in audit situations on the West Coast to challenge appraisals for ESOP transactions involving minority interests when a marketability discount is zero or deemed too small.

Because the absence of marketability discounts results in higher values, it is not difficult to see how the marketable minority interest concept came into being. However, the sellers of minority holdings are not hurt by the application of a marketability discount versus what they could obtain from a third party. In fact, because many are selling to an ESOP with the intent of obtaining Section 1042 tax-deferred treatment—often allowing them to permanently defer capital gains taxes—the sellers are already receiving a bonus value over what they would receive by selling to a hypothetical third party. It is inappropriate to induce them to sell their minority interests by offering what amounts to a premium price by not reflecting the shares' inherent limited marketability in the valuation of those shares.

The Appraiser's Role

The work product of the qualified independent appraiser should provide assurance to the plan fiduciaries that the ESOP is not acquiring employer securities in excess of their fair market value. In fact, the appraiser should help the ESOP fiduciary to pay as little as it can for the shares it is acquiring.

In this sense, the appraiser acts as financial advisor to the ESOP fiduciary. Even if the ESOP fiduciary is sophisticated in ESOP valuation issues, it still relies on the appraiser to do what needs to be done in order to affirm that the ESOP is not entering into a prohibited transaction when it acquires shares. It is the appraiser's obligation to stay informed and to keep the clients informed on important developments that can affect their decision to rely on the conclusions contained in the appraisal.

This role is not played properly when the appraiser writes into the engagement letter a provision that the appraisal will be determined on the so-called "marketable minority interest basis" and then writes a limiting condition into the appraisal report that the appraiser has been directed to determine the value on a "marketable minority interest basis."

In fact, given the IRS position in the *Eyler* case, a valuation opinion rendered on a marketable minority interest basis is reckless and puts the fiduciaries in a precarious position, one in which they ought not be.

Role of ESOP Fiduciaries

ESOP fiduciaries should be proactive and in close contact with their legal counsel to obtain advice as to whether the valuation opinion has been prepared in accordance with rules, regulations, and case law on the issue. Fiduciaries, as made clear in the *Eyler* case, are not protected simply by "acting in good faith" or by obtaining an independent valuation. The fiduciaries have the ultimate responsibility to know and understand what a valuation should contain and ascertain that theirs has been prepared in conformity with the highest current standards.

Department of Labor Rules Are out of Date[2]

The dual issues of liquidity and marketability were addressed in the 1988 proposed adequate consideration regulation of the U.S. Department of Labor (DOL).[3] The proposed regulation, which is now about 10 years old, indicates that in the conduct of an independent appraisal, one may apply a lower-than-average marketability discount in cases where there is a put option and sufficient liquidity to make repurchases. The regulations use the words "diminish" and "reducing" and avoids the word "eliminate," at least indicating official prohibition at the time of their issuance against using a zero discount to reflect the limited marketability of the shares being valued.

It appears that the Department of Labor misunderstood the definition of "fair market value" as it relates to the necessity to construct a valuation with the hypothetical investor in mind. It is highly probable that when (or if) the DOL finalizes its regulations the words "diminish" and "reducing" may come out and there will be emphasis on the hypothetical investor issue. But whether or not the DOL finalizes the regulations, the IRS is likely to continue to concentrate on the inclusion and appropriate size of a discount for marketability. Accordingly, it is unwise for the appraiser to rely on the proposed regulations (as they were originally issued and currently exist) as a rational to exclude or minimize a discount for the limited marketability of closely held shares for purposes of an ESOP's acquisition of a minority interest.

Quantifying the Discount for Limited Marketability

Liquid publicly traded (i.e., marketable) securities are the standard upon which the selection of a discount for limited marketability can be based. Before applying the discount for limited marketability, the independent appraiser needs to be familiar with the several studies examining the discounts associated with corporate securities that lack marketability. These studies provide empirical evidence regarding investors' required discounts for the lack of a liquid market.

Generally, as indicated above, discounts applied in the context of a hypothetical investor purchasing closely held shares have ranged from 25% to 40%. There is a great deal of subjectivity in the selection of the actual percentage to be applied, and the final number could be above or below this range.

The widely used text *Valuing a Business, The Analysis and Appraisal of Closely Held Companies*[4] devotes a chapter to the subject of discounts for limited marketability. It discusses many studies that attempt to define in different ways the range of possible marketability discounts. Generally, they found mean discounts ranging from approximately 23% to approximately 45%.

As recently as June 1998, in a (non-ESOP) tax court case (*Estate of Davis v. Commissioner*) the taxpayer's expert appraisal witnesses (including one of the authors of the above-referenced text) testified for a discount for limited marketability ranging from 23% to 35%.

Considering all of this, whether it is referred to as a "discount for limited marketability," "liquidity adjustment," or "allowance for illiquidity," it is difficult to see how a discount of 5% or 10% is anything more than window dressing, especially when most appraisers would agree that these percentages are within a reasonable margin of error in an opinion of fair market value.

Fair Market Value Presupposes a Hypothetical Buyer

Clearly, the *Davis* estate tax valuation should comport with the long-held definition of fair market value as "the amount at which property would change hands between a willing seller and a willing buyer when neither is acting under compulsion and when both have reasonable knowledge of relevant facts."[5] As alluded to earlier, this definition presupposes the willingness and ability to buy and thereby presupposes a hypothetical buyer.

A hypothetical buyer in an ESOP situation should not pay more for the same security at the same point of time than would a hypothetical buyer conjured up for an estate tax valuation. If the discount for limited marketability is smaller in the ESOP scenario than in the estate tax scenario, then the ESOP presumably would be paying more for the same stock than would the conjectural estate tax buyer.

Discounts far outside of the lower end of the range of those considered normal will result in the ESOP paying more than it should and may cause a prohibited transaction under ERISA.

Conclusion

The only time the appraiser knows with certainty whether the opinion rendered is correct is when the company is sold or if a court renders a decision on value. Absent a sale of the firm or a court decision, it is the obligation of the independent appraiser to determine a fair and reasonable price upon which ESOP purchases can occur. As part of this process, the independent appraiser needs to determine and include a marketability discount that takes into account the full definition of fair market value including the assumption of a hypothetical investor before the opinion should be relied upon by the fiduciaries of the ESOP.

Notes

1. Shannon P. Pratt, Robert F. Riley, and Robert P. Schweihs, *Valuing a Business: The Analysis and Appraisal of Closely Held Companies,* 3rd ed. (McGraw-Hill, 1996), 358.
2. In May 1988, the Department of Labor (DOL) issued a proposed draft of a *Regulation Relating to the Definition of Adequate Consideration* (29 CFR Part 2510). However, the DOL has acknowledged that it is not actively working to finalize the regulations.
3. Proposed Regulation Relating to the Definition of Adequate Consideration, 29 CFR Part 2510.
4. Pratt et al., 332–335.
5. American Society of Appraisers, Business Valuation Standards, Definition.

12

Shifting Control in an ESOP Context

David R. Johanson
Gregory E. Kniesel

For many years, legal and financial advisors have counseled companies, selling shareholders, and fiduciaries regarding the appropriate use and structure of multi-stage transactions in which an employee stock ownership trust (ESOT) purchases a controlling interest of company stock over a period of time. Such transactions have resulted in a substantial number of employees becoming employee-owners through participation in employee stock ownership plans. This article examines situations in which the ESOT's control, or lack thereof, may shift over time, how it might shift, and some of the legal and valuation implications inherent in such shifts. It focuses on the issues involved in multi-stage ESOT transactions and provides an appropriate practical and contractual framework for accomplishing such transactions. It also provides empirical support from a number of perspectives for an ESOT paying a controlling interest premium in the initial stage of a multi-stage transaction in which the ESOT owns less than 50% of a company's issued and outstanding company stock but ultimately owns a controlling interest within a reasonable period of time after the initial transaction.

Owners of closely held corporations are often disappointed to learn that the fair market value of the company stock that they intend to sell to an employee stock ownership trust (ESOT) set up under an employee stock ownership plan (ESOP) is independently appraised at significantly less than they anticipated. This is often the case because an ESOT's independent appraiser (and its board of trustees) must discount the value of the company stock that the ESOT acquires if the ESOT does not own a controlling interest (more than 50% in some jurisdictions, more than 66⅔% in other jurisdictions, and possibly including other elements of control) in the corporation after the ESOT's stock purchase. The discounts applied may include a discount for minority interest and an additional discount for lack of marketability. Such discounts are likely to reduce the controlling interest or enterprise value by 25% to 45% in the aggregate.

David R. Johanson is an attorney and counselor at law with Johanson Berenson LLP, which has offices in Napa and San Francisco, California; Washington, D.C.; Arlington and Great Falls, Virginia; and Cary, North Carolina. At the time this article was written, Gregory E. Kniesel, ASA, was managing director of FMV Opinions, Inc., and also ran the firm's Atlanta office and directed the firm's national ESOP practice. Mr. Kniesel currently is managing director of Libra Valuation Advisors and directs the firm's national valuation practice.

If a business owner sells company stock to an ESOT, and the ESOT's independent appraiser does not take such discounts into consideration for purposes of the ESOT board of trustees good faith determination of fair market value, there is a substantial risk that the Internal Revenue Service (IRS) or the U.S. Department of Labor (DOL) may determine on audit that the ESOT purchased the company stock for more than fair market value.[1] If the seller to the ESOT is the corporation that created the ESOP and the ESOT, an employee or member of the board of directors of such corporation, a 10%-or-more owner of such corporation, or other "parties-in-interest" or "disqualified persons," the result will be a "prohibited transaction"[2] under the Code and ERISA. A "prohibited transaction" can give rise to a substantial (15% to 100%) nondeductible excise tax by the seller (and other parties involved) and both a refund by the seller to the ESOT of the amount of the purchase over fair market value and disgorgement of profits by the seller.[3] A "prohibited transaction" also can result in (1) a possible undoing of the ESOT transaction, (2) the imposition by the DOL of a 20% penalty on the ESOT's board of trustees, (3) the loss or diminution of related tax benefits to the corporation that established the ESOP and the ESOT, and (4) personal liability on the part of the ESOT board of trustees with respect to the amount of the purchase price in excess of fair market value.

ESOT ownership percentage changes (and changes in elements of control) over time also are significant in that annual update valuations of the sponsoring corporation stock held by the ESOT after such a change in ESOT ownership may be affected. This article examines situations in which the ESOT's control, or lack thereof, may shift over time, how it might shift, and the legal and valuation implications inherent in such shifts.

Situations in Which Control May "Shift"

Transactions and Events That May Bring the ESOT's Ownership from Minority to Control

After the initial transaction in which the ESOT acquires stock of the sponsoring corporation, changes in stock ownership might occur that actually change the elements of control held by the ESOT by way of its stock ownership. If the ESOT starts with a non-controlling interest, which typically means less than 50% of voting control, it may end up with a controlling interest, which typically, but not always, means more than 50% of voting control. One means by which the ESOT's level of control might shift from non-controlling to controlling is by way of a purchase of stock by the ESOT from either the sponsoring corporation or one or more of its shareholders. Another means by which the ESOT's level of control might shift from non-controlling to controlling is by way of a redemption of stock held outside the ESOT by the sponsoring corporation.

Transactions and Events That May Bring the ESOT's Ownership from Control to Minority

After the initial transaction in which the ESOT acquires stock of the sponsoring corporation, changes in stock ownership might occur that actually change the elements of control held by the ESOT by way of its stock ownership from control to non-control. If the ESOT starts with a controlling interest, which typically, but not always, means more than 50% of voting control, it may end up with a non-controlling interest, which typically means less than 50% of voting control. One way in which the ESOT's level of control might shift from controlling to non-controlling is by way of repurchases of departing ESOP participants' stock over time by the sponsoring corporation. Another way in which an ESOT's level of control might shift from controlling to non-controlling is by way of a one-time sale of stock by the ESOT to another party. The ESOT's level of control also might shift from controlling to non-controlling through issuance of stock by the sponsoring corporation for purposes of a merger or acquisition or for purposes of raising equity capital. In any of these cases, all pre-issuance shareholders, including the ESOT, will be diluted.

Transactions and Events That Bring the ESOT's Ownership from 50% to Control

If the ESOT starts with 50% of the voting stock of the sponsoring company, such an interest is neither a fully controlling or a non-controlling interest—it possesses elements of each. Although a 50% interest possesses, in essence, veto power, it does not possess total control. Furthermore, a 50% interest is below the 80% or 90% level required to "squeeze out" minority shareholders in several states. The ESOT's level of control might shift from 50% to controlling by purchasing stock from either the sponsoring corporation or one of its shareholders. The ESOT's level of control also might shift from 50% to controlling by way of a corporate redemption by the sponsoring corporation of stock held outside the ESOT. Conversely, of course, the ESOT's interest also could shift from a controlling interest to an interest represented by 50% of the voting stock of the sponsoring company.

Transactions and Events That Bring the ESOT's Ownership from 50% to Minority

If the ESOT starts with 50% voting control, such an interest is neither a fully controlling or a non-controlling interest—it possesses elements of each. The ESOT's level of control might shift from 50% to non-controlling in the same ways described above. Of course, the ESOT's interest also could shift from a minority interest to an interest represented by 50% of the voting stock of the sponsoring company.

Summary of Appropriate and Required Considerations Regarding Various Shifts in Control

In the four scenarios discussed above, the ESOT's ownership percentage and incidents of control are assumed to change over time, the result of various possible occurrences. In the examples above, the ESOT either gains ownership percentage and elements of control or loses them, depending on the circumstances. What is consistent in each of the above scenarios is that the ESOT is assumed to consistently possess a certain ownership interest, with its inherent incidents of control, until events occur which increase or decrease that ownership interest and, therefore, the inherent incidents of control. The multi-stage transaction discussed below differs in that a shift in the ESOT's ownership percentage and, therefore, the ESOT's inherent elements of control, is anticipated at the time of the initial ESOT stock purchase transaction. In fact, this anticipated shift in control is incorporated into the initial transaction structure and documentation.

This article primarily addresses the multi-stage scenario described below. The four scenarios discussed above, however, whereby the ESOT's ownership percentage and incidents of control are assumed to change over time, the result of various possible occurrences that were not anticipated at the time of the initial ESOT stock purchase transaction, warrant further consideration. What are the ongoing ESOP valuation issues that arise under these or other scenarios? The primary questions that must be answered are whether or not such changes in the ESOT's ownership percentage and, therefore, the ESOT's inherent elements of control, dictate a change in the level of control premium and/or discount that might be appropriate to apply in the valuation of the ESOT's ownership interest, and, strictly from a fiduciary perspective, what impact such changes might have on various classes of ESOP participants (such as existing participants, terminated vested participants, those about to retire, and younger participants) and the fair market value of the company stock held by the ESOT.[4] If the ESOT's interest shifts from control to non-control, and future departing ESOP participant stock repurchases are subsequently transacted at a discounted fair market value, resulting from newly applied discounts for lack of control and lack of marketability, such departing ESOP participants will have effectively acquired company stock through the ESOT at a control level of value (presumably undiscounted) only to be later bought out at a discounted value. This not only appears to be inherently unfair but also may be grounds for potential future litigation initiated under ERISA by the departing ESOP participants.

What about the opposite scenario? If the ESOT's interest shifts from non-control to control and future departing ESOP participant stock repurchases are subsequently transacted at an undiscounted fair market value, resulting from the elimination of previously applied discounts for lack of control and/or lack of marketability, such departing ESOP participants will have effectively acquired company stock through the ESOT at a non-control level of value (presumably discounted) only to be later bought out at an undiscounted value. This may appear to be inherently unfair to the remaining shareholders of the sponsoring company, including the ESOT, because of the resulting dilution, as well as to previously terminated ESOP participants who were bought out at a discounted fair market value before the ESOT's shift from non-control to control. It also may be grounds for potential future litigation initiated by the remaining shareholders (including the ESOP's participants) and/or the previously terminated ESOP participants who were bought out at a discounted fair market value before the ESOT's shift from non-control to control.

It may be that the best solution to this valuation discount/premium dilemma is to apply discounts and/or premiums consistently throughout the life of the ESOP.[5] What about the case of a subsequent stock purchase by the ESOT, which was not anticipated at the time of the initial ESOT company stock purchase transaction and which changes the ESOT's level of control and elements of ownership?[6] For example, if the subsequent stock purchase by the ESOT increases the ESOT's ownership percentage from 40% to 60%, the ESOT acquires incremental elements of control. Can the ESOT pay some level of control premium in this case, particularly if the selling shareholder(s) will not sell at a lower value? From a financial perspective, some level of control premium can be justified. From an ESOP fiduciary perspective, the DOL's regulations on adequate consideration (discussed at length below) provide a regulatory basis for the ESOT to do so, provided that the ESOT's fiduciaries exercise an appropriate level of prudence and due diligence in making the investment decision. The implications for future ESOP update valuations are the same as those described in the preceding paragraph.

Conversely, what about the case of a subsequent stock sale by the ESOT, which was not anticipated at the time of the initial ESOT company stock purchase transaction and which reduces the ESOT's level of control and elements of ownership? For example, if the subsequent stock sale by the ESOT decreases the ESOT's ownership percentage from 60% to 40%, the ESOT relinquishes substantial elements of control. Can the ESOT sell at a value that does not include some level of control premium in this case, particularly if the buyer will not pay a value that includes some level of control premium? From a financial perspective, it may be difficult to justify a sale under these conditions, particularly if the original ESOT stock purchase transaction included some level of control premium. The same holds true from an ESOP fiduciary perspective.[7]

"Multi-Stage Transaction" Whereby the ESOT Originally Acquires 30%, with a Binding Unilateral Right to Acquire Controlling Interest Within Reasonable Period of Time

Background It is possible to structure a transaction whereby the ESOT does not initially acquire a controlling interest in the sponsoring company but still pays a purchase price whereby the discounts for lack of control and lack of marketability have been reduced, provided that the ESOT enters into a properly structured multi-stage transaction in which at the time of the initial ESOT transaction, the ESOT executes a binding written contract that ensures that the ESOT will own a controlling interest, at its discretion, in the corporation within a reasonable period of time after the initial transaction.[8] Transactions in the public marketplace often occur whereby the acquiring entity obtains control by way of a series of purchases of the stock of the target entity. The motivations and strategies behind these "multi-stage transactions" involving publicly traded entities are varied, as are the motivations and strategies behind "multi-stage transactions" involving closely held entities. One of the primary reasons that ESOTs acquire the stock of closely held entities on a "multi-stage" basis is that a purchase of enough company stock to obtain control of the sponsoring corporation in a single transaction is often not financable on favorable terms. By executing a binding written contract at the time of the initial ESOT transaction that ensures that the ESOT will own a controlling interest in the company stock of the sponsoring corporation within a reasonable period of time after the initial transaction, the ESOT is able to eventually obtain control at its discretion.

Negative Considerations The negative implications to the ESOT regarding this transaction structure might include the fact that future acquisitions of the company stock of the sponsoring corporation will be at the fair market value of such stock at the time of such future acquisition(s) and the fact that there will be uncertainty regarding financing availability for such future stock acquisitions (although the ESOT and its advisors should carefully negotiate this second point at the time of the initial transaction). This uncertainty regarding financing availability can be mitigated by incorporating seller financing, for example, into the transaction documentation as a last resort to the ESOT. Many of these "multi-stage transactions" involving ESOTs are structured such that the ESOT initially acquires 30% of the stock of the closely held sponsoring corporation and, simultaneously, obtains the unilateral right to acquire a controlling interest (at least another 21%) in the company stock of the sponsoring corporation within a reasonable period of time after the initial transaction. The interpretation of a "reasonable period of time after the initial transaction" can vary, but often is five to seven years. Important transaction terms to consider in determining what is "reasonable" include anticipated debt on the sponsoring corporation and anticipated cash flow in the years following the initial ESOT stock purchase.

Adequate Consideration Regulations The DOL's 1988 Proposed Adequate Consideration Regulations, albeit brief with respect to this subject matter, provide the only real guidance on "enterprise value" or "controlling interest value" in a multi-stage ESOT transaction. Paragraph B.5. of the preamble to the DOL regulations provides, in relevant part, as follows:

> Similarly, if the plan purchases employer securities in small increments pursuant to an understanding with the employer that the employer will eventually sell a controlling portion of shares to the plan, a control premium would be warranted only to the extent that understanding with the employer was actually a binding agreement obligating the employer to pass control within a reasonable time.

The DOL's Proposed Regulations also specifically address this subject matter, again briefly, by including as a factor in determining the fair market value of company stock held by a qualified trust like an ESOT, the following:

> Whether or not the seller would be able to obtain a control premium from an unrelated third party with regard to the block of securities being valued, provided that in cases where a control premium is taken into account:
>
> (1) Actual control (both in form and in substance) is passed to the purchaser with the sale, or will be passed to the purchaser within a reasonable time pursuant to a binding agreement in effect at the time of the sale, and
>
> (2) It is reasonable to assume that the purchaser's control will not be dissipated within a short period of time subsequent to acquisition.[9]

Based upon these provisions in the DOL's Proposed Adequate Consideration Regulations, it is reasonable to conclude that even if an owner sells less than a "controlling interest" in a corporation to an ESOT in an initial transaction, he or she may still be able to sell in the initial transaction at a "controlling interest" or "enterprise" value provided he or she commits to allow the ESOT to purchase a sufficient amount of additional company stock to bring the ESOT's ownership to a "controlling interest" within a reasonable period of time of the initial transaction. State law, the corporation's articles of incorporation or bylaws, or shareholder agreements (among other matters) may dictate that an ESOT purchase substantially more than 50% of a company's issued and outstanding company stock in order to obtain a "controlling interest" after an initial ESOT transaction.

Appropriate Transaction Structure A number of factors should be addressed in the initial transaction in order to ensure that an owner may sell company stock to an ESOT in such transaction at a "controlling interest" or "enterprise" value without the ESOT obtaining "control" in such transaction. In addition to such factors, the overall transaction involving the ESOT must occur on an "arm's length" basis. In other words, the ESOT's board of trustees should evaluate the initial transaction and the subsequent transactions on the basis of whether a non-ESOT purchaser would enter into the same agreement to purchase company stock on the same terms, including, but not limited to, the same purchase price. Furthermore, the ESOT's board of trustees should be able to demonstrate that the owner would not have sold at any other price. This can be supported by the negotiation and execution of a cross purchase and redemption agreement by and among the corporation, the owner, other shareholders, and, possibly, the ESOT (as a beneficiary only) providing for redemption of the owner's company stock at a "controlling interest" or "enterprise value" basis. Finally, the ESOT must be treated consistently with the owner(s). For example, if the ESOT purchases company stock from an owner at a particular purchase price and on a particular basis of valuation, then (all things being equal) ESOP participants and beneficiaries should have their vested ESOP account balances of company stock repurchased on the same basis upon appropriate triggering events (i.e., retirement, death, disability, or termination of employment after vesting).

Although this is not intended to be an exhaustive list, the factors to be considered in an initial transaction in order to ensure that an owner may sell company stock to an ESOT in such transaction at a "controlling interest" or "enterprise" value without the ESOT obtaining "control" in such transaction are as follows:

- In addition to the company stock that the owner sells to the ESOT in the initial transaction, the ESOT should receive a gratuitous contractual right to purchase a "controlling interest" in the company. The right should be gratuitous in that the ESOT should not pay for it in the initial transaction. This will help to avoid a claim by the IRS or the DOL that the right was not an "employer security" and, therefore, that the ESOT entered into a "prohibited transaction" under Section 4975(d) of the Code and Section 406(d) of ERISA for which there is no available exemption. The ESOT should be able to exercise the right in whole or in part to ensure that it is reasonably possible for the ESOT to exercise such right.
- The written contract should permit the ESOT to exercise the right within a reasonable period of time after the initial transaction. The DOL Proposed Regulations specifically reference this concept. "Reasonable"

needs to be interpreted under the specific facts and circumstances. If a substantial period of time passes in which the ESOT fails to exercise the right, the ESOT board of trustees may be subject to a cause of action by disgruntled participants or by the DOL or the IRS. The written contract should include a contractual remedy of specific performance so that the ESOT can enforce the right, if necessary.

- The corporation that establishes the ESOP and the owner who is selling to the ESOT in the initial transaction should commit to guarantee or otherwise facilitate the ESOT's financing of its exercise of the right to purchase "control." This may be done by having the owner commit to use his or her best efforts to cause the corporation to obtain the financing necessary for the ESOT to exercise the right or provide seller financing on a promissory note basis (on reasonable repayment terms). Without a reasonable means of financing the ESOT's exercise of the right, the DOL, the IRS, and/or a court may determine that the right lacks substance. This may provide ground for unwinding the initial transaction and subjecting the corporation, the owner, and other responsible parties to adverse financial consequences.
- Some independent appraisers and legal advisors have required the ESOT to obtain a voting proxy at the time of the initial transaction, thereby permitting the ESOT to exercise "control in fact" at such time. Although this has been done in response to the language in the DOL's Proposed Adequate Consideration Regulations about "voting control," this focus is misplaced. There may be limited circumstances in which a voting proxy is necessary at the time of the initial transaction but the use of such proxy normally does not make sense. Such proxy would give the ESOT voting control at the time of the initial transaction. It would make no sense for the ESOT to have a right to purchase "control" because it already would have "control." The language in the DOL's Proposed Adequate Consideration Regulations make it clear that the ESOT does not have to acquire "control in fact" in the initial transaction in order to justify paying "control or enterprise value" in such transaction, provided that the ESOT acquires the right to purchase control described in this article and that the ESOT's board of trustees satisfies its fiduciary responsibilities with respect to such transaction (as described here).
- The ESOT also should obtain "tag-along" rights in the event the controlling owner sells the corporation to a third-party before the time that the ESOT exercises its right to purchase "control." The owner should not be allowed to sell to the third party unless such purchaser agrees to purchase all of the ESOT's company stock at the same purchase price and on the same terms as the owner. The owner and the ESOT should negotiate at "arm's length" with respect to the disposi-

tion of the ESOT's right, the owner's ability to market the corporation, and the ESOT's other alternatives in the event of intervening events of this nature.

- The ESOT should receive "anti-dilution" protection of some kind in the initial transaction documentation. This will protect the ESOT from exercising its right to purchase "control" and then having the corporation either issue additional shares of company stock or redeem company stock from terminated ESOP participants that results in the ESOT's ownership declining to less than a "controlling interest."

Empirical Support Substantial empirical data supports the application of a control premium in an initial transaction of the nature described above. In order to better understand such empirical data, it is helpful to understand that there are actually varying degrees of control that an investor might possess through stock ownership. For example, an investor owning 100% of the stock of an entity possesses complete control of that entity and its cash flows. On the other hand, an investor owning 51% of the stock of an entity does not possess complete control of that entity, even if only a majority vote is required to pass any action requiring a vote. This is because that investor has, at the very least, certain fiduciary responsibilities under applicable corporate law to the remaining 49% shareholder(s). This fiduciary responsibility limits what the investor owning 51% of the stock of the entity can do regarding the assets and cash flow of that entity. In many, if not all, states throughout the United States, a majority shareholder(s) has a fiduciary responsibility not to oppress the minority shareholder(s) and has a duty of loyalty to such shareholder(s). Furthermore, a 50% interest possesses, in essence, veto power, but it does not possess total control. For example, a 50% interest is below the 80% or 90% level required to "squeeze-out" minority shareholders in several states. Finally, of course, an investor owning less than 50% of the stock of an entity certainly does not possess complete control of that entity and may not possess any elements of control.

To definitively answer whether an ESOT may pay a control premium in a properly structured and negotiated initial ESOT stock purchase transaction that is part of a multi-stage transaction in which the ESOT will execute a binding written contract at the time of the initial ESOT transaction to ensure that the ESOT will own, at its discretion, a controlling interest in the corporation within a reasonable period of time after the initial transaction, FMV Opinions, Inc. performed an analytical study (the "FMV Control Premium Study") involving approximately 150 transactions initiated and completed from 1993 through July 1999 in which an entity acquired a non-controlling interest in a publicly traded company (the "target" or "targets") and later acquired a controlling interest in the target.[10] The final database, comprised of those transactions for which sufficient information was available, includes 13 such multi-stage transactions. The initial interests in the targets that the acquirers purchased ranged from 20% to 49.4%. In each case, the acquiring entity ended up, through subsequent acquisitions of stock in the target, with 100% of the stock of the target. In all cases except one, the multi-stage acquisition occurred in two stages. The other multi-stage acquisition occurred in three stages. Excluding one multi-stage transaction which was initiated in 1985, the length of time between the first target stock acquisition and the final transaction ranged from approximately five to approximately 52 months, with an average of approximately 21 months. The calculated control premiums for the initial target stock acquisitions for the 13 multi-stage transactions in the database ranged from zero to 47.2%, with an average of approximately 22% and a median of approximately 19%.[11]

The calculated control premiums for the final stage target stock acquisitions for the 13 multi-stage transactions in the database ranged from 7.4% to 49.9%, with an average of approximately 29% and a median of approximately 32%. The data does reflect that, for the initial target stock acquisitions in the 12 multi-stage transactions in the database for which the initial stage ownership percentage acquired is available, the initial stage control premium was higher, on average, when higher percentages of total target stock outstanding were acquired. All initial stage target stock acquisitions involved purchases totaling under 50% of the target's outstanding stock. The data also reflects that for the multi-stage transactions that were completed in their entirety in shorter periods of time (the data was split down the middle and excluded the multi-stage transaction, which was initiated in 1985), the initial stage control premiums were significantly smaller on average, but the final stage control premiums were significantly larger on average. The data also reflects that for final stage target stock acquisitions in the multi-stage transactions which occurred over longer periods of time, the control premiums were actually lower on average in the final stage than they were on average in the initial stage. What is particularly interesting is that the weighted average control premium (weighted by percentages acquired in each stage) for each multi-stage transaction did not differ significantly as a function of the time it took to complete each multi-stage transaction in its entirety. As a final note, the level of control premium for an initial stage target stock acquisition relative to the level of control premium for a final stage target stock acquisition appears to be effected by agreements that are in place between the target and the acquirer at the time of the initial stage target stock acquisition.

The data derived from the FMV control premium study indicates that an ESOT may pay some level of control premium in a properly structured and negotiated initial ESOT stock purchase transaction, which is part of a multi-stage transaction in which the ESOT executes a binding written contract at the time of the initial ESOT transaction that ensures that the ESOT will own a controlling interest in the corporation, at its discretion, within a reasonable period of time after the initial transaction. The level of control premium appropriate at the time of the initial ESOT stock purchase transaction might be the same, lower, or higher than the level of control premium appropriate at the time of a subsequent ESOT stock purchase transaction that would give the ESOT a controlling interest, but it appears that the weighted average control premium applied should not be substantially different than that which would be appropriate if the target were being acquired by the ESOT in a single stock purchase transaction. The relative control premium to be applied in each respective stage of a multi-stage ESOT transaction, therefore, appears to be a function of several things, including the percentage acquired by the ESOT in each respective stage, the agreements in place between the ESOT and the selling shareholder(s) at the time of the initial ESOT stock purchase transaction, and the time between each respective stage.[12]

General Background Regarding Control Premiums, Discounts for Lack of Control, and Discounts for Lack of Marketability

The relative control premium applied in each respective stage of a multi-stage ESOT transaction also is a function of generally accepted concepts of control premiums, discounts for lack of control, and discounts for lack of marketability. This section summarizes those general concepts for purposes of rounding out the knowledge basis required in order for ESOP fiduciaries and their advisors to properly evaluate the appropriate level of control premiums in such multi-stage ESOT transactions.

Control Premiums and Discounts for Lack of Control

A controlling interest in a corporation has the power to effect changes in overall corporate structure and corporate policies. A minority interest, on the other hand, does not have the power to effect changes in the overall corporate structure or corporate policies. When determining the value of a minority interest in a company, a discount for minority interest must be applied to the controlling interest value conclusion to reflect the diminution of value. Because publicly traded companies inherently trade at a minority interest level of value, the discount for minority interest is often determined by analyzing control premiums paid when companies are acquired in the public marketplace. Because the discount for minority interest is a function of and inversely related to the control premium, the selection of the appropriate control premium indirectly determines the minority interest discount. As an example, a 25% control premium equates to a 20% minority interest discount (1-[1÷(1+0.25)]). Control premiums typically range from 20% to 50% with an average of approximately 30% to 40%. Accordingly, discounts for lack control typically average approximately 23% to 29%.

Even after a minority interest discount is applied to adjust a controlling interest level of value to a minority interest level of value, an additional discount for lack of marketability must be applied because a minority interest investment in a closely held company still represents an illiquid investment. Investments that lack the liquidity of publicly traded securities are less attractive even if otherwise identical. Accordingly, it is logical to discount the value of illiquid interests to reflect this liquidity disparity.

Discounts for Lack of Marketability

Several studies have examined the discounts associated with corporate securities that lack marketability. These studies, which are further discussed below, provide empirical evidence regarding investors' required discounts for lack of a liquid market. Typically, the empirical studies focus on two types of transactions: restricted stock transactions and pre-IPO transactions. The pre-IPO transactions measure the difference between the price at which a company's stock goes public, with the earlier (in some studies as much as three years earlier) negotiated price for the same company's stock. Restricted stock studies are regarded as a more appropriate measure of discounts for lack of marketability because they measure directly the difference between the contemporaneous prices of two otherwise identical securities: one fully marketable and one less than fully marketable.

Restricted securities are generally subject to severe marketability restrictions under Rule 144 of the Securities Act of 1933. In order to establish an objectively determinable "safe harbor" for purchasers of restricted securities, the Securities and Exchange Commission (SEC) adopted Rule 144 in 1972. To prevent a seller from purchasing unregistered securities with a view to resale, Rule 144 requires a holding period of some length of time. Under the rule, all unregistered securities must be held for at least one year, measured from the time the securities are purchased from the issuer or an affiliate, before any resale. In addition, after the initial one-year holding period, such securities may be sold only according to certain "dribble out," or volume limit, provisions. According to these provisions, to qualify for the exemption, the total amount of securities sold in any three-month period could not exceed the greater of 1% of the total number of the company's outstanding shares or the average weekly reported trading volume during the four weeks preceding the sale. Rule 144 also specifies that any person or entity which is not an affiliate of the issuer of the securities may sell all remaining securities, without volume limits, after a holding period of at least two years, measured from the time the securities are purchased from the issuer or an affiliate of the issuer.

In 1990, the SEC amended the "tacking" concept of Rule 144. Before the amendment, if a purchaser of restricted stock were to sell his or her holdings in a privately negotiated transaction (not in the public markets), the required holding period would restart. The amendment allowed the purchaser of restricted stock to "tack" the holding period of the previous owner (or owners) of these securities to his or her own holding period, as long as the previous owner was not an affiliate of the issuer. The 1990 amendment had the effect of increasing the liquidity of restricted stock. Furthermore, the outgrowth of new financial derivatives, such as equity swaps, and trading techniques, such as "selling short against the box" (disallowed after 1997), has similarly affected the market for restricted stock. In 1997, the SEC amended Rule 144 once again, this time to shorten the initial holding period from two years to one year and the ultimate holding period for non-affiliates from three years to two years. Most of the studies discussed here were performed on transactions taking place before the 1990 amendment; none of the studies includes transactions from after the 1997 amendment.

The IRS has issued Revenue Ruling 77-287, which sets forth valuation guidelines in the determination of discounts for lack of marketability for securities restricted under Rule 144. Revenue Ruling 77-287 outlines two major factors that a purchaser of restricted securities must consider: (1) "The risk that the underlying value of the stock will change in a way that, absent the restrictive provisions, would have prompted a decision to sell" and (2) "The risk that the contemplated means of legally disposing of the stock may not materialize."

Furthermore, because of the resale restrictions of Rule 144, Revenue Ruling 77-287 recognizes that the value of a restricted security is less than the value of its freely traded counterpart and gives the following guidelines in determining a discount for lack of marketability for restricted securities:

- No automatic formulas should be used to determine the discount for lack of marketability.
- The discount is a function of the earnings, net assets and sales of the underlying entity.
- The discount is a function of the trading market for the equivalent freely traded stock.
- The discount is a function of the resale constraints applicable to the restricted security.

The Institutional Investor Study (SEC Study)

The basis for Revenue Ruling 77-287 is the Institutional Investor Study Report[13] (the "SEC study"). The SEC study empirically examined discounts in transactions involving securities that were restricted under provisions

similar to Rule 144. Based on more than 300 transactions, the SEC study found the following relationships ("MM" = million(s)):

1.	*Companies Ranked by Sales*	*Discount Range*
	$20 MM–$100 MM	10%–20%
	$5 MM–$20 MM	10%–20%
	$1 MM–$5 MM	30%–40%
2.	*Companies Ranked by Earnings*	
	$1 MM–$10 MM	10%–20%
	$0 MM–$1 MM	20%–30%
3.	*Companies Ranked by Exchange*	
	NYSE	10%–20%
	ASE	20%–30%
	OTC—Reporting	20%–30%
	OTC—Non-reporting	30%–40%
4.	*Overall Mean Discount*	24%

The SEC study includes transactions in stock with certain resale provisions, often referred to as registration or "piggyback" rights. The SEC study notes that the presence of such resale provisions "assuages, but by no means eliminates the illiquid character of restricted securities." The SEC study does not separate the data for shares with resale provisions from those without such provisions. Unlike most published studies of restricted stock transactions, which report only the range of discounts and the average discount to use as a "benchmark," the SEC study provides a comparative framework for determining a lack of marketability discount. However, shares in a closely held company should typically be considered less marketable than the unregistered stock of a publicly traded company sold in a private placement, indicating a higher discount for the stock of the closely held company. This is because the stock of a closely held company has no market, whereas the publicly traded company has an already established trading market for its shares and its unregistered shares will eventually become fully tradable in that market, simply with the passage of time. Furthermore, shares in a closely held company are even less liquid than those included in the SEC study (as opposed to several other studies), due to the inclusion of shares with resale provisions in the SEC study. This also indicates a higher discount, all else being equal, for closely held shares than the average discounts in the SEC study.

Other Studies

Several other studies have also examined discounts for lack of marketability. The most recent Emory study analyzed 91 private stock transactions that had occurred within the five months before an initial public offering of the company's stock. The average discount determined in the study was 43%, consistent with the overall study of 310 transactions since 1980. The Willamette pre-initial public offering (IPO) studies, based on transactions as much as three years before the IPO, typically indicate approximately 50% to 60% discounts (adjusted for the passage of time). The Gelman study examined 89 restricted securities transactions and found that the average discount from the publicly traded price was approximately 33%. The Maher study also examined restricted securities transactions and found that the average discount was approximately 35%. The HLHZ study, the Management Planning, Inc., study, the Moroney study, the Standard Research Consultants study, the Trout study, and the Willamette Management Associates study are each based on private placement transactions and have found average discounts from the publicly traded price ranging from 30% to 45%. The Solberg study was based on fifteen court cases and found that the average discount for lack of marketability was 37.4%.

The SEC study provides a comparative framework for the determination of discounts for closely held stock. The other studies discussed above, while providing less detail than the SEC study, act as a benchmark and shed further light on the issue and indicate higher discounts than the SEC study. However, in order to make more relevant specific comparisons with more recent data, FMV Opinions, Inc., has performed its own study of transactions in restricted stock.

The FMV Restricted Stock Study

In addition to the SEC study, FMV Opinions, Inc., has examined 163 actual transactions involving restricted securities of publicly traded companies from 1982 through early 1996 (the "FMV restricted stock study"). This study analyzed in detail the annual reports of all companies included in order to identify and remove any transactions involving shares with resale rights. The study generally supports the results of the SEC study. The discounts found in the FMV restricted stock study, however, are slightly lower than the discounts in the SEC study. This is most likely due to some of the changes that have taken place in the market for restricted stock (discussed above), which have tended to increase the marketability of restricted stock. This again indicates that discounts appropriate for minority interests in the common stock of closely held companies are likely higher than discounts typically found in recent empirical studies, such as the FMV restricted stock study. Also, as previously mentioned, studies of restricted stock transactions will typically indicate discounts lower than the discounts appropriate for stock in a closely held company because closely held companies have no established market for their stock.

The mean discount in the FMV restricted stock study is approximately

20%. The study analyzes the individual companies and their financial statements in great detail and provides insights that are not typically available in other studies. Some of the main conclusions of the FMV restricted stock study are that the magnitude of a discount for lack of marketability is:

- Negatively correlated with the absolute dollar level of the subject entity's revenue;
- Negatively correlated with the total assets of the subject entity;
- Negatively correlated with the aggregate market value of the subject entity as represented by its publicly traded price; and
- Positively correlated with the percentage size of the block of the ownership interest to be traded, described as a percentage of total ownership.

In general, both the SEC study and the FMV restricted stock study indicate that discounts for lack of marketability are greater for smaller entities. The FMV study provides additional insights that the SEC study does not. In particular, the FMV study found that large percentage blocks of restricted stock (equal to or greater than 30% post-transaction) had a mean discount of 30.2% and a median discount of 34.2%. This comparison is particularly relevant because restricted stock has varying degrees of liquidity depending on the percentage size of the block. Large percentage blocks of restricted stock are less liquid than smaller percentage blocks because large percentage blocks take longer to "dribble out" under the provisions of Rule 144 and are, therefore, more comparable to minority interests, such as the subject interest, in small, closely held entities which have limited liquidity.

The discounts typically found in empirical studies range from 20% to 45%, with the FMV restricted stock study, the most comprehensive of all the studies, indicating a median 34% discount for the most illiquid larger block sizes. Shares in closely held companies, all else being equal, are less marketable than the shares covered by the empirical studies. In addition, investors will incorporate certain factors in determining the elements of value associated with a non-marketable investment. Those factors include the expected holding period, the expected return in value and distributions, and the expected growth.

Eyler Decision

One decision over the last few years best underscores the importance of considering appropriate discounts (for lack of marketability and lack of control) for purposes of determining fair market value for purposes of an ESOT transaction. In *Eyler v. Commissioner* (July 2, 1996), the U.S. Court of Appeals for the Seventh Circuit affirmed the U.S. Tax Court's 1995 decision that Gary L. Eyler is liable for 5% (now 15%) and 100% excise taxes imposed under Section 4975 of the Code on the *full* amount of proceeds in connection with his sale of stock of Continental Training Services, Inc. (CTS) to the CTS ESOT because he failed to establish either that (1) the sale price to the CTS ESOT was no greater than the fair market value of such stock or that (2) any fiduciary named in the ESOP made a good-faith determination of the purchase price. The *Eyler* decision illustrates the types of discounts for lack of marketability (and by implication lack of control) that an ESOT board of trustees (and its independent appraiser) should consider in making a good faith determination of fair market value for purposes of an ESOT transaction.

The Seventh Circuit concluded that Mr. Eyler failed to establish that the purchase price paid by the CTS ESOT was no greater than the fair market value of the CTS stock for the following reasons:

- Eyler relied on a valuation conducted by underwriters in connection with an anticipated initial public offering (IPO). The valuation did not purport to determine the fair market value of the CTS stock at any specific point in time, nor did it purport to be a final determination of the stock price.
- The lack of public interest in the CTS stock after marketing efforts for the proposed IPO also weighed against Eyler's reliance on the underwriter's valuation.
- The change of conditions from when the prospectus for the IPO was filed to the sale of Eyler's CTS stock to the CTS ESOT indicated that the purchase price should be lower than the price suggested in the IPO valuation. For example, the underwriters assumed that the CTS stock would be publicly traded and readily marketable and that the IPO would bring in positive cash flow for CTS. Instead, CTS's cash flow worsened because CTS had to make ESOP contributions. In addition, the establishment of the CTS ESOT itself negatively affected the balance sheet of CTS. CTS guaranteed a loan to the CTS ESOT that was required to be classified as debt on CTS's balance sheet and a charge to shareholder's equity. This obligation subjected CTS to several restrictions that the underwriters did not consider. For example, CTS agreed not to distribute dividends until the entire loan to the bank was repaid. CTS was also limited in its ability to borrow money, grant liens, and make capital expenditures.

The Seventh Circuit asserted that applying a lack of marketability discount was not inappropriate in determining the value of the CTS stock to be sold to the CTS ESOT. The Seventh Circuit rejected Eyler's argument that the requirement that put options be granted to ESOP participants renders a marketability discount unnecessary because as of the date of the sale of Eyler's stock to the CTS ESOT, there was no history of making ESOP distributions in cash, and the put option had no fixed price and payments could be made over five years under the terms of the CTS ESOT.

The Seventh Circuit rejected the purchase of CTS stock by several directors for the same price as Eyler's sale price to the CTS ESOT as a basis of establishing fair market value. Although the Seventh Circuit indicated that Eyler was correct in stating that the best method for determining fair market value of non-tradable stocks was by reference to actual sales made in reasonable amounts, at arm's length, in the normal course of business, and within a reasonable time before or after the valuation date, Eyler failed to demonstrate that the sales to the directors were sufficiently arm's length. The transaction here involved a purchase of CTS stock from a minority shareholder by CTS's directors whereby Eyler provided unsecured bridge loans to six of the seven directors who were involved in the purchases.

The Seventh Circuit also concluded that the fiduciaries of the CTS ESOT did not make a good-faith determination of the fair market value of CTS for purposes of the purchase price due of the following reasons:

- The trustee and the plan administrator of the CTS ESOT did not play any role in pricing the CTS stock for the CTS ESOT.
- There was no evidence that the plan committee of the CTS ESOT conducted any investigation to determine the fair market value of the stock.
- CTS's board of directors may be considered fiduciaries of the CTS ESOT. A fiduciary of an ESOP is required to act with the care, skill, and diligence that a prudent person would undertake in a like capacity, with the same degree of familiarity with the facts, and with similar aims. In this case, the minutes of the board meetings revealed that the board members were not acting as ESOP fiduciaries. Further, the board of directors did not make any independent inquiry regarding the current fair market value of CTS stock for the CTS ESOT transaction. Rather, the board of directors merely relied on the underwriter's valuation for an IPO, which was four months old. Although the board of directors was aware that the lack of public interest and the cyclical nature of IPO markets would have further reduced the value of the sale price, it ignored these factors. The board of directors also failed to consider the financial impact of implementing an ESOP. Reliance on the financial consultant or law firm to CTS without conducting independent evaluation also is not an excuse. Informal opinions of various investment banking firms that indicated that the value of CTS ranged from $50 million to $120 million should also have put the fiduciaries on notice that an independent valuation should be conducted. The time con-

straints on the board of directors also call into question whether the board of directors had sufficient time to independently evaluate the fair market value of CTS stock.

In 1997, the IRS began citing the *Eyler* case as authority in challenging valuations used in connection with purchases of closely held company stock by ESOTs. The IRS has asserted that an ESOP's acquisition debt must be taken into account in determining fair market value and that the "put option" applicable to shares of stock distributed by an ESOP does not eliminate the need to apply a discount for lack of marketability.

Impact of "Put Option" Requirements

Although the existence of a "put option" applicable to shares of stock distributed by an ESOP does not necessarily eliminate the need to apply a discount for lack of marketability to the value of shares purchased by an ESOT, it does mitigate the magnitude of the discount for lack of marketability. This article demonstrates that substantial discounts for lack of marketability are appropriate for minority interests in the stock of closely held companies. To what extent is the discount for lack of marketability reduced in light of the "put option" typically included in an ESOP plan document? The magnitude of the reduction is a function of a number of things, including liquidity inherent in the sponsoring company and within the ESOT itself. The magnitude of anticipated future cash flows and the sponsoring company's unused borrowing capacity also should be considered. It must be remembered that one of the primary purposes of annual update valuations is for the determination of the price at which departing ESOP participants' stock might be repurchased by either the sponsoring company or the ESOT. This, then, presupposes a possible liquidity event for the departing ESOP participant. The ability to force a repurchase upon termination as a participant from the ESOP creates an element of liquidity for the departing participant that would not exist if not for the ESOP.

Some may argue that the "put option" does not justify a reduction in the discount for lack of marketability for minority interest purchases of stock by the ESOT at the time of the initial ESOT stock purchase transaction because the ESOT itself obtains no "put option" for the block of company stock that it owns and because cash payouts to departing ESOP participants can be spread over time. It is true that the ESOT itself obtains no "put option" for the block of stock that it owns, but the fact remains that the ultimate goal of the ESOP is to get stock into the hands of employees upon their termination as participants in the ESOP, at which time the "put option" can be exercised. To disallow a reduction in the discount for lack of marketability based on this argument would be to ignore the obvious liquidity advantage afforded by the put option. This argument, however, provides a strong basis for limiting the extent to which the discount for lack of marketability should be reduced as a result of the put option.

With respect to the argument that cash payouts to departing ESOP participants can be spread over time and that the discount for lack of marketability should, therefore, not be reduced as much as a result of the put option, this argument also provides support for limiting the reduction in the lack of marketability discount. There are a number of ways in which ESOP companies can delay the distribution process for former ESOP participants and thereby extend their repurchase obligations. First, the Code provides that "financed shares" need not be considered a part of an ESOP participant's account while acquisition debt for such financed shares is outstanding.[14] Sections 411(d)(6)(C) and 409(o) of the Code permit ESOP companies and their fiduciaries to defer distributions to former ESOP participants in a nondiscriminatory manner so that they occur over a period of six to eleven years after such participants' termination of employment. Third, Section 409(h) of the Code permits an ESOT to distribute company stock to former ESOP participants and the ESOP company or the ESOT to repurchase such company stock with a promissory note, the payment of which is adequately secured, payable with a reasonable rate of interest over a five-year period of time. These circumstances in which the ESOT's and the ESOP company's repurchase obligations can be extended over time should be considered in the determination of the appropriate discount for lack of marketability.

In the final analysis, the very nature and unique qualities of an ESOP leave no definitive answer to certain questions related to the ESOP structure. One such question is whether or not the "put option" indeed mitigates the discount for lack of marketability appropriate for minority interests held by the ESOT. The best answer is probably that the existence of the "put option" does increase the liquidity of shares of company stock held by the ESOT, but does not make such shares completely liquid. Accordingly, the discount for lack of marketability appropriate for a minority interest held by an ESOT should be reduced from what it would be if not for the ESOP but the level of reduction depends upon the particular facts and circumstances.

Conclusion

For many years, ESOP companies and their legal and financial advisors have structured transactions whereby the ESOT does not initially acquire a controlling interest in the sponsoring company, but still pays a purchase price whereby the discounts for lack of control and lack of marketability have been reduced. The ESOT usually enters into a properly structured multi-stage transaction in which the ESOT executes a binding written contract at the time of the initial ESOT transaction ensuring that the ESOT will own a controlling interest, at its discretion, in the corporation within a reasonable period of time after the initial transaction. This article has met one of its objectives of providing empirical support for the financial viability and fairness of such transactions to ESOPs and their participants from a number of perspectives—valuation, ERISA fiduciary responsibility and legal/regulatory. It also has met another significant objective, that of providing one view of appropriate standards for structuring such transactions. It also should serve as a resource and an analytical framework for those ESOP companies and their advisors who are faced with circumstances in which control shifts over time.

2003 Update

As of June 2003, it now appears that after remaining largely silent for over 14 years, the DOL has broken its silence regarding multi-stage ESOP transactions. Recently, the DOL has conducted investigations of a small number of multi-stage ESOP transactions. Throughout these investigations, the DOL's representatives have made a number of troubling observations regarding the feasibility of multi-stage ESOP transactions under any circumstances.

Whether these sentiments are shared by the entire DOL and will be followed in subsequent investigations is unknown, although the DOL's national office has privately indicated that some of its offices may be taking positions that are not entirely consistent and may be unreasonable in certain respects. What is known is that until recently, the DOL has never directly commented regarding the specific elements that may be necessary for structuring a successful multi-stage ESOP transaction. Absent specific DOL guidance other than the DOL's Proposed Adequate Consideration Regulations, ESOP professionals and consultants had believed they could defend their transactions based on supporting evidence in the public marketplace, common sense, and a good-faith interpretation of the Proposed Regulations.

As a result of the statements recently made by the DOL's investigators in three cases, ESOP professionals and consultants may now have to ponder whether such transactions will be subject to targeted prosecution by the DOL based on the DOL's theories concerning multi-stage ESOP transactions, theories that in the eyes of many ESOP professionals and consultants bear no relation to financial reality, the public market, and/or a good-faith interpretation of the DOL's Proposed Adequate Consideration Regulations. Future articles will address this issue in depth as the situation evolves.

Notes

1. See, e.g., *Eyler v. Commissioner* (7th Cir., July 2, 1996).
2. Section 4975(d) of the Code and Section 406(d) of ERISA.
3. Section 4975(a) and (b) of the Code; Section 409(a) of ERISA.
4. U.S. Department of Labor Interpretive Bulletin 94-2 describes certain fiduciary

responsibilities of ESOP fiduciaries that, in relevant part, require them to take actions that might maximize the fair market value of company stock held by the ESOT. It may make sense from a prudence perspective (and require careful consideration) under ERISA for an ESOT's fiduciaries to accept dilution to below 50%, and hold on to company stock rather than sell it, in anticipation of a future transaction that might maximize the fair market value of such stock for the ESOP's participants. This may affect various classes of ESOP participants in varying ways that the fiduciaries must consider.

5. *Charles S. Foltz, et al. V. U.S. News & World Report, Inc., et al.* and *David B. Richardson, et al., U.S. News & World Report, Inc. et al.*, U.S. District Court, District of Columbia, Civil Actions Nos. 84-0447 and 85-2195, June 22, 1987.
6. Ibid.
7. Paragraph B.5. of the preamble to the DOL Proposed Regulations under Section 3-18 of ERISA and DOL Proposed Regulation Section 2510.3-18(b)(4)(I).
8. DOL Proposed Regulations Section 2510.3-18(b)(4)(I).
9. The initial target stock acquisition for one of the multi-stage transactions in the database occurred in 1985, with the second and final target stock acquisition for that multi-stage transaction occurring in 1997.
10. In only one of the multi-stage transactions was the initial stage calculated control premium equal to zero. The next lowest initial stage calculated control premium was 9.4%. It is interesting to note that, if the multi-stage transaction in which the initial stage calculated control premium was zero is removed, the calculated control premiums for the initial target stock acquisitions for the other 12 multi-stage transactions in the database ranged from 9.4% to 47.2%, with an average of approximately 23% and a median of approximately 19%.
11. It should be noted that the data in the FMV Control Premium Study indicates that control premium differentials from initial stage to final stage target stock acquisitions were not, to any large extent, a function of the overall level of control premiums from one point in time to the next for each respective transaction in the database. The data in the FMV Control Premium Study also indicates that control premium differentials from initial stage to final stage target stock acquisitions were not, to any large extent, a function of the overall level of control premiums from one point in time to the next sorted by the SIC codes of the respective targets or sorted by companies of similar size (as measured by revenue) to each of the respective targets.
12. Institutional Investor Study Report of the Securities and Exchange Commission, H.R. Doc. No. 64, Part 5, 92nd Congress, 1st Session, 1971, pp. 2444-56.
13. Section 409(o)(1)(B) of the Code.

13

How to Appraise an Appraiser

Idelle A. Howitt

The selection of a business appraiser to determine the fair market value of employer securities is one of the pivotal decisions to be made when considering an ESOP. Not only will the conclusion of value figure prominently in the feasibility of the plan from an economic perspective, but it can effectively determine the value of the life's work of an entrepreneur.

When considering an employee stock ownership plan (ESOP) for a closely held company, either your own or that of a client, you may be approached by a number of ESOP consultants who hope to provide you with their services. They will offer advice on many different issues. For example, should the attorney or the benefits consultant draft the plan documents? Should a repurchase obligation study be performed? Which vesting schedule is more appropriate? However, whatever their respective specialties, one matter all of these consultants will agree on is the pivotal importance of the selection of the business valuation consultant, also known as the business appraiser. In an ESOP, the business appraiser determines the fair market value of the company's stock, thus effectively calculating the value of what may be the life's work of an entrepreneur.

Further, if the value is ever challenged, whether by an employee or by either of the two federal agencies that have enforcement responsibility for ESOPs, the Internal Revenue Service (IRS) and the U.S. Department of Labor (DOL), the appraiser may be called upon to defend the value. If you are the entrepreneur, how do you evaluate the ability of such a person? If you are an advisor, such as an attorney or an accountant, to the entrepreneur who seeks your counsel on this matter, what is the basis of your recommendation?

Why an Appraiser Is Needed

When a statutory framework for ESOPs was created in 1974 by the Employee Retirement Income Security Act (ERISA), there was no legal requirement for an independent appraiser to determine the fair market value of the stock to be acquired by the ESOP. For example, the company's financial officer could calculate the value of the employer securities the ESOP would purchase. However, because of real or perceived abuses, Congress subsequently enacted Section 401(a)(28)(C) of the U.S. Internal Revenue Code

---

Idelle A. Howitt is the founder and managing director of Howitt & Associates, a financial consulting firm based in New York City that specializes in financial valuations of closely held businesses for legal and tax purposes.

(the "Code"), which requires an independent appraiser to determine the fair market value of closely held employer securities acquired by an ESOP after December 31, 1986. This value becomes the basis for the negotiations, and in some cases becomes the actual price for the stock.

Fair Market Value

Under an exemption from ERISA's prohibited transaction rules, ESOPs are permitted to acquire employer securities from a "party-in-interest," such as the plan sponsor, if the purchase price is no more than "adequate consideration." If the ESOP acquires publicly traded stock, adequate consideration is the generally recognized market price. However, if the stock is closely held, by definition it does not have a generally recognized market price; here, adequate consideration is considered to be the fair market value of the stock as determined in good faith by the named fiduciaries according to the provisions of the plan. The fiduciary can determine the fair market value if he or she is independent and qualified to do so. If the fiduciary is not so independent or qualified, he or she should hire a qualified advisor, namely an independent business appraiser.

Fair market value for closely held securities is defined in the estate and gift tax context as the price at which the stock would change hands between a willing buyer and a willing seller, neither being under compulsion to act and both having reasonable knowledge of relevant facts. The guideline used by business appraisers to determine fair market value is Revenue Ruling 59-60, which was promulgated by the IRS in 1959. After the passage of ERISA in 1974, the business valuation community adopted Revenue Ruling 59-60 for ESOP valuations as well.

The DOL, which has simultaneous enforcement responsibility for ESOPs with the IRS, issued its own interpretation of fair market value in its proposed regulations for adequate consideration in 1988. While essentially incorporating the existing definition and Revenue Ruling 59-60, the language and requirements of the proposed DOL regulation are not identical with those of the IRS. Although the proposed DOL guidelines technically are not legally enforceable until adopted, many business appraisers nonetheless began to follow them. When interviewing an appraiser, you should determine if the appraiser is familiar with the requirements of both Revenue Ruling 59-60 and the proposed DOL regulations (discussed below).

The Appraisal Industry and Professional Standards

The Appraisal Industry

The business appraisal profession is a fragmented industry. Unlike attorneys and accountants, business appraisers are subject to neither state examinations nor state licensing boards for business appraisers. Neither are they subject to any federal examinations or licensing boards.

A handful of firms in the United States are multi-disciplinary organizations with full- and part-time staff members who appraise all kinds of assets (including real property, machinery and equipment, and business interests) for a variety of reasons, such as for estate and gift tax matters, divorces, mergers, and ESOPs. There are many small consulting firms and partnerships whose primary or only business is business appraisals. Many were begun by people who once worked for the larger valuation consulting companies.

In addition, there are several other types of businesses that have specialized groups or individuals who spend some or all of their time performing business valuations; these businesses include investment banks, commercial banks (often in their trust departments), and especially accounting firms. In recent years, as accounting firms, including the Big Six, have diversified their practices, they have developed appraisal departments that include business appraisers. Finally, there are individuals in other or related professions who perform business appraisals on a part-time basis, such as college professors of finance.

Regulation of Business Appraisers

The business appraisal industry is essentially self-regulating. There is one multi-disciplinary appraisal organization of which the business valuation division forms a growing part. The American Society of Appraisers (ASA), headquartered outside of Washington, D.C., is a 6,000-member organization that offers education and professional accreditation in many appraisal disciplines such as gems and jewelry, appraisal review and management, real property, machinery and technical services, personal property, and business valuations. The ASA sponsors a series of exams in each discipline to test competency and establish proficiency in each field. Its Business Valuation Committee, formed in 1981, emphasizes techniques for appraising closely held businesses and professional practices, or a partial interest therein.

To achieve the ASA's professional designation of Accredited Member (AM), one must have two years of experience in the field, pass the ASA's examinations, and submit two appraisal reports that meet the standards of its examining committee. To achieve its professional designation of Accredited Senior Appraiser (ASA), in addition to achieving the requirements of an AM, one must have five years of experience in the field. As of 1994, there are almost 600 members who have achieved the designations of AM and ASA. The American Society of Appraisers also holds national professional meetings in business valuation plus course offerings and local meetings.

A smaller organization founded in 1978 specializes in business appraisals. The Institute of Business Appraisers (IBA) is based in southern Florida and has approximately 2,000 members. The Institute offers a designation known as a Certified Business Appraiser (CBA) that is achieved after successfully completing a comprehensive examination and submitting two business appraisal reports before its examination committee. There are approximately 200 members who have achieved the CBA designation. The IBA also holds annual national professional meetings.

Educational and Professional Credentials

Nearly all business appraisers today have at least a college degree. Relevant undergraduate majors may include finance, accounting, or economics. Many believe that a Masters in Business Administration (MBA), especially with a major in finance, is highly desirable. Among other virtues, an MBA provides a broad understanding of business, which is helpful because valuing a closely held business should involve more than simply analyzing financial statements.

Another professional credential held by some business appraisers is Chartered Financial Analyst (CFA). Sponsored worldwide by the Association for Investment Management and Research (AIMR), a nonprofit organization, this designation is achieved after passing a series of three examinations that test proficiency in accounting, economics, analyzing equity securities and fixed income securities, quantitative analysis, investment portfolio management, and professional ethics. The CFA program focuses on analyzing minority interests in publicly traded companies, rather than valuing minority or majority interests in closely held companies. However, the basic financial analytical skills, as well as the knowledge of the public securities markets, can be fundamental to the education and training of a business appraiser. There are almost 16,000 CFA charterholders worldwide.

As mentioned above, the accounting profession has become proactive in diversifying its revenue base to include business appraisals. Until recently, there was no specialized business valuation training within the accounting profession. However, the American Institute of Certified Public Accountants (AICPA) has adopted an educational program developed by the Illinois Institute of CPAs. This program of eight one-day courses leads to a Certificate of Educational Achievement (CEA) in Business Valuation, but it is not a specialty designation.

Training for ESOP Appraisals

Until recently, the only national effort to establish some uniformity among business appraisers regarding ESOP valuations had been by the Valuation Advisory Committee of the ESOP Association. The Valuation Advisory

Committee is limited to 25 members of the ESOP Association who are active in ESOP valuations. They have published a booklet titled *Valuing ESOP Shares* that discusses the major issues to be resolved in the ESOP valuation process and indicates where a difference of opinion exists. The ESOP Association, which consists of almost 2,000 members, and its Valuation Advisory Committee conduct annual meetings each spring in the Washington, D.C., area, as well as regional presentations.

The Business Valuation Committee of the American Society of Appraisers recently developed a four-day business valuation course, *Employee Stock Ownership Plans,* to be offered for the first time in the spring of 1995 in the Washington, D.C., area.

The AICPA offers a course called *Employee Stock Ownership Plans: Practical Applications.* However, rather than being a course in ESOP valuation per se, this course focuses on qualification, reporting, and disclosure requirements for ESOP companies.

There is no legal requirement that the business appraiser have experience in providing ESOP appraisals per se. A point of reference could be the regulations for charitable contributions, which define a "qualified appraiser" as one "qualified to make appraisals of the type of property described." One could interpret this phrase to include "experience," yet that term is not defined. Common sense suggests that retaining a business appraiser who has performed ESOP appraisals previously can add the incremental value to the engagement that experience provides.

Requirements for an ESOP Appraisal

A business appraisal is essentially a financial research project. The written report is the summary of the research and analysis performed to reach the conclusion of value. It should be clear enough so that the plan fiduciary and other interested parties can understand it, and it should be sufficient to withstand the scrutiny of a federal audit or a challenge in a court of law.

Revenue Ruling 59-60

Many ESOP valuations involve determining the fair market value of a minority interest position of closely held stock. The factors the IRS wants to be considered, which were originally developed for estate and gift tax purposes, are enumerated in Revenue Ruling 59-60. They are:

- The nature of the business and the history of the enterprise from its inception.
- The economic outlook in general and the condition and outlook of the specific industry in particular.

- The book value of the stock and the financial condition of the business.
- The earnings capacity of the company.
- The dividend-paying capacity of the company.
- Whether or not the enterprise has goodwill or other intangible value.
- Sales of the stock and the size of the block to be valued.
- The market price of stocks of corporations engaged in the same or a similar line of business having their stock actively traded in a free and open market, either on an exchange or over the counter.

The DOL's Proposed Adequate Consideration Regulations

In its proposed regulations, the DOL set forth a two-part fair market value test: (1) the value assigned to the stock must reflect its fair market value determined according to the DOL's regulations, and (2) the determination must be made by a fiduciary in good faith.

Determining Fair Market Value The first part of the test has two requirements: (a) fair market value must be determined as of the date of the transaction, and (b) the determination must be reflected in written documentation meeting certain content requirements.

Because the "date of the transaction" is not defined, it could mean the date of the purchase or the date of the closing. Practically speaking, most ESOPs are created over a period of several months, and the value used in the planning process is initially determined at the beginning of the process. That value may change before the closing date. Hence, when retaining the appraiser, one must be certain to contract with the appraiser to update the valuation as of the date of closing.

The DOL's proposed regulations essentially adopted Revenue Ruling 59-60. However, as previously mentioned, it did include a few more specific requirements, some of which had become part of ESOP valuation reports through custom and usage. They include:

- The methodologies used to determine value, and the basis for the valuation in light of those methods.
- The relevance or significance accorded to the valuation methodologies.
- The factors taken into account in performing the valuation, including any restrictions, understandings, or obligations limiting the use or disposition of the asset.

- Other special factors including the marketability or lack thereof of the security, and the basis for payment of a control premium.

Good Faith The second part of the two-part fair market value test, the good faith requirement, establishes an objective standard of conduct, a standard that involves an examination of all relevant facts and circumstances. The proposed regulations state that two key factors must be present to establish that a fiduciary acted in good faith: (a) the fiduciary must apply sound business principles of evaluation and conduct a prudent investigation of the circumstances prevailing at the time of the valuation, and (b) either the fiduciary making the valuation must be independent of all the parties to the transaction, or the fiduciary must rely on the report of an appraiser who is independent of all the parties to the transaction.

Independence

The appraiser must be independent of all parties to the transaction (other than the plan), a determination made in light of all the relevant facts and circumstances. An appraiser is considered independent only if the plan's fiduciary retains the appraiser, has the right to cancel the relationship, and establishes the plan as the appraiser's client. Practically speaking, this requirement can be awkward, especially for smaller companies trying to minimize the cost of creating the ESOP.

For example, when a plan sponsor is considering an ESOP, he or she often retains a business appraiser to provide a determination of the fair market value of the stock to help decide if an ESOP is feasible for the company. Assuming that an ESOP is feasible, the plan sponsor will proceed to the next step, which often is to appoint a temporary trustee as the plan's fiduciary, who also is often an employee of the company. It is then the responsibility of the temporary trustee to select and retain an appraiser. The temporary trustee can begin to search for another appraiser or use the one initially retained by the plan sponsor. An advantage of using the same business appraiser is that he or she may provide the valuation in a more efficient and cost-effective manner than another appraiser. However, the matter of a possible conflict of interest, or appearance thereof, may exist. A practical solution is to have the proposed temporary trustee, rather than the plan sponsor, retain the business appraiser at the very beginning of the process. There is, however, a practical problem with this practical solution.

At the beginning of the process, neither the temporary trustee nor the plan (which technically does not yet exist), has funds to pay the appraiser's fee. The plan sponsor has the funds. Yet, traditionally, the party who pays the fee is the appraiser's client. If the plan sponsor pays the appraiser's fees, the appraiser's independence, at best, might appear to be compromised. Footnote 3 of the proposed DOL regulations tries to address at least this part of the situation by stating that the independence of the appraiser is not affected solely because the plan sponsor pays the appraiser's fee.

Footnote 4 of the proposed DOL regulations continues the circular discussion of independence when the DOL notes that the Code section that requires closely held stock to be valued by an independent appraiser for ESOP purposes defines an appraiser similarly to the Code requirements for charitable contribution purposes. The DOL states that its requirements are not the same as the requirements of the IRS, but does not say how.

Hence, the definition of independence remains unclear and questions remain unanswered. For example, it remains unresolved whether the outside accountant, banker, or other financial advisor for the company or plan sponsor can be considered independent for purposes of performing an ESOP valuation for his or her client. Not surprisingly, attorneys have expressed somewhat differing views on the matter. Over time, the general feeling seems to have evolved that although it may not be expressly prohibited for a company to use its outside accountant or other financial advisor to determine the fair market value of the company's stock, the risks involved may not be worth the potential cost savings of using someone with prior knowledge of the company's operations. Indeed, a number of accounting firms, including some of the Big Six, have established internal policies to refuse ESOP valuation assignments from audit clients. Commercial banks uniformly do not seem to permit their trust departments to appraise the stock of a company if the bank will be financing the transaction.

Practical Matters

Fees

As with any profession, fees vary widely in the business appraisal profession. Generally speaking, fees are a function of the amount of time it takes to perform the appraisal. Appraisal fees should be negotiated and agreed upon at the beginning of the engagement. They also should be in writing. Many business appraisers will request the most recent five years of the subject company's financial statements before they provide a fee quotation so that they can estimate the amount of time necessary to perform the valuation.

Basing the fee for an appraisal on the valuation result is prohibited. The Internal Revenue Code, when defining a qualified appraiser in Section 170(c)(5)(B), states that an appraisal shall not be treated as a qualified appraisal if all or part of the fee paid for such appraisal is based on a percentage of the appraised value of the property. Further, Section 7.2 of the Principles of Appraisal Practice and Code of Ethics of the American Society of Appraisers expressly states that "it is unprofessional and unethical for the appraiser to contract to do work for a fixed percentage of the amount of value . . . which he determines at the conclusion of his work." A challenging problem occurs in fee negotiations when a client requests a lower fee because the subject company is a small company. Clients of appraisers may not be aware that not only does a small company take the same amount of time to evaluate as a large company, it sometimes takes longer.

Annual valuations of ESOP stock are required by federal law, although the law does not require the ESOP to use the same appraiser each year to perform annual updates. Fee-sensitive trustees might consider negotiating with the appraiser for a contract covering a term of years to achieve some cost savings. Most business appraisers do not prepare the same type of reports for annual updates as they do when ESOPs are created. A brief written report that includes the conclusion of value and the factors considered in determining the conclusion is generally provided. If less time is necessary for report writing, the fees for annual updates may be less than for the original valuation. If, however, there is a material change in the operations of the company or its industry, a complete valuation study and report may be required. Also, most business appraisers recommend a complete valuation study every five years.

Liability

The fiduciary for any ERISA plan or IRS qualified plan, including an ESOP, is required to act prudently and in the best interests of plan participants. If the qualifications of the business appraiser, the conclusion of value, or the quality of the report are challenged by the DOL or IRS, substantial financial liabilities could accrue to both the company and the fiduciary. For example, the proposed DOL regulations provide that if the determination of fair market value is outside an acceptable range of reasonable values, including a calculation error or an honest failure to consider certain information, the adequate consideration test would not have been met. Hence, a prohibited transaction may have occurred which could impose financial liability and civil penalties on the fiduciary who could otherwise demonstrate that his or her decision was based on prudence and good-faith conduct. In addition, parties in interest who engage in prohibited transactions with a plan are subject to excise taxes and correction requirements.

Contracting with an Appraiser

When retaining a business appraiser, the arrangement should be committed to in writing. When the ESOP is created, the contract or engagement letter should be between the ESOP fiduciary and the business appraiser or appraisal firm, and should include:

- The purpose of the valuation.
- The number and type of shares or percentage of the company to be valued.
- The valuation date.
- The premise of value, fair market value, and the definition of fair market value.
- The delivery dates of the valuation conclusion and the written report.
- An indication of the items to be included in the written report.
- The amount of the fee or the fee range and the payment schedule.
- The qualifications of the person or persons performing the work.
- Any special restrictions or considerations.

Conclusion

The selection of the business appraiser is one of the most critical decisions in the creation of an ESOP. The business appraiser should understand the requirements of both the IRS and the DOL, and be both qualified and independent. The conclusion of value must be documented in a thorough narrative report that describes the information collected, the valuation approaches used, and the restrictions and limiting conditions considered in the analysis leading to the conclusion of value.

14

Valuation Ethics

Corey Rosen

The ESOP appraiser faces a variety of ethical dilemmas that have not adequately been discussed. Should the appraiser be clear with clients about the assumptions and approaches that will be used? Should the appraiser accept as reasonable assumptions that just because the ESOP has a majority ownership interest, it therefore has control, even if the trustee acts at the direction of management? Is a legal right for a put option really enough to eliminate the need for a marketability discount? Is there a tendency to line up assumptions in favor of the seller? There are no data on these issues, but there is and should be concern that at least some appraisers may try too hard to please their clients.

Imagine this very common ESOP scenario. There are four owners of a company, three of whom own 30% each and one (the company's president) who owns 10%. The 30% owners are no longer active in the business and want to sell "at the highest price possible as soon as possible." It's not that they are being unfair or greedy. In fact, they want to see the business continue, and they like the idea of employees being owners. But they also have other business interests and would like to have the funds available for those or for some liquidity not now available to them. It's only natural that they want to get the best price they can.

The company might be able to buy out all three, allowing them to get a control price. If the company's appraiser agrees that the requirement for the company to repurchase shares from terminated ESOP participants eliminates a "lack of marketability" discount, then the selling owners may not have to face the lower sales price that shareholders in private companies often face because their shares are harder to sell than public company shares. If the company cannot buy out all three shareholders at once, then the shareholders have two options. Each can sell a portion of his shares, or one can sell first, then the other two down the road. But this raises some tricky issues. If the ESOP borrows money to buy their shares, the added debt will reduce the price of future transactions because the value of the company after the first transaction will reflect the loan obligation. Then there is the control issue. If the ESOP buys, say, 30% of the company's stock in 1995, then another 30% five years later, and then the last 30% a few years after that, will only the second seller get a control premium?

Let's add another layer of complexity. What if the president, who wants to stay with the company, wants to buy another 20% of the equity as part of the transaction? He's putting up cash; the ESOP is using nonrecourse

Corey Rosen is the executive director of the National Center for Employee Ownership.

debt, with the company repaying the loan. To help make it possible for the ESOP to pay the debt, the company is scrapping its current profit-sharing plan to which it had been making contributions of about 7% of pay. The new ESOP would make it possible for the company to contribute somewhat more than that, although its investments would be much more risky.

The owners want to select a valuation consultant who will help them negotiate through this maze in a way that will maximize the value they can receive without jeopardizing the transaction. At some price level, they will decide it would be better to sell the company to someone else. So they want to interview valuation consultants with a view towards finding someone who will make the most favorable assumptions that can be defended.

Legally, of course, the sellers are not hiring the valuation consultant; the trustee is. The trustee, not the seller, is the valuation consultant's client. In theory, there should be a clear separation of interests between the seller and trustee. The trustee wants to assure the ESOP gets the lowest price possible; the seller usually wants the highest. In many ESOP transactions, the trustee is an outsider, often a professional trustee, or at least is someone other than the seller (the company's CFO, for example). Often, the trustee does work to obtain a price that is fair, or better yet, the lowest price possible. Assuming all parties are well advised by professionals, this is about as "clean" a process as can be expected. But in other transactions, the seller is also the trustee, or the trustee is acting at the seller's direction. Even without this conflict of interest, the valuation consultant knows that in most cases the appraisal bill is paid by the company, which is run by the seller.

This scenario raises some very difficult ethical questions. The owners are sophisticated enough about valuations and ESOPs to ask good questions about assumptions such as discounts for minority interests, lack of marketability, and equity allocation, as well as the impact on stock price of additional ESOP debt (an impact that some people count more heavily than others). The valuation consultant is smart enough to know that if too many answers are not what they want to hear, he or she won't get the engagement, and even if he or she does, if the sellers decide the price is too low, there won't be the chance to do repeat valuations. But the valuation consultant also has a personal and professional code to follow. What happens now?

Should valuation consultants even discuss what assumptions they make on these issues or does that allow valuation shopping? Should they tell the client what to expect when the ESOP takes on debt? What about all the other myriad issues of valuation that the clients haven't even considered, such as whether to rely more heavily on price/earnings ratios or on discounted cash flow?

There are no data to answer how valuation consultants deal with these questions, but I have some impressions from talking to hundreds of ESOP companies and listening to hundreds of valuation presentations over the last 18 years. Some valuation experts simply say that they are experienced, capable, and independent, and that it would be inappropriate for them to discuss methods. Some are willing to discuss the assumptions, but fear that if they do they could be implicated as a fiduciary. Still others believe they should discuss these issues so the client can fulfill its fiduciary obligation to make an intelligent choice about valuation. Finally, at least some valuation people do what they can to help clients justify the price they want. It's not necessarily that they are explicitly trying to cheat. They have a strong rationale for why what they are doing is really ethically acceptable, and after so many years of doing it, it seems OK, especially if potential clients will just pick other appraisers who will do it anyway.

What Should Be Discussed?

The issue of what should be discussed with a valuation consultant creates something of a quandary. There are three parties to this discussion: the person paying the bills, the ESOP fiduciary (who may or may not be the same person who pays the bills), and the valuation consultant. The Internal Revenue Service and the U.S. Department of Labor could get involved as well. The person paying the bills usually wants the best (i.e., the highest) price possible. He or she naturally wants to discuss the assumptions being used in order to choose someone who will tend toward a higher valuation conclusion. The trustee is supposed to act on behalf of the ESOP to assure that it gets at least a fair price; many would argue that the trustee should be pushing for the best deal possible (i.e., a lower valuation conclusion). In itself, that is quite a dilemma if the trustee and bill payer are the same. The valuation consultant may hope to dazzle both, although legally he or she should impress only the trustee, who is supposed to be unconcerned about whether the price that is arrived at is acceptable to the seller.

In the scenario above, the sellers could reasonably hope to find a valuation consultant who would make the following assumptions:

- If the ESOP is not buying control right away, but is given an option to buy it five years from now, all transactions will be at the control price, including the final transactions for the remaining 30%. It is true that in many cases, the valuation consultant does not decide this issue. The trustee, with advice of counsel, directs the consultant to base the appraisal on a control or non-control price. In other cases, however, the consultant may decide what is most appropriate. Even in the first scenario, however, the valuation consultant must decide whether a control price is justifiable. If the company gives the ESOP an option to buy shares seven years down the road, is that still control? What if there are conditions attached to the option that make it effective only if certain targets are met? Given that there is no regulation or any clear consensus on when a gradual acquisition merits a control price, the valuation consultant will always have some role in this decision.

- No marketability discounts will be taken because of the ESOP put option, even though the company has not yet shown it has the resources to satisfy those obligations.
- Future share prices will not take into account the magnitude of the ESOP repurchase obligation because it is simply theoretical. Maybe the company will go public or be sold to satisfy the obligation. Or perhaps the valuation consultant is not sophisticated enough about ESOPs to even know that should be done. After all, the repurchase obligation does not appear on the balance sheet or income statement, except perhaps as a footnote, and then only to state the current size of the ESOP holdings.
- The ESOP trustee should not be able to bargain for part of the Section 1042 rollover tax benefit, if the sellers decide to use that, even though the ESOP is bringing that benefit to the table.
- If there is an equity investor, the allocation of shares to that investor will reflect the greater risk and investment that person undertakes, meaning the ESOP will get proportionally fewer shares for each dollar of its purchase. While ESOP participants are giving up their profit sharing in return for the ESOP, this will not be considered an investment on their part because the benefits, after all, are "free."

Every one of these assumptions can be defended, and every one has been by various valuation consultants I have heard make presentations. Because many of these assumptions involve potential discounts of 10% to 50% each, their cumulative impact can be huge.

So should these assumptions be discussed? When I talk with companies, I tell them they absolutely should ask questions about the assumptions. If you do not know the basis for an appraisal, you cannot possibly make a good choice to meet either the seller's desires or the fiduciary demands of the ESOP, or both. But when I ask this question of consultants, many (but not all) say it would be improper for them to discuss these issues. Some fear that such a discussion would make them a fiduciary. Advisers are shielded from fiduciary liability to the extent they are just providing advice; if they get involved in making a recommendation for the ESOP to purchase stock, they may be considered fiduciaries. Not answering questions about assumptions may be more a way to avoid giving unpleasant answers than to avoid getting sued. There is no case in which a valuation consultant has been sued successfully as a fiduciary. The stunned client who thought his business was worth $1 million—and it is—but who finds that the 30% stake he is selling to a leveraged ESOP is only worth $120,000 is not going to be happy that he paid a bill without knowing these things in advance. And the ESOP trustee who selects a consultant who lines up all favorable assumptions for the seller and pushes them to their maximum has arguably done a lousy job of representing the participants. Clearly, the seller should not negotiate with a valuation consultant to arrive at the "right" assumptions; however, it would be foolish to avoid asking what the consultant's assumptions are.

Is There a Bias Toward Finding the Right Price for the Client?

Most of the valuation people I know say that they usually disappoint the client, reporting a lower number than the client hoped. But there also seems to be a systematic bias from some appraisers to make very favorable assumptions.

For example, several well-known appraisers have said they regard the legal obligation of a put as enough to eliminate the lack of marketability discount. When I asked one about the difference between a legal obligation and practical ability, he said that was not an issue. But, I asked, even if the company does have the practical ability, does not the very commitment of those funds reduce the company's cash flow and earnings and thus reduce its price? He had not considered that issue, he said. Another said no because who knew what would happen to the company down the road. Similarly, there is an issue whether the block of stock the ESOP owns would be marketable. While the company may be able to buy back stock in the small portions that come from departing employees, it may not be able to buy the entire block without forcing a sale under less than ideal circumstances that would lower the price.

More broadly, few valuation consultants have seriously considered whether *any* consideration for the ESOP participant put option is appropriate. After all, the appraisal is assessing the price the ESOP should pay, and the ESOP itself does not have a put option.

Or take the issue of control. Imagine in our example that the ESOP buys 59% of the stock. A control price for sure, right? But DOL guidelines talk about control in fact, not just form. What if the president is the trustee and directs the voting of the shares? True, the president has a theoretical (one might say formal) obligation to vote those shares for the interests of participants, but only on the most limited of issues, those that are likely never to come up. On issues that really matter, such as electing the board that sets the president's pay and decides whether the company continues the ESOP or not, participants have no control. Should the ESOP really pay for control? This is a controversial issue, and many people argue the regulations refer only to the ESOP trust having control, not the individual participants. But even granting this argument, would an outsider really pay a control premium if given the same option the ESOP often has, namely of having decisions made by an insider?

To be sure, there are heated counterarguments (I can hear them now). And they have merit. The problem is the cascading of favorable assumptions. When every issue cuts against a lower price for the ESOP, it seems to me a serious question is raised about the relationship between the appraiser and the client.

Before You Throw Rotten Tomatoes

I certainly do not mean to impugn the ethics of the whole industry here. Far from it. In fact, ESOP professionals strike me as having more integrity than might be found in other fields. I think it is the fortunately rare appraiser who knowingly sets out to do whatever it takes to get the "right" (i.e., the highest) price for the seller. Still, if your livelihood depends on getting owners to hire you (I know, it's technically the ESOP trustee, but they don't pay the bills), and if you see other people finding ways to make deals happen, it is easy to become comfortable with favorable assumptions. All of us rationalize things we do in this way. Take the extreme case of tobacco company executives. When asked by the *New York Times* how they justify spending their lives selling a product they know is dangerous (most did not want their kids to smoke), they talked about their pride in providing a good product for those consumers who made a free adult choice to smoke. Or the corporate attorney I met who defended Hooker Chemical of Love Canal fame. He had no doubt of their guilt, he said, but they too deserved representation. Did it concern him that those with resources are more able to insure their rights to good representation? Of course. But his firm represented Hooker, and his duty was to do the best he could to defend the client.

On a less dramatic scale, all of us make compromises like these all the time. Should we at the NCEO, for instance, continue to list someone in our *Resource Guide* if we suspect that person does not have the high competence we would like our members to acquire? Well, we do clearly say that the guide does not represent a judgment on people's qualifications. But we also know that people see a name in writing listed by a reputable organization and that confers a credibility that would not otherwise be there. Rather than continually face tough issues with no easy answer, all of us tend to put them off, or to construct ethical rationalizations. If we do that too much, however, it is easy to slip from behavior that is within normal bounds of ethical ambiguity to marginal or unethical acts.

I suspect that valuation consultants sometimes end up in a similar place. If that place becomes too uncomfortable, too unquestioned, it can easily lead to appraisals that, while perhaps technically defensible, really do not accomplish what the law envisions: protecting the best interests of plan participants.

In theory, the solution is for the ESOP trustee to aggressively pursue the best possible deal for the ESOP. It is, after all, the trustee's responsibility to do that, not the seller's or the valuation consultant's. If the consultant makes too many assumptions that are favorable to the seller(s), the trustee should challenge those assumptions. In practice, however, the trustee is often not independent of the seller, or is the seller or an employee of the seller. And while the valuation consultant's client is the trustee, the seller or the seller's company pays the bill and says "no deal" if the appraisal is too low (meaning no repeat engagements for the consultant). The ESOP's legal advisors should be watching out for all this too, but they face similar conflicts of interest. For all of us in the ESOP community, it is in our interest to insist on the highest ethical standards. While that may mean some individual transactions do not happen, that is far better than having too many failures and undermining the public support that makes ESOPs possible.

About the NCEO

The National Center for Employee Ownership (NCEO) is widely considered to be "the single best source of information on employee ownership anywhere in the world" (*Inc.* magazine, August 2000). Established in 1981 as a nonprofit information and membership organization, it now has well over 3,000 members, including companies, professionals, unions, government officials, academics, and interested individuals. It is funded entirely through the work it does.

The NCEO's mission is to provide the most objective, reliable information possible about employee ownership at the most affordable price possible. As part of the NCEO's commitment to providing objective information, it does not lobby or provide ongoing consulting services. The NCEO publishes a variety of materials—such as this book—explaining how employee ownership plans work, describing how companies get employee owners more involved in making decisions about their work, and reviewing the research on employee ownership (see the list of selected publications on the following pages). In addition, the NCEO holds dozens of seminars and conferences on employee ownership annually. These include "introduction to ESOPs" seminars, seminars on equity compensation, meetings on employee participation, and a large annual conference. The NCEO's work also includes extensive contacts with the media, both through articles it writes and through interviews with reporters. Finally, the NCEO has written or edited five books for outside publishers: *The Equity Solution* (Lexington Books, 1986); *Taking Stock: Employee Ownership at Work* (Ballinger, 1986); *Employee Ownership in Public Companies* (Quantum, 1990); *Understanding Employee Ownership* (Cornell I&LR Press, 1991); and *Employee Stock Ownership Plans* (Harcourt Brace, 1996, 1999).

Membership Benefits

NCEO members receive the following benefits:

- The bimonthly newsletter, *Employee Ownership Report*.
- Access to the members area of our Web site, including a searchable database of over 200 service providers, a searchable directory of ESOP lenders, a searchable newsletter archive, and other resources.
- Substantial discounts on publications and events produced by the NCEO (such as this book).
- The right to email or telephone the NCEO for answers to general or specific questions regarding employee ownership.

NCEO Annual Membership Fees

$80	*Associate* (non-employee ownership companies, organizations, and consultants not listed in the members area referral service)
$265	*Consultants* (listed in the referral service)
	Employee Ownership Companies:
$80	1–50 employees
$140	51–100 employees
$265	101–500 employees
$380	Over 500 employees

Add $10 to any of the above amounts if your mailing address is outside the U.S.

Regardless of the above subcategories (such as the $380 rate for large employee-owned companies), an introductory one-year NCEO membership is only $80 ($90 if outside the U.S.), or $35 for full-time students or faculty members who are not employed in the business sector ($45 if outside the U.S.). Ordering information is at the end of this section.

Selected NCEO Publications on ESOPs

The NCEO offers a variety of publications on all aspects of employee ownership and participation, from ESOPs to stock options, as well as how to communicate these plans to employees and build a more productive corporate culture. Below are descriptions of our main publications on ESOPs.

We publish new books and revise old ones on a yearly basis. To obtain the most current information on what we have available, visit our extensive Web site at *www.nceo.org* or call us at 510-208-1300.

- *The ESOP Reader* is an overview of the issues involved in establishing and operating an ESOP. It covers the basics of ESOP rules, feasibility, valuation, and other matters, and then discusses managing an ESOP company, including brief case studies. This book is for both private and public companies as well as anyone with a general interest in ESOPs and employee participation.

  Cost: $25 for NCEO members, $35 for nonmembers

- *Selling to an ESOP* is a guide for owners, managers, and advisors of closely held businesses. It explains how ESOPs work and then offers a comprehensive look at legal structures, financing (including self-financing), and other matters, especially the tax-deferred Section 1042 "rollover" that allows owners to indefinitely defer capital gains taxation on the proceeds of the sale to the ESOP.

  Cost: $25 for NCEO members, $35 for nonmembers

- *Leveraged ESOPs and Employee Buyouts* discusses how ESOPs borrow money to buy out entire companies, purchase shares from a retiring owner, or finance new capital. It is applicable to both public and closely held companies.

  Cost: $25 for NCEO members, $35 for nonmembers

- The *Employee Ownership Q&A Disk* gives Microsoft Windows users (any version from Windows 95 onward) point-and-click access to over 500 questions and answers on all aspects of ESOPs in a searchable hypertext format. Distributed on a 1.44 MB 3.5-inch diskette.

  Cost: $75 for NCEO members, $100 for nonmembers

- *The Journal of Employee Ownership Law and Finance* is the only professional journal solely devoted to employee ownership. Articles are written by leading experts and cover ESOPs, stock options, and related subjects. The *Journal* appears quarterly.

  One-year subscription:
  $75 for NCEO members, $100 for nonmembers

- This book, *ESOP Valuation,* brings together and updates where needed the best articles on ESOP valuation that we have published in the *Journal.*

  Cost: $25 for NCEO members, $35 for nonmembers

- The *Model ESOP* contains a sample ESOP plan, with alternative provisions given to tailor the plan to individual needs. It also includes a section-by-section explanation of the plan and other supporting materials.

  Cost: $50 for NCEO members, $75 for nonmembers

- The *ESOP Committee Guide* describes the different types of ESOP committees, the goals they can address, alternative structures, member selection criteria, training, committee lifecycle concerns, and more.

  Cost: $25 for NCEO members, $35 for nonmembers

To join the NCEO as a member or to order any of the above publications, mail or fax the order form on the following page, use the secure ordering system on our Web site at *www.nceo.org,* or telephone us at (510) 208-1300 with your credit card in hand. If you are not already a member but join at the same time you order publications, you will receive the members-only publication discounts.

Order Form

To order, fill out this form and mail it with your credit card information or check to the NCEO at 1736 Franklin Street, 8th Floor, Oakland, CA 94612; fax it with your credit card information to the NCEO at 510-272-9510; telephone us at 510-208-1300 with your credit card in hand; or order securely online at our Web site, *www.nceo.org*. If you are not already a member, you can join now to receive member discounts on the publications you order.

Name

Organization

Address

City, State, Zip (Country)

Telephone Fax E-mail

Method of Payment: ❑ Check (payable to "NCEO") ❑ Visa ❑ M/C ❑ AMEX

Credit Card Number

Signature Exp. Date

Checks are accepted only for orders from the U.S. and must be in U.S. currency.

Title	Qty.	Price	Total

Subtotal	**$**
Sales Tax	**$**
Shipping	**$**
Membership	**$**
TOTAL DUE	**$**

Tax: California residents add 8.25% sales tax (on publications only, not membership)

Shipping: In the U.S., first publication $5, each add'l $1; elsewhere, we charge exact shipping costs to your credit card, plus (except for Canada) a $10 handling surcharge; no shipping charges for membership or for Journal subscriptions

Introductory NCEO Membership: $80 for one year ($90 outside the U.S.)